Who Am I and Why Am I Here?

Who Am I and Why Am I Here?

The Universal Spiritual View of the Meaning and Purpose of Our Human Life on Earth

William Rosek

Channeled by
Cathy and Bill Rosek

Credits:

Cover Design: Saint Germain and William Rosek

Text Design and Composition: Graphics West, Inc., Colorado Springs, Colorado

Edited by: Sharon Green, Graphics West, Inc.

Back Cover Photography: the Family studio, Colorado Springs, Colorado

Library of Congress Cataloging-in-Publication Data

Rosek, William A.
Who Am I and Why Am I Here?: The Universal View of the Meaning and Purpose of Our Human Life on Earth
William A. Rosek
p. cm.
ISBN 0-9711772-0-1
1. New Age 2. Spiritual 3. Metaphysical 4. Self Help
2001-132606
CIP

This First Edition printing by arrangement with Kendall Printing, Greeley, Colorado.

Published by

Universal View Publishing

P.O. Box 2458, Monument, Colorado 80132
cathy@universalspiritualview.com
Website: www.universalspiritualview.com

Dedication

I dedicate this book and the information in this book, provided by the Archangels, the Ascended Masters, and other Beings of Light (those minions of God in the heavenly realms of the Hierarchy of God, whose missions are to assist humankind's spiritual evolution back to conscious Oneness with God), to the souls of all students in the Earth School.

Who Will Be Helped by This Book?

Excerpt from a reading by Cathy from Saint Germain on 03/11/01.

✦ Who will be helped by this book?

This book was not written for a particular group. It is for all seekers. It is for lightworkers and starseeds and wayshowers, but also for those who are just waking up to the idea, to the awareness, the concept, that there is something far greater in life than the third-dimensional experience. This volume addresses a large, inclusive, holistic description of the Universal Spiritual Picture from almost the very beginning levels of understanding to the very high levels of awareness and growth on humankind's evolutionary spiral. It will bring different aspects to different individuals. The audience is large because it is not aimed at any specific area.

Many will find much that is of value.

The Cover Illustration "Our True Identity"

The cover illustration, offered by Saint Germain, shows the physical human body (with its personality), the attached soul (and its Body of Light), and the divine Spark of God that lives within the soul of every human on Earth.

To reach conscious Oneness with God requires only that we bring the personality of our physical body into *harmony* with our attached soul and with the Spark of God that lives untainted within our soul. We thus refine and spiritualize our human personality, raising its consciousness upward to the level of our soul. We become one with our soul and we begin to identify with our soul again rather than with just our body and personality. We live our lives at the higher level of consciousness, understanding, and intuitive knowing associated with the higher perspective of our soul selves again.

Creating this inner *harmony* and *conscious Oneness* allows us to bring the innate power and abilities of our soul and our Spark of God Within into our harmonized personality and into our third-dimensional lives. This inner harmony allows our personality to receive divine inner guidance from our soul and our Divinity Within (and from the Angels and other Beings of Light in the higher realms of the Hierarchy of God) through our soul's natural, intuitive path.

With this inner harmony and the divine intuitive guidance it brings, we may manifest the divine light, divine love, and divine will of our soul and Divinity Within into our own little third-dimensional worlds as we discover and fulfill our soul's purpose. This is how and where we find true and lasting joy, peace, unconditional love, wholeness, completion, and fulfillment while still having a physical body on Earth. This is how we return to the state of conscious Oneness with our God within and therefore with God, the All That Is. This is how we complete our spiritual journey in the third dimension and return home.

Contents

PART II An Overview of the Spiritual Realms

The view of human evolution as seen from above

PART III The Priceless Value of Divine Feminine Energy

Five readings

PART IV The Spiritual Path Itself

Creating harmony among the Personality, the Soul, and the Spark of God Within the Soul

PART V Our Changing Perspectives, Seeing From Above

Viewing the Earth School from the perspective of our soul and our Divinity Within

Preface

An introduction follows this preface and makes it clear that much of the higher information presented in this book has been provided by Archangels, Angels, Guardian Angels, Ascended Masters, Higher Guides, and other Beings of Light received in readings by Cathy or journaled by myself. It indicates that the information we seek from above is transmitted to the Spark of God within our souls (through our crown, brow, throat, and heart charkas) and verbalized or written by ourselves. It discusses how the book came to be and how we receive our information. In this preface I would like to describe the book itself, as it has co-creatively evolved.

This book presents an overview of the Universal Spiritual Picture that lies above (behind and within) everything that we ordinary humans call "life" in the third dimension. To those readers who have not consciously had a great deal of interest in spiritual matters, most of this information will be new and different. To those who have been interested in spiritual matters for some time, perhaps fewer concepts will be new, for much of this information (sometimes called the Ancient Wisdom) has always been around. Either way, sufficient new information has been offered by the Archangels and Ascended Masters, dealing with the monumental, divine changes soon to evolve in the nature and character of humankind in the Golden Age, to satisfy all spiritually interested readers.

The Ancient Wisdom (in many esoteric volumes) has always been made available through the writings of individuals with seemingly special talents and abilities to lift their consciousness to a higher level and to open and receive the information that comes from the Hierarchy of God as answers to their inner philosophical questions. There always have been and there always will be such individuals around to keep the spark alive, to keep the flame of spirit burning among evolving humankind for this, too, is part of the design, part of the plan for the inhabitants of Earth.

For the past five or six years I have had a very strong feeling in my heart that the greatest need of humankind at this time is for a single book that condenses and makes clear the Universal Spiritual Picture of the origins of human life on Earth and the meaning and purpose of that life, as it has been provided to Cathy and me by Angels, Archangels, Ascended Masters, and other Beings of Light in the divine dimensions of the Hierarchy of God above us.

Until now, to capture a meaningful glimpse of a somewhat holistic Universal Spiritual Picture required one to read dozens or perhaps even hundreds of books, each dealing with seemingly separate aspects of the larger picture, and then to put their contents together to form a meaningful whole. This one volume has sufficient information to awaken any reader who is ready, to an understanding of the Universal Spiritual Picture as provided by the Archangels and Ascended Masters.

However, to provide a comprehensive picture of such a vast subject in a single volume means reducing each subject area to a single chapter rather than an entire book or several books. An overview simply cannot be all-encompassing. Therefore, each chapter of this book will contain only the essentials of the subject rather than all the details available from above or in the Ancient Wisdom teachings. Given an overview of the Universal Spiritual Picture, of the meaning and purpose of life as lived in the physical dimension of planet Earth, the reader can then choose to explore in greater detail any specific area that happens to be of special interest (due to her or his unique set of past life experiences).

Many humans on Earth today understand and feel, deep inside, through the evidence provided by their personal experiences, that our material life on Earth has no real meaning or purpose in and of itself as it is being lived today. The understanding of the meaninglessness of third-dimensional life on Earth causes in many an internal feeling of generalized depression. The Archangels and Ascended Masters describe this generalized depression as a very natural symptom of feeling consciously separated from God. We may know or believe that there is such a thing as God but, in general, we do not yet know and feel that we *are* souls, parts of God, in harmony with God, consciously One with God, communing with God, and fulfilling our soul's purpose. If we had achieved this state of conscious Oneness, we would not have the feeling of depression.

However, this natural feeling of depression can have the very positive effect of providing us humans the motivation to seek *within* and thus to find the way back to harmony with our soul and the Spark of God within. It is our creation of this inner harmony among our personality, our soul, and our Divinity Within that brings us the permanent feelings of conscious Oneness, and the joy, peace, and unconditional love that derive from it.

We are told by the Ascended Masters that an individual's awakening to the larger spiritual picture, or even awakening to the *possibility* of the existence of a meaningful Universal Spiritual Picture, is the first step in the fulfillment of his or her soul's life purpose on Earth. The remaining steps are along the spiritual path of harmonizing our personality with our soul and with the Spark of God within our soul. It is this harmony among the three aspects of our Beingness which brings all humans (back) to conscious Oneness with God, to lasting inner feelings of inner peace, joy, unconditional love, the understanding of our higher soul purpose in this life and the divine experience of fulfilling our purpose.

The information provided to us from the Archangels and Ascended Masters describes, in an understandable way, the Universal Spiritual Picture of the origins, meaning, and purpose of physical human life as it is being lived on Earth today. It describes why God and the many Divine Minions of God have designed, created, and maintained the Earth as it is. Encapsulating this description into a single book makes it possible for all interested readers to quickly and easily awaken to a rather comprehensive understanding of the Universal Spiritual life that offers them a heavenly potential that might otherwise have taken many more lifetimes of experience to discover.

All my text is journaled from the highest level of consciousness that I could attain at the time (mostly from the soul level). It is written from that level so I could see and understand, from my soul's perspective, the holism of the Universal Spiritual Picture, described by the Archangels and Ascended Masters as a context into which all of our Earth life can be placed, as I wrote about the different portions included in this volume.

If questions arise as you read, my best suggestion is to continue reading, for the answers will usually be found in the following paragraphs. If you have doubts about the validity of any of this material, just remember, it is provided from above for your *soul,* not your personality. If you still have doubts, put the book down. However, do not be surprised if something inside you causes you to pick it up again later, after your offended personality calms down and your soul has had the opportunity to indicate to you its wishes for you to know more about the Universal Spiritual Picture.

If you find yourself to be somehow touched (especially) in the area of your heart region while assimilating this Archangel and Ascended Master information and inwardly feel the desire to chose to move along the spiritual path back to conscious Oneness with God, know that the appropriate Beings of Light in the Heavenly Realms above are instantly aware of your feelings and intentions and will immediately begin their assistance within the bounds of Universal Law.

The spiritual path now, at the beginning of the Golden Age, is easier to tread than it has ever been since creation. Extremely efficient and effective spiritual tools have been created by the Archangels and Ascended Masters and are now available to assist us all in making smooth progress along the path, if we choose to make use of them. These spiritual tools may seem quite amazing to many readers since humankind in general currently knows so little about the larger Universal Spiritual Picture. For more on the new spiritual tools, see chapter 21 and appendix A.

Many, whose souls are ready and who feel a deep inner response to the awesome potential the Universal Spiritual Picture presents, may at first have personalities that feel somehow unworthy to choose the path. To avoid any such misunderstanding, the Ascended Masters have repeated dozens of times that, "All who commit to the spiritual path back to conscious Oneness with God are worthy." There are no exceptions! Regardless of what we may presently feel and think of our personal past, there are no exceptions. The spiritual path is available to each and all of us down here on the Earth plane.

The reason that such a broad statement can be made without exception is that the entire Earth planet was designed and created as a school, an educational environment that would provide all its inhabitants with the type of experiences needed to eventually bring them to their (free will) desire and choice to return to the state of conscious Oneness with God from whence we all came. When you understand that the only purpose of this planet, the home of the Earth School, is to provide each of us humans (having an attached entrapped soul) with an evolutionary path back to conscious Oneness with God, you will also understand why, from the higher perspective of the many minions of God in the heavenly realms above, "all who commit to the spiritual path are worthy".

The Ascended Masters have also repeated over and over that the most appropriate and efficient attitude for those who choose the spiritual path is one of lightheartedness! It is from a lighthearted perspective that the presence and love of the Beings of Light in the Angelic Realm can most readily be experienced and felt. A heavy, overly serious, or depressed feeling only makes it more difficult to raise the consciousness upward to the soul level where divine communication is made easier. So, while the natural depression of our personality (caused by our feelings of the meaninglessness of third-dimensional life and simultaneously feeling consciously separated from God) may be an excellent motivator to cause one to *choose* the spiritual path, as soon as that choice has been made the lighthearted feelings of the soul are much more beneficial to swift movement along the path.

From the perspective of the Ascended Masters, awakening to the existence of the Universal Spiritual world, discovering the true purpose of life, and choosing to move along the path takes us on a meaningful journey toward lasting inner joy, unconditional love, completion, wholeness, and fulfillment. The spiritual path is also a journey of empowerment for, as we harmonize our personality with our soul, we regain our soul's innate abilities to receive divine guidance and we also begin to remember our soul's innate powers of divine creation (when in conscious Oneness with the Spark of God within it). When we choose this journey, the Archangels and Ascended Masters have repeatedly recommended that we maintain an attitude of good humor and lightheartedness.

We are just beginning the millennium that is to become the Golden Age. The New Age will bring into the Earth School the beginning of the manifestation of a new paradigm, a new model for life, a new way of "being" for all those remaining on Earth. What is the amazing change to take place in the nature and character of humankind that will have an impact so powerful that it will bring about an entirely new way of *Being* for humans in the Golden Age? It is the ability for each of us to receive divine guidance from the divine Spark of God that lives within our soul, *through our natural intuitive path.*

After an as yet undetermined period of time, approximately twenty years or so, all entities remaining on Earth will be those who have evolved themselves consciously to the point of beginning to manifest their higher soul-level awareness and higher-level consciousness. All humans who awaken to the larger spiritual picture, commit to the spiritual path, and grow in harmony with their soul's higher state of consciousness will regain their soul's innate ability to communicate with the Spark of God that lives within their soul.[1] Each human, through its progress along the spiritual path, will be re-awakened to its soul's inherent abilities to receive divine guidance from within. This means that any information we wish to know that is divinely appropriate and in harmony with the higher good of all life will be readily provided to each of us.

These abilities are for *everyone*. The skills and abilities are already there, in our soul. They were part of our soul's experience before the "fall" and they still remain within our eternal soul. To regain them, we are required only to raise our personality's consciousness to the higher level of our soul's consciousness, and our innate soul skills will be ours again. This we do by creating harmony between our personality and our soul. The harmonizing itself raises our consciousness (and our heart) upward. Harmonizing the personality with the soul is the true purpose of the spiritual path and the divine purpose of the Earth School.

This is an excerpt from a reading by Cathy, for the purpose of obtaining editing suggestions on this part of the book, received from Sananda on 10/02/99.

*You may wish to include here, that this (*ability to receive divine intuitive guidance*) is something that is well within the capability* ***of every entity.*** *You may even suggest that those who have been drawn to read this book are already being influenced by their own souls and higher selves to open to the greater awareness of the Divinity Within, of their* ***power*** *to create lives of beauty, harmony, peace, love, and abundance. Let your reader know that*

---

1 Those who do not yet desire to choose the path back to Oneness with God will no longer be able to sustain life in the higher vibrations present on Earth at that time. These souls will be given another place, another planet, another school, (together with others of similar vibrational rate who also are not yet ready) in which to carry on their evolutionary paths.

this is written for him or her and that within himself or herself exists all the awareness and all the tools that are required for spiritual development and for achieving a conscious awareness and connection with the higher realms. And we recommend that you use the words, "with the higher realms."

So for those of you whose personalities currently believe that you cannot do this, you now have heard, from the living soul of the one who was called Jesus in his last incarnation, that you can. This is for all souls on Earth—all of us.

The new millennium will bring the beginning of the manifestation of a new world wherein each remaining human will grow to know itself to be a soul which has a body, rather than a body which may or may not have a soul, depending upon the adopted personal belief system. Each human will have evolved consciously and know itself to be a soul, a part of God, with a Spark of God inside. Each human will know that the Spark of God within its soul is a part of God, the All That Is. All will come to know that all other souls are also parts of God and that as parts of God, parts of the whole, all souls are connected to each other. Because each soul is part of the whole, all are connected. Each soul will evolve itself into the full conscious awareness of the Universal Spiritual Picture of the immense spiritual life that fills the entire Cosmos, not just the Earth School environment.

Everything is in place. All is in divine order. Just as the birth of Christ was known beforehand by those who were in touch with the minions of God at that time, so it is now known that humankind in general has evolved in consciousness to the point where many are ready to awaken to the Universal Spiritual Picture and to move along the spiritual path to the inner peace, harmony, joy, unconditional love, and fulfillment that lies in our return to conscious Oneness with God.

The heavens are ready. All the Angels, Archangels, Ascended Masters, and other Beings of Light that live in the heavenly realms above our third-dimensional existence have been waiting for each of us on Earth to ***Awaken*** to the Universal Spiritual Picture. They have been waiting for us humans to ask for their assistance (of our own free will) so that they in turn may help us, as individuals, to move along our path back to conscious Oneness with God. When it awakens, the majority of the population remaining on Earth will transform itself and grow to become sentient, loving beings, sensitive to inner divine guidance, aware of their true identity as souls, and aware of being parts of God. All remaining humans will be living in harmony with their own inner divine guidance and, therefore, in harmony with each other.

This book consists of five parts, three appendices, and a glossary. The **boldface terms** in the text are further defined in the glossary in order to provide information for quick and easy reference and also to show relationships between various entities and terms. The glossary may prove interesting in and of itself to many readers.

- Part I provides an overview of the Universal Spiritual View of the immense, magnificent spiritual life that lies above, within, and behind all that we ordinary humans call "life" in the third dimension. It describes the creation of our perfect, divine, eternal, and etheric souls, and the origins of physical life on Earth. It details, for all of humanity to understand, who we are, what we are doing down here, and the meaning and purpose of life in these conditions. Part I includes a chapter on each of the nine most important elements, systems, and Universal Laws that were designed and created by God as part of our educational Earth School environment. An understanding of how each of these elements presently impact upon all of us Earth School students is critical to finding our way back to conscious Oneness with God.
- Part II presents an overview of the spiritual realms, beginning with a description of the three parts of our individual beingness, our physical body with its personality, our soul (and its Body of Light), and the Spark of God that still lives within our soul. It describes the divine dynamics behind the ability to obtain information from the higher realms in a way that may help to remove the mystery present in the minds of most of humankind living on the Earth today. Part II makes clear that this ability is available to all humans as a normal part of the spiritual path and that this is a skill that already exists in each of our souls, not something that we must learn anew. It includes a portrayal of some of the common changes toward higher consciousness and expanded awareness that may be noticed by those choosing to take the spiritual path back to harmony with the soul, to conscious Oneness with the Spark of God within the soul, and therefore also to Oneness with God, the All That Is.

  Part II concludes with a brief description of the vast heavenly collection of divine Beings of Light (Angels, Archangels, Ascended Masters, and others) whose individual and combined missions are to assist all of humanity on its path of spiritual evolution back to conscious Oneness with God.
- Part III is perhaps the most amazing and most important part of this book (to all but a very few human personalities on our planet at this time). It deals with the incredible value of integrating divine feminine energy into the lives of any choosing the spiritual path. It portrays the general population of the Earth today, male and female, as extremely overbalanced in masculine energy and details

the negative effects that this masculine imbalance has had on our world today.

Part III expresses the Universal, spiritual requirement for a balance of divine feminine and divine masculine energy within each of those who choose the spiritual path. It describes what is meant by divine feminine and divine masculine energy and makes clear that one of the priceless benefits resulting from the creation of such a balance within an individual is his or her ability to receive divine guidance and information from within and above through our natural intuitive path.

Part III also includes some of my personal experiences with the feminine energy information (as specifically requested by the Beings of Light).

- Part IV details aspects of the spiritual path itself. It defines the spiritual path as that of creating and maintaining increased harmony among all three aspects of our Beingness (our personality, our soul, and the Spark of God that lives untainted within our soul). It provides examples of attachments to our personality's adopted (learned and conditioned) outer world habit patterns that are the cause of disharmony among our three aspects. It then describes in detail how we can release the habits that create *disharmony* and replace them with those that create inner *harmony,* using some of the spiritual tools designed and created by the Archangels and Ascended Masters to speed humankind's spiritual progress on the path back to conscious Oneness with God.

  Part IV includes a brief description of a simpler way to understand dreams in context with the Universal Spiritual Picture. It portrays dreams as messages from our soul provided nightly to indicate to our personality how it can create and achieve greater inner harmony with the soul and the Spark of God within. From this viewpoint or perspective, our soul provides our personality with a nightly picture of how it *feels* about our personality's daily activities. This it does for the purpose of making clear which of its personality's daily activities reflect habit patterns that are in complete harmony with the soul and which are not. Then we, as our personalities, can use our free will either to change ourselves to increase our inner harmony or to ignore these messages, but at least our soul has offered our personality the understanding.

- Part V consists of four brief chapters showing how our perspectives change as we move our personality's consciousness along the spiritual path upward to the higher level of consciousness of our soul. It emphasizes the dramatic differences in *values* between our personality's and our soul's perspectives, while placing them in the context of the Universal Spiritual Picture.

- Appendix A offers more information on spiritual tools created and maintained by the Archangels and Ascended Masters to assist all humans in the process of releasing and replacing disharmonious habit patterns with new habits which are in harmony with our soul.
- Appendix B includes a list of books and other materials recommended by the Archangels and Ascended Masters in our readings, but they cautioned me to state that this is not an all-inclusive list.
- Appendix C provides an abbreviated, eight page version of the Universal Spiritual Picture in case someone needs a review now and then.
- The glossary is included to provide definitions provided by the Archangels and Ascended Masters. Some of these may provide new insights and understandings, in and of themselves, to the interested reader.

This book provides an overview of the Universal Spiritual Picture that lies above our limited, physical world life. This picture is the summarized result of information obtained from hundreds of Cathy's readings and perhaps thousands of my own journalings (accumulated since 1989), not just those quoted in the book. It is a picture that all souls can understand. Overall, it presents a kind of map (as the Archangels and Ascended Masters intended), appropriate for all of humanity, showing each of us how to find our way back to conscious Oneness with God. Again.

Acknowledgments

First of all I wish to express my gratitude to all the Beings of Light in the Hierarchy of God who have assisted me in any and every way to awaken to the Universal Spiritual Picture of the meaning and purpose of human life on Earth. I thank my Higher Self, my Soul, my Divinity Within, my Guardian Angels, my Higher Guides, the Archangels, the Ascended Masters, and all other groups of humankind's evolutionary assistants—truly too numerous to mention.

These Beings of Light not only provided whatever I asked or needed for the souls of the readers of this book but also tutored me along my own spiritual path toward bringing my personality into greater harmony with my soul and with the Spark of God within my soul.

My task was not merely to listen and pass on this higher information, but to use it in my own life. My job was to **use** this higher information to grow and expand to the point where I could speak of its validity from personal (and impersonal) experience. I needed to grow and to progress along the spiritual path to where I could bring my personal experiential understanding—from my soul's perspective and level of consciousness—to the souls of all readers. I was required to grow so that I could first understand for myself and then describe to others the Universal Spiritual Picture of life on Earth and the spiritual path back to conscious Oneness with one's soul and with the Divinity that lives within the soul. It was essential that I provide this understanding from **my own** experiential, pragmatic perspective. I am a **plain ordinary human being** who successfully used this extraordinary, divine information to move along my own spiritual path, to discover my own soul's purpose, and to begin to fulfill that purpose in my lifework in world service. This is important for it shows that the information is useful to all humans. It shows that one need not in any way be special or different to make progress along the spiritual path.

This is why I am so grateful to all the Beings of Light in the Heavenly Realms who are still helping me in any and every way. This is also why it took so long to complete the book (slow learner).

Down here in the third dimension, I also wish to thank two editors—the one in Indiana who has had so many direct experiences with members of the Angelic Realms in her own personal life, but who wishes to remain anonymous—and Ms. Sharon Green, in Colorado, who helped me (tremendously) to refine the final product. Resolving the questions arising from the perspectives and perceptions of these two provided me with one of the greatest challenges I have experienced in this lifetime. However, meeting this challenge has no doubt led to an exponential increase in the clarity of the message for the souls of all readers.

INTRODUCTION

How This Book Came About

Who am I and how dare I voice my understandings and knowings about such esoteric spiritual matters as are included in this book?

I am an ordinary guy named Bill, with an ordinary wife named Cathy. I have had a consuming interest in spiritual matters and spiritual philosophy since we were married in 1968.

Introduced to a book about Edgar Cayce soon after we were married, we read all the Cayce material and all the Ruth Montgomery information and wanted more. We both thought the ability to receive information from the Creative Forces of the Hierarchy of God's minions, from the Angelic Realm, and from the Ascended Masters was possibly the greatest spiritual gift in the world.

Cathy and I pursued our respective spiritual paths for years until in 1989 an unusual thing happened. Cathy read a new book,[1] tried a few of the exercises in it, and learned that she could receive clear information from her Higher Guide, Jacob. The process involved stilling her personality mind, lifting her level of consciousness to the highest plane possible, and opening to receive higher information from the divine dimensions above (through the crown chakra, the brow chakra, the throat chakra, and the heart chakra). That was the beginning of quite a change in our lives that continues today and holds great promise for the future.

Within a few months Cathy's first Higher Guide was replaced by another called Jonathon. About a year later Otheus replaced Jonathon. Otheus stayed around for several years until various Archangels and Ascended Masters began coming into our readings.

---

[1] For a list of books and other materials that were recommended by the Archangels and Ascended Masters in our readings, see Appendix B.

Our questions focused primarily upon spiritual philosophy. We desired to know more about our personal spiritual paths, and we desired to understand all we could learn of the Universal Spiritual Picture from the viewpoint of the Archangels and Ascended Masters in the Hierarchy of God above. Over a twelve-year period, the information and knowledge received in answer to our questions have provided a higher, broader, and more comprehensive understanding of the view from above—of the Universal Spiritual Picture, of the origins of human life on Earth, of the purpose of our life in the physical world, and of the understanding of humankind's way back to conscious Oneness with God.

For the first few years we used and tested the information in our own lives (our spiritual lives and our material lives) and found it to be good, valid, true, and helpful. It was consistently offered to us in a kind, patient, gentle, and loving way.

To say we tested the information is neither sufficiently accurate nor on point. In fact, the idea of testing in the usual third-dimensional sense is a rather shallow concept compared to the truth. In today's world a human personality, using his or her personality's mind, might simply formulate a finite series of questions that he or she believed would present a sufficiently convincing argument to cause other humans to believe, feel, and think the same as the tester intends to "prove." This is superficial and simply will not do the job.

To know, to truly *know*, the truth behind the information, one must experience it in her or his life, and through that experience feel it, understand it, know it to be the truth for her or him at a higher level of consciousness (the soul level of consciousness). A bit of bizarre information first received may seem too far out, too distant from what the personalities of the general public have been taught and conditioned to believe, to be readily assimilated or adopted. However, tentatively using the information in one's own life and finding it to be consistently positive, good, valid, true, and helpful in very pragmatic ways provides the personal evidence needed to encourage further testing. As one uses the information over time and experiences an expansion of consciousness and an increase in inner harmony and peace while moving forward and upward along the spiritual path, he or she grows to know it as good for him- or herself. Individual, long-term experience at the higher-level consciousness of the soul becomes the never-ending test. Cathy's and my testing of the information received from above is of the never-ending, individual, long-term "experiencing" type, and after twelve years there has never been the slightest hint of anything fearful or negative in any reading.

In a reading by Cathy for the purpose of editing this portion of the book, Sananda, the soul name of the one called Jesus, suggested that I might wish to add an incident that early on gave us both confidence that higher information was flowing through.

This is an excerpt from that reading by Cathy received from Sananda (see glossary) on 10/02/99.

The tractor incident is an excellent example for this intuitive reader herself that the information coming through her was coming from a unique and higher source.

Remember to include the fact that as the information was coming through her she was actually being guided to walk through the internal workings of the tractor. Everyone will be able to see that as evidence.

✦ A convincing argument.

Correct. For there is no entity more difficult to convince than the channel herself or himself in these cases, and you may want to include that as well.

The incident to which Sananda alluded occurred only a few months after we each learned the process of stilling our busy personality minds, lifting our level of consciousness to the highest degree possible, and opening to receive higher information from the divine dimensions that exist above our physical world. At that time we lived in Virginia on fifty-six very beautiful, secluded, and heavily wooded acres situated more than a mile from our nearest neighbor. This location provided a great deal of privacy in a beautiful, natural setting. The price for the privacy was in the maintenance of the mile-long dirt road entrance that would wash out after any heavy rainfall. One day, after just such a gully-washing downpour, the tractor that I used to pull a drag box to smooth out and maintain the road suddenly would not start. Cathy did a reading and I asked Jonathan, her guide at the time, why it wouldn't start.

Cathy verbalized what Jonathon was giving her, and from my end it was just a verbal description of his view of different parts of the tractor. He could see no problem with the electrical system or wiring or other parts of the tractor until he came to the fuel system. He then said there seemed to be some sort of gel around the fuel filter at the bottom of the fuel tank. That information in itself was great for me to know, but I'm not much of a mechanic so I also asked if this was a problem that I could repair myself without calling for distant and expensive professional help. He replied that it was indeed something I could do and that I would have no trouble fixing it. He was right. The following day I had no trouble at all removing the twenty-gallon fuel tank, cleaning it in the most environmentally correct way recommended by Jonathon, and replacing it. The fuel tank never gave us a problem again.

After completing the reading, Cathy told me that Jonathon had not only given her the verbal information I had heard, but also had simultaneously taken her along with him on a microcosmic journey through all the parts of the tractor. She could see it all as they moved through the electrical system, through the fuel lines, and into the bottom of the fuel tank where the problem became apparent. She could see it all at the same time she was verbalizing it to me while we were sitting in our living room.

This was definitely information from a higher source related to a mundane physical-world problem. Because it afforded us with irrefutable evidence of the validity of what was received, it was of special importance to both of us. You have no idea of how little understanding Cathy's personality mind had about the inner workings of a diesel tractor, but I certainly did. This incident helped us both to understand that we had a source of information, coming from within and above, that could at the very least bring us true information relating to mundane situations about which neither of us knew anything.

However, tractors in general have never been one of my main interests in life. The questions of greatest interest to me personally (and impersonally) have been those of an esoteric nature relating to:

- the meaning and purpose of life on Earth
- the nature of the higher realms
- the difference in nature between Angels and Ascended Masters
- the nature of the spiritual path and how we can move most swiftly along it
- what is coming in the Golden Age
- and so on.

It is the bringing of this type of information into our own life experience for over twelve years that has been and remains our never-ending, individual, experiential, pragmatic type of testing. This kind and gentle leading has caused us to know it all as good, true, helpful, and coming from a divine source.

We asked the reason for the changes in Higher Guides and the coming in of the Ascended Masters and were told it was caused by progress on our respective spiritual paths.[2] We also asked why Cathy was able to learn to receive information so quickly and easily; we were told that this was due to the experience of her soul in previous lifetimes. According to the information given, she had gained her channeling experience in the days of Atlantis, in Egypt, and in Ancient Greece.

---

[2] Useful here is the Earth School analogy that a Ph.D. is not needed to teach kindergarten students. In the structure and order of the hierarchical heavens above, all Beings of Light are competent to fulfill their respective positions, responsibilities, and missions. Should information suddenly be requested that calls for a higher perspective or a deeper understanding, then a new Higher Guide or Angel may be enlisted. If the

Cathy receives the information from and through her higher self, soul, and Divinity Within (right-brained activity), translates it into English, and speaks it aloud (left-brained activity). The Guardian Angels, Higher Guides, Ascended Masters, Archangels and other appropriate minions of God, bring the information to Cathy's highest self for the higher good of those whose questions are being answered. The primary mission of these Beings of Light, who are part of the Hierarchy of Godness, is to assist humankind in its evolutionary spiritual path back to its original state of conscious Oneness with God, as eternal etheric souls.

While doing a reading, Cathy is in a light trance state, as in meditation. She is always conscious and aware of what is going on around her, even though later she has only a dim recollection of the information that came through her. She describes it as similar to the situation in dream recall where a short time after awakening one may not remember all the content that was readily available immediately upon waking. However, all the readings are recorded on tape so nothing is lost.

Cathy also has the ability to receive information in other ways that are preferred by certain individuals or organizations. She can receive it directly, without a trance, through her intuitional path. In this case she is often aware of Angels and Higher Guides, both hers and her client's, who are present in the environment as she verbalizes. She is also aware, at times, of the presence of deceased relatives who may have messages for the client.

Personal and organizational preferences of this nature signify to me how very little is known today about the dynamics of intuitive reception of information stored in the Akashic records of souls. It also speaks of how little is known about the existence, nature, mission, and purpose of those divine minions of God in the higher realms who have evolved themselves to the ascended state and subsequently volunteered to assist humankind in its evolutionary return to its original and natural state of conscious Oneness with God.[3] However, this information will be more commonly known in the new millennium.

While doing her readings, Cathy is aware that her last Higher Guide Otheus is still nearby even though the sessions we do for ourselves are now attended mostly by Archangels and Ascended Masters: Archangel Michael, Archangel Uriel, Sananda, Saint Germain, Lady Mary, Kuthumi, and Melchizedek. Other Beings of Light may come in depending on the nature of the subject area in which we seek understanding.

---

intentions of those seeking higher information are consistently for a higher purpose and the questions asked are regularly of a higher nature, then again a Higher Guide or Angel of a higher echelon may be enlisted. This is discussed more thoroughly in later chapters.

[3] I have placed some of this information in chapter 13, if you care to skip to it now.

Each of these Beings of Light has its own specialty areas. And yes, they know in advance what area our questions will cover. For example, Athenarious and Thenous made themselves available for the specific purpose of providing information on the universal requirement for and the priceless value of integrating a balance of divine feminine energy into the personal lives of all humanity. Divine feminine energy is their specialty area.

All the information that has come through these Higher Guides, Ascended Masters, and Archangels has been unfailingly magnanimous. These are all divine Beings of Light, many of whom have had the experience of living in physical human bodies and going through the spiritual evolutionary process to Ascension, as did Christ.

Angels and Archangels have never known the experience of being born into physical bodies, of having the veils of consciousness dropped, or of knowing the feeling of conscious separation from God. Through their evolutionary development, those in the angelic realms are able to manifest or materialize temporary bodies whenever needed to carry out a mission to help others, but when they do this they do not take on a lower consciousness.

Other minions of God have all volunteered for their current mission of helping humanity in its evolution back to Oneness with God because of their own personal experience on Earth with the evolutionary birth-death-reincarnation process and their desire to help others evolve toward and achieve Ascension too.

Conducting one of Cathy's sessions with these fifth-dimensional (and higher) Beings of Light affords me the opportunity to have a conscious verbal dialog with them. Since I am fully conscious and generally in the higher conscious state of my higher self, or my soul self, I am able to indicate to these Beings of Light what I can or cannot understand. In the latter case, I can immediately ask additional questions until I comprehend the message or understand the dynamics behind the information given.

In our readings the categories of our questions are not necessarily confined to a single subject. We can ask spontaneous questions on any number of subjects, in any order, at any time. Questions on subjects ranging from the physical health of humans or pet animals, mundane third-dimensional matters, esoteric spiritual philosophy, the meaning of dreams, the content of previous lifetimes, higher realm structure, spiritual dynamics, and the meaning and purpose of life on Earth can all be fully addressed in a single session.

This is all neat stuff to me. For over twelve years I have had the opportunity, through conducting hundreds of Cathy's readings, to have a direct and conscious dialog with Higher Guides, Ascended Masters, Archangels, and other Beings of Light to discover and learn anything I desired to know and understand. It has been most enlightening in every way.

But that's not all!

Immediately after seeing Cathy's excellent results, I tried it too. On the first day that I attempted to call in my Higher Guide (as an exercise to learn his name), I was successful. It took me three separate sessions or attempts that day, but on the third try I clearly received his name, Jason. Apparently Jason has been my Higher Guide for many lifetimes, whenever I have been down here in lesson. Between incarnations, depending on a particular soul's development, it can either choose or be assigned a Higher Guide to help it find its God/Goddess within in its next Earth lifetime. Apparently we tend to stay with a guide who knows us best. Within a year I learned that I had three Higher Guides in addition to my permanent Higher Guide Jason. Their names were Kron, Paramell, and Ashtobar, and their roles were slightly different from those of Jason.

I tried to verbalize my information like Cathy but had poor results. Why? I did not have the past life background experience that she had. I could ask questions (silently) and receive answers internally all right, but when I tried to verbalize the understandings and knowings that came to me, I would immediately refocus my attention on what I was saying and mentally critique it, judging whether that was the best way to express the information I had received. This simply won't work! To receive well, whether one is receiving information directly from her or his higher self, soul, or Spark of God Within, or from other Beings of Light *through* one's higher aspects of self, it is important to stay focused on receiving the incoming information.

Even as a youth I had known I had the ability to "write out" an understanding of any personal problem that was bothering me, from a higher perspective, but I had no knowledge of the nature of this ability. I was aware that my ordinary mind was pretty dumb sometimes, but at other times I had this very wise and knowing part inside. "It" had a much larger vocabulary, a much greater grasp of my problem areas, and a much higher perspective than "I" did. "It" was also much more impersonal and objective in its insights and understandings. I only wished that it had been available whenever I needed it. There were no books describing the different levels of consciousness that exist within each of us on the market back then, so I never thought this ability was anything important. Except for the "writing out" of my personal problems for my own increased understanding I seldom used this ability to my advantage. Now and then it helped me in taking tests and scoring top-notch grades but only when I accidentally happened to be in that zone at the time.

However, now this ability came in handy. I found that I could internally ask silent questions of my higher self, receive the knowing and understanding I desired, and write out the answers without the mental problem of judging the phrasing and changing my focus of attention as I wrote. The Higher Guides and Angels called this "journaling." For me it was and is quite natural and easy to do. I still have thousands of old journaled pages in boxes to remind me of where my focus of interest was in the old days. Looking through them is like going through old dream journals, and it is enlightening at times to realize how long it has been since I received a specific piece of information. The only trouble with journaling is that writing is very slow as opposed to speaking the awareness or understanding that comes to my higher self. Of course, for quick personal answers and understanding there is no need to speak or write; the entire process is silent and internal, there is no need for hardcopy.

As I was going through this entire discovery process I thought, "At last! Now I will be able to do something unique, something that few others can do." But, in one of Cathy's earliest readings, when I asked for verification of my ability to access valid information from my higher aspects in this way, I was told that:

- My understanding was correct.
- I could certainly ask for and receive valid information from my higher self, my soul, and/or my Divinity Within.
- Anyone and everyone on Earth has the innate soul ability to do it too.

Now, ten years later, I know that this ability to ask for and receive information and divine guidance from one's higher self, soul, and Spark of God Within, is simply a natural part of everyone's spiritual, evolutionary path. Oh well, so much for my "unique" ability.

My understanding at this moment is that all so-called psychic abilities of every kind will soon be understood to be very natural and normal for everyone when the new millennium is more fully underway because we will all[4] be living at the higher level of soul consciousness. All psychic skills are simply the innate skills that our souls used before we became involved in physical life. We can regain or reactivate them by stilling our personality's mind and shifting our focus of attention upward to our soul's level of consciousness, which is a higher, finer, more expanded, sensitive, and aware level of consciousness (than that of our personality's mind). This is the evolutionary expansion of consciousness to which the spiritual path will take all humans, if we choose it and persevere.

But back to business. I receive any information or understanding that I focus upon or ask about from or through my higher self, my soul, or the Spark of God that lives within my soul.[5] My Guardian Angels (Philithion, Alphion, Lily, and Anna), my new Higher Guides (Almetron, Bressalus,

---

[4] At least all those who are still around in a physical form.

[5] The higher self at any moment in time may be at any one of these three levels of consciousness. Higher self is a relative term and always refers to the next higher level of consciousness from the point where one's consciousness is at the moment. In other

Gregorious, and good old Jason), and other Beings of Light that I may invite to assist me when I am writing, may and will obtain any information, knowing, or understanding I am seeking (if it is not already in my higher self's repertoire) and present it to my higher self. I journal it from there. Unless I make a point of asking which of these Beings of Light brought it to my higher self, I would have no idea, but I am always under the protection of the white light of the Christ Spirit and the violet light of Saint Germain.

The only time any misinformation enters is when I allow my consciousness to slip down to the level of my personality mind as opposed to remaining at the level of my higher self, my soul, or the Spark of God that lies within my soul. This is most likely to happen if one of my loving and faithful dogs would suddenly bite me on my backside, or my loving and faithful wife would ask me to take out the trash in the middle of a chapter. In such cases (and a few others perhaps) the results are immediately noticeable and those Beings of Light who have a vested interest in this book are very (divinely) honest about telling me of such instances and helping me to correct them.

I am very interested in the validity and helpfulness of this information. However, one of the most painful and difficult lessons I have learned since beginning this book is that it is not possible to achieve perfection in such an offering. Part of the difficulty stems from the requirement of using a limited vocabulary of man-made words (created to describe physical world things) while attempting to describe the dynamics of an etheric or spiritual nature.

But a larger part of the problem is that I had long held a personal desire for perfection and a personal belief that it would be possible to make the words perfectly understandable to all readers. Toward this end I continued to ask questions of the Archangels and Ascended Masters relating to the fine-tuning of certain parts of what I had already written. However, after spending uncountable hundreds of hours on this effort, which amounted to months and years of calendar time, I finally gave up. I finally surrendered to the feeling experience that it now no longer seemed possible to accomplish perfection, and that even if it were possible it would not be worth the effort or the time because the resulting changes had proven over time to be so subtle or insignificant that very little was gained in what I wanted to describe to the world. I finally understood that I was spending a thousand dollars for a ten-cent item that really wasn't needed in the first place.

---

words one always looks "up" internally for guidance or information, from whatever level of consciousness she or he may be in. The three levels of human consciousness, personality, soul, and the Divine Spark of God that lives within the soul, are discussed more thoroughly in part II.

In frustration I finally asked the question in another reading.

This is an excerpt from a reading by Cathy, on the subject of editing, received from Saint Germain on 02/12/2000.

✦ Are there any more efficient ways to edit this book?

There are two aspects to this. One is that you will be given anything that you ask, and the other is that you must look at why you ask as much as you do. Does this not come from a belief perhaps that you can achieve perfection in offering this up? And indeed we are certain that this has been indicated previously.

You cannot make what you offer perfect in physical terms, in third-dimensional terms, for each reader who will read your book. Each reader will take the information a little differently. The most important thing is to have the book so filled with the light and the vibrations, the love and the intensity of the higher planes that as the reader reads he or she will be drawn into an experience of the higher planes, not just of the written word. And so then the document, in its entirety, will be experienced (felt) *by the reader. And whether the words are what you would consider perfect or not, the information that is necessary to open that reader, to bring that reader to the next level of understanding and enlightenment, or to inspire that reader to pursue more, will come through because we and that reader's personal guides will be working in that scenario to make certain that that which is needed is given. If you seek detailed editing in a desire to have greater perfection, you will receive answers and the responses will be correct, but perhaps unnecessary.*

✦ Okay. My second question is, am I to change my way of believing that it must be perfect in the eyes of an Ascended Master?

The book is not being written for the eyes of an Ascended Master. It is being written to facilitate every level of need there is in the entity who is reading, and you can rest assured that that facilitation ***will not*** *come entirely from the printed page. But the printed page will be used as a key, as a catalyst perhaps, so that the individual's guides, and those in the Angelic Realm, and other Ascended Masters will be able to then open the entity more perfectly.*

✦ Thank you. I'll call this a good lesson.

Something that was important for you to experience and to learn because you would not have merely believed the words, but now you see that it is not possible.

✦ It is not possible!

*Correct. But now you **know** that, through your experience and not just through words that were given to you. And so now the issue is solved, resolved.*

This is just one example of how a personally held belief learned from the outer world can cause more trouble on the spiritual path than it was ever worth.

This is my first large effort toward the fulfillment of my soul's mission, contract, or purpose. It turns out that my soul's purpose in this life is first to awaken to the Universal Spiritual Picture, to choose the spiritual path for myself, and then to help others to help themselves back to Oneness with God. More specifically it is to begin by making this information, received from above through Cathy or myself, available in this book to anyone who desires it. It is the beginning of my lifework in world service. (Actually though, the Ascended Masters have told me that any work that anyone does on their spiritual path is the beginning of the fulfillment of their soul's purpose and the beginning of their lifework in world service.)

I have included excerpts from Cathy's readings of the Archangels and Ascended Masters wherever I felt they were appropriate and effective for the subject at hand. These are set apart from my own journalings as you can see immediately below. My journaling includes all relevant knowledge assimilated from the hundreds of Cathy's sessions obtained over a twelve-year period, plus information provided by or through my higher self, soul self, or Spark of God Within, my own Guardian Angels and Higher Guides, and the Archangels, Ascended Masters, and other Beings of Light who have had a special interest in co-creating this book. For the first five or six years these sessions were focused largely on questions I had about my own personal spiritual path. Then I began to receive nudges from within and above indicating that this information might be of value and interest to others.

There is one more important point. In answer to my questions I was told to target this book to the souls of the readers who would be drawn to it, not to their egos or personalities. This I have done to the best of my ability.

This is an excerpt from a reading by Cathy, on miscellaneous subjects, received from Saint Germain on 01/18/99.

✦ Okay. To address that to the ordinary human—.

*You need to recognize here that that which you are writing is not addressed to the mental body of the ordinary human. Rather it is put forth to allow the **soul** of each entity to have greater input, to make greater contact, to have* *greater influence, and the greater opening; and so what you write is that which would touch the* ***soul****, that which would allow an opening in the consciousness, for if there is the question, "Can this be true?" then the* ***soul*** *has that opening, that opportunity to move in to whatever degree, small or large, and make itself known. If you think that you can teach merely the personality or the ego, then that perspective does not serve you for it is not accurate.*

To take that which you offer, that which is offered through you, for the path of spiritual development and to ask an ego to embrace it, is to ask the impossible, to ask that which will never occur. For the ego, no matter whose it is, strives valiantly to keep the entity away from the desire to move forward on the spiritual path. It is driven by fear to maintain control.

What you really offer is an opportunity to experience something different, to experience peace and harmony; and believe me the souls of the entities incarnated on your planet today by and large are very restless and are making themselves known in ways that are not comfortable to the consciousness, to the egos of the entities with whom they are connected.

✦ I see.

And it is this restlessness of the soul that you serve. It is the soul itself that you serve. It is not the ego. A part of the plan of the ego is to maintain a level of inner turmoil. Enough to keep an entity uncomfortable, enough to keep an entity believing that there must be fear, that there must be strife, that there are those things that must be resisted and fought against and that the ego is the strength. This is the picture that the ego (personality) *offers.* ***It*** *is the strength.* ***It*** *is the "savior."*

The ego is closely connected to the mental body. Indeed it has great control, often, over the mental body and uses it to its own ends. The ego walks a tightrope, for if it pushes the entity into a sense of turmoil too great, then the entity will feel and experience being overwhelmed; and it is in this state of experiencing "overwhelmedness" that the entity will seek the God Within, seek the spiritual, for it feels that it cannot fight successfully any longer. And it is at this point of surrender, and often it is fleeting, but it is at the point of surrender that there is the great need for those objects such as your book, such as visitations from the Angelic Realm or from spirits who are deceased and who are greatly concerned for the entity. It is at this time that these activities can be of service.

Often the restlessness of the soul comes slowly, as a wearing down, and there are the flashes of desire for more. And when that desire is experienced then the teacher must be there; and if the teacher is there in the presence, or in the form of a book that is offered, that is given, then there is the great assistance. Do not write for the ego. Do not ever think that you are writing to convince or to bypass an ego.

✦ Then need not the ego understand before any movement can be made?

If making the ego understand, bringing the ego to awareness, were the only path to bringing an entity to spiritual development, this experiment, this grand experiment, would have long since failed.[6]

One of the most noticeable differences between the soul and the personality (or ego) is the soul's ability to experience higher, more divine emotions (feelings of an extremely profound nature and a very high vibrational level). The soul can experience divine love, unconditional love.

The personality's basic mode of operation in today's world is that of thinking with the busy, left-brained, logical mind (as opposed to Being and feeling). This means that the average personality has no good way to grasp, to experience, or to understand the divine feelings relating to the innate need in every incarnated soul to receive and transmit (and therefore to experience) the unconditional love of God that it knew before the fall. The personality mind has no true way to understand the innate soul-need to receive divine unconditional love in order to achieve an inner sense of completion, fulfillment, wholeness, and joy. Instead, the personality, extremely outer world oriented, seeks to find unconditional love from other physical world humans (who are also living at their personality level of consciousness) where it cannot be found.

The soul, however, does have an expanded, experiential, and intuitive understanding of the need for receiving and transmitting unconditional love and all the divine feelings associated with it. This understanding comes from the soul's experience before it became involved in physical life forms. Our eternal soul already knows the beautiful and exquisite feelings of receiving and transmitting unconditional, unselfish love from its own past experience in harmony and Oneness with God and with the other minions of God in its original, natural soul state. It is the faint memory of our soul's previous divine feelings that provides all of humanity with the motivation to seek to find them again. When we have become totally disillusioned in our uncountable attempts to find divinity in the third-dimensional, outer world around us, we are then ready to seek within by creating harmony and conscious Oneness among our personality, our soul, and our Spark of God Within our soul. The point here is: it is through your heart, your soul's feeling center that your soul will respond to this information, if it is ready.

---

[6] The word experiment is explained in chapter 1, How It All Began.

If while you are reading this you happen to feel a very high, loving vibration in the region near your heart, it may be your soul responding in a positive way to what it knows is the truth behind this information. Any such inner feeling of this information ringing true to your higher aspects may be an indication that you are now ready to awaken to a conscious understanding and awareness of the Universal Spiritual Picture that lies behind and above our human, third-dimensional, physical world existence.

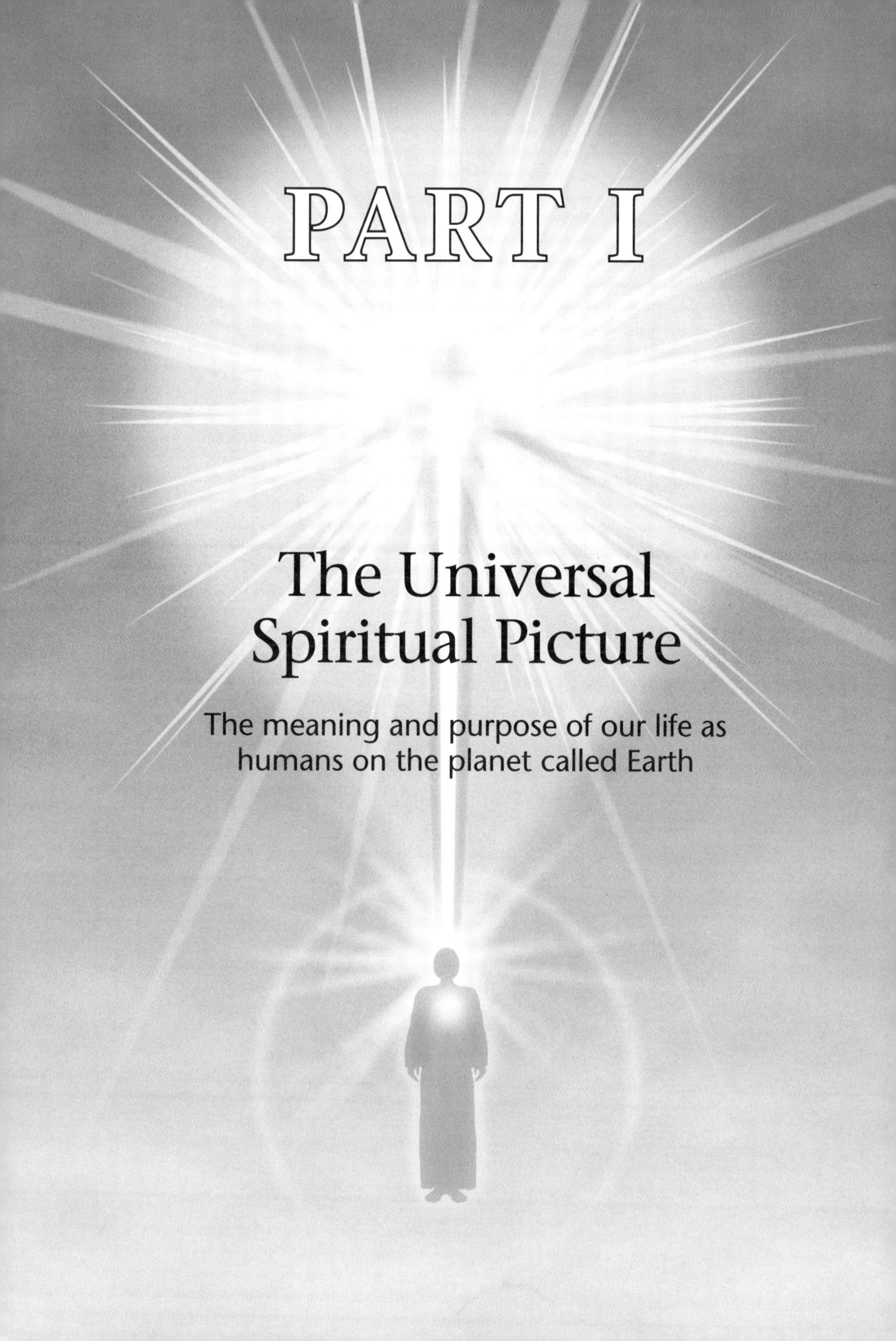

PART I

The Universal Spiritual Picture

The meaning and purpose of our life as humans on the planet called Earth

CHAPTER 1

How It All Began

Creation of the Earth School

In the beginning there was only **God**, the All That Is. God was spirit; God was everywhere, in all Galaxies and all Universes within the entire Cosmos, not just planet Earth. God was everything. There was only God.

Excerpt from a **reading** by Cathy, on the subject of the original creation, from Archangel Michael on 04/28/01.

All of creation occurred in the days of creation as described in the Bible, as you call it. All came before the individuation of souls. The individuation of souls was the last part of the creative acts of the Deity.

The Earth as a planet existed, had been created, before the individuation of souls, before the Deity individuated itself into multiple souls. And the Earth contained the vegetable, the mineral, and the animal kingdoms as well. All of creation had already occurred, and not just on the Earth, understand?

✦ Yes. So individuated souls were the last of the major creations.

Correct, because what occurred is that the Deity created all of this and still found it unsatisfying. Still found it not to be enough.

✦ Ohhhh!

Because it had no companionship!

✦ No Beings of like mind, like hearts, and so forth.

Correct. And then the individuation of souls came about so there could be companionship. Perhaps the ideal is to explain that after the Deity completed creation, It was still not satisfied, and so chose to individuate souls. That allows everything to be in place.

✦ Yes, it does. Thank you.

God's creation of all souls, placing in each a divine spark of Itself and providing each of us with the gift of free will to experience life as we choose

For the purpose of companionship, God created souls. Because there was only God, God created all souls from God's Beingness so all souls, yours, mine, and everyone's, have a divine **Spark of God**, of **Godness**, of **Goddessness**, of **Absolute Goodness** at the center of their beings. All souls were perfect. All souls knew themselves each to be a part of God. All were completely aware of the Spark of God within them and lived in perfect harmony with that Divinity Within. All were aware of their individual connection to God and also to all other minions of God. All souls were etheric, spiritual, not having physical bodies. They were complete and whole in their bodies of Light.

At the time of individuation, God gave all souls free will. Many of those who were given free will so loved the blissful etheric experience of their conscious Oneness with God in their bodies of Light that they chose to remain always attuned to God. They chose to remain always in harmony with their inner divine guidance and always consciously aware of being parts of God. To them, God was and still is the source of all they desire or need. All the divine light (knowledge and information) and all the divine love (complete, unconditional emotional fulfillment) they desire are available to them simply by extending their love to God and then opening to receive it back. Higher frequencies of vibratory senses, together with feelings of bliss and ecstasy far above what we humans can presently experience, are available to them at all times. Souls who live in harmony with the Spark of God within them resonate with the eternal, fully mutual, reciprocated, and unconditional love of God.

Some souls, choosing to play with their new creative powers, inhabited existing animal bodies to experience what physical life might be like, how it would feel to be physical

However, some of the etheric souls who were given the gift of free will to experience life as they chose, in their zest to experience more and more of life, began to insert themselves into the physical animal forms that already existed on the planet we now call Earth. At first this experimenting with physical life was just a temporary experience, a temporary sensation, a jumping in and out of animal bodies to see how physical life felt.[1] It was as if these souls were playing a harmless new game.

Nevertheless, some souls inhabited the bodies too long, and after a while personal attachments to the bodies developed and animal habit patterns grew. It became more and more difficult to remember how to return to being their eternal, etheric, divine soul selves again.

As these souls continued to focus on the obvious sensations of physical existence, they gradually became less and less consciously aware of being etheric spiritual souls attached temporarily to physical bodies. This decrease in awareness continued until finally they lost *all* conscious awareness of being souls, of having a direct connection to God, and of how to return to their original state.

> *In time, souls who had playfully inhabited existing physical bodies became totally entrapped in the lower consciousness of those physical bodies, with no awareness either of their entrapment or of their way back*

As they lost awareness of their true identities, these souls began to identify with, to see, to feel, and to believe themselves to *be*, the physical bodies they now inhabited. With the loss of all conscious awareness of having any connection to God, these souls began to believe that the body and its **personality** or **ego**, were the true self and the only self.

Excerpt from a reading by Cathy, on the subject of the original creation, from Archangel Michael on 04/28/01.

When the animals were created, they were created with group souls. The connection of the animal life-form to the Hierarchy, to the higher realms, was a group soul. And when the individuated souls created life-forms, the same

---

[1] If you object to the term animal being used to describe our physical bodies and their personalities, please consider that there are only three generally recognized categories of physical existence, animal, vegetable, and mineral. However, for the purposes of this book, we humans are distinguished from true animals and we now have our own human evolutionary spiral. It was God's creation of involution and evolution that separated humans from true animal life and provided us with our own way out of the entrapment. Wherever I use the term animal, I do so to make a clear distinction between our current false identity as a physical body (with its personality mind) and our true identity as a soul, which has much higher consciousness and a body of Light. See Appendix C for more detail.

connection was true. In other words, there was no such thing as creating an animal in the Earth plane that was connected to nothing in the heavens.

The Difference Between True Animals and Humans

The playful activities of some of the newly individuated souls had caused their entrapment in the bodies of existing true animals. However, the existing animal life had a much lower level of consciousness than that of the individuated souls in their bodies of Light with their direct connection to God.

True animals are created with group souls. For example, the group of all beavers shares one "beaver" soul. The group of all elk shares a common "elk" soul. True animals do not have individuated souls.

By inhabiting existing animal life to the point of becoming consciously entrapped, these individuated souls had not only lowered their level of consciousness, they had also created a new form of animal life—animals with *individuated souls*. Prior to the entrapment there were only animals with group souls. This is the main difference between true animals and humans.

Later in Earth time, when the Hierarchy of God's minions saw the hopelessness of the situation, they designed and created a way out. They created a new type of evolutionary cycle for the entrapped souls that was very different from the evolutionary cycle of the existing true animals. It was God's creation of a new path of involution and evolution that clearly separated humans from true animals. Our new evolutionary path provided us with a way to spiritualize our bodies (and personalities) and return to life as individuated souls in conscious Oneness with God.

The Ways of True Animals

With their new perception of themselves as physical beings, entrapped souls began to learn from the outer world what the existing true animals already knew—animal ways. In general, true animal ways are quite fearful, selfish, self-centered, and parochial. Survival of the mortal body is key in the animal world. True animals focus *all* their attention upon the external environment to avoid danger. They learn from their experience in the outer world. They learn from other animals. They are taught by other animals.

Through their intuitional connection to the group soul of their particular species, animals may be told to gather nuts for the winter, to find a quiet hiding place in which to hibernate, to go south because it will soon be too cold to live, or to be aware that a human, perhaps a hunter, is coming near. These are things they need to know in order to survive in the physical **dimension** of Earth.

However, following intuitional guidance to gather nuts, true animals will gather yours, mine, or any others they may find. Do they have an understanding of the more divine concepts of creating abundance and sharing? No, they are quite beyond or beneath the idea of unselfishness. They are at the evolutionary state of knowing what is necessary for survival of their mortal life, and that's it. The evolutionary path for true animals is far different from that of entrapped, eternal souls.

True animals are not concerned with the concept of a higher good or how their actions may affect the lives of others. Bigger, stronger, faster, and more aggressive animals tend to kill smaller, weaker, slower, and gentler ones, and eat them to stay alive. And these were just some of the things these early humans began learning from their outer world environment as a result of identifying with their new physical bodies rather than with their souls.

Entrapped souls, no longer having an awareness of being parts of God, developed 'human' personalities (or egos) using the physical body's brain mind

The early entrapped souls began to learn to think with their new physical body's brain, the personality mind of the mortal body to which they had attached, rather than using the higher soul mind with which they were once familiar while in their souls' higher etheric state. Previously, the soul's higher mind had allowed each soul to receive divine intuitional guidance, divine knowledge, and divine love at all times and in all circumstances, but now they had even lost conscious awareness of being souls. Losing this awareness cut them off from all divine guidance including how to get out of this situation. This is the essence of the catch-22 entrapment and/or the fall in consciousness of some of the individuated souls created by God.

Entrapped souls learned to feel fear for the first time because they now identified with their physical bodies (which they soon learned were mortal, grew old, and died) as opposed to identifying with their souls (which they once knew were etheric, eternal, and could never die). It is easy to be fearless when you know you cannot die.

These new humans also learned to develop *personal* feelings, thoughts, attitudes, beliefs, and actions (through the evolution of their physical body's new personality mind). These personal ways were based upon what they learned from their outer world environment, pertinent to survival in their particular part of the world.[2]

---

[2] In their previous natural divine state, these soul's feelings consisted of an impersonal, unconditional love for all life. Their thoughts were for the higher good of all life, and the desires of their higher wills were to carry out whatever actions and missions were beneficial to all life.

The personalities of humans, reared in different types of environments, different climates, or under different immediate personal circumstances, learned unique sets of survival habits. Different types of habitual feelings, thoughts, attitudes, beliefs, and actions became "natural" or "unconscious" to them. They therefore developed quite different personalities, for these things now were all learned from the outer world. These behavioral patterns were learned from other humans who had their own conditioned biases and favorite ways of doing things. In the third-dimensional, physical world, all such learning and conditioning came from the outer world environment as opposed to receiving divine intuitive guidance and unlimited true information from their Sparks of God Within as they formerly did as souls in conscious Oneness with God.

Total Entrapment

So it is that we souls (who had temporarily attached ourselves to the bodies of existing physical beings of our own playful, free will choice) gradually became totally involved in physical, third-dimensional existence. In doing so we had unintentionally moved our consciousness from that of our higher, divine, soul mind down into our lower vibrational, third-dimensional, physical body's *personality consciousness.* As personalities we became totally engrossed in the outer world physical aspects of life until we lost all conscious awareness of ever having been souls consciously connected to God. We stayed too long in our play. We reached the point of not knowing who we were or why we were here. We no longer felt One with God, and we had lost awareness of how to return to conscious Oneness with God.

This was *not* part of God's original plan!

The original plan was simply to create souls, to give those souls their free will, and to allow them to experience life as they chose while remaining in harmony with God. Because we were given free will, this unfortunate situation was known to be a possibility, but it was not a part of God's plan for companionship.[3] Thankfully, not all souls chose this path.

God's subsequent design of the Earth School, with involution and evolution, provided a way back to conscious Oneness with God

Seeing the sad state of affairs in which we playful souls had unintentionally entrapped ourselves, God (the upper echelons of the **Hierarchy of God**), in order to make the best of the situation, formulated a plan, a way out, for us. God, and the many minions of God who remained in Oneness

[3] Self-centered personalities make much less desirable companions than divine souls.

with God, designed and created a way that would enable entrapped souls to extricate themselves from the physical world's personality state of feeling consciously separated from God. The newly created way would allow all humans to move back to our original blissful and natural state of conscious Oneness with God as divine souls again.[4]

The way out of our conscious entrapment required God's creation of the cycles of involution and evolution placed within an educational environment (the Earth School) that would allow us humans eventually to learn, through our own free will and personal experiences, whether we prefer a life with third-dimensional self-centeredness or a life that is divine.

Involution is the path of increasing involvement and attachment to all aspects of the material, physical life with which we humans choose to experiment. Evolution is the path of awakening to the larger Universal Spiritual Picture followed by the ever-decreasing attachment to outer world life and the increasing involvement with our inner world spiritual growth back toward conscious Oneness with God.

A reading to validate the above description of creation, and the meaning and purpose of human life

---

This is an excerpt from a reading by Cathy from Saint Germain on 10/25/98, which begins with the usual greeting.

Welcome beloved and blessings be upon you. This is St. Germain.

✦ I have questions to help me with what I have already described in the first part of the book and I am looking for corrections, additions, or anything else that I may have omitted which from your perspective would be beneficial for others to have and to read. Is that okay?

That is excellent.

✦ In describing involution as souls choosing to become part of existing physical animal life to a greater and greater degree and then finding themselves entrapped in the physical body and consciously feeling separated from God, losing awareness of their true nature and

[4] The emphasis here is on the fact that while it is true that these entrapped souls chose of their own free will to play with their creative powers in this way, it is also true that they were *not aware of any long-term negative effects of their playful actions.* Their fall in consciousness was quite unintentional. They really intended no permanent harm to anyone, including themselves.

character as divine beings, can you and will you tell me what I am leaving out that you feel would be beneficial to add?

Be certain that it is clear that this was a ***natural*** *process.*

✦ Oh! It doesn't seem very natural.

Well it was quite a natural process for the souls who became involved.

✦ But they were aware that they were doing it, that they were—

Not entirely. You must understand that they were aware that they were ***playing****. Perhaps that they were enjoying a new experience, a new challenge, that they were having great sport, if you will. And the game went too far for they became so involved and they stayed so long in the denser vibratory rate that they lost consciousness. At first they did not lose total awareness, but they lost awareness of how to return, how to be free. And after time they lost all awareness of their connection* (to God).

Truly it was the desire to exercise their own creative natures as they began to create beings that were part animal and part man. And their consciousness became trapped because their focus of attention became so long and fully directed toward the denser vibrations.

✦ Was the primary attraction that held them sex, sexual ecstasy?

The experience of the ***physical****. Eating physical food.*

✦ That too!

Indeed! Indeed! Everything that had to do with being involved in a third-dimensional body, in being physical, was new and different and attractive.

✦ Okay. Well, I tell you what, that almost answers my next question.

Well, you may wish to offer it and see if there is something additional.

✦ Okay. Does anyone know, at the level of Archangels or Ascended Masters or anything near there (those levels of higher consciousness, those levels of higher frequencies of vibration), whether this "fall" was part of God's original plan to expand Godness into all dimensions or was it made part of the plan only after the fall. In other words, was the fall itself a surprise? From the terms you just used it doesn't really sound like it would have been much of a surprise, given that souls were given free will.

In actuality the goal, the primary impetus was to give souls free will and have them return to the Godhead of their own free will and have them return with experiences that could not be attained if they were not given free will. In other words, there was the desire for them to become aware of their power, their ability to create and to know themselves. So indeed it was not a surprise, but neither was it the plan!

✦ Ahhh! I see!

The plan of ***involution and evolution*** *was created as the way of escape, was that which was devised when it became clear that there were those who were so trapped that they could not release themselves. And so the plan of involution and evolution was devised as a path, as a method of returning. It did not exist in the beginning.*

✦ It was not a milepost on a schedule, on a development schedule.

Correct! The giving of free will took away all ability, perhaps all clarity, in knowing what would occur or how it would occur.

✦ And is there an explanation or an understanding of why God chose to divide "Itself" in that way?

In order to have companionship! And companionship with those who chose, who had the opportunity to choose, to be One with the Father, One with the Creator.

This reading shows how very interested the Ascended Masters are in conveying to us that this entire process is *not* to be seen by us humans in any sort of a negative light, but rather as a natural, playful scenario that unintentionally led us into a catch-22 dilemma. It was perhaps analogous to a child playing in an abandoned farmyard, having great fun, but accidentally falling into an open dry well. God's resolution of the dilemma, from which there was at that moment no probability of escape, involved choosing to create an educational school environment for entrapped souls.

God's further design and creation of the Earth School as an educational environment that provides us humans with a path back, a method of returning to conscious Oneness with God

For the purposes of this book, let us say that the planet Earth was selected as the location for the new school. In addition to the processes of involution and evolution, Universal Laws and other new systems and features (i.e., free will, reincarnation, karma, et cetera) were designed and included as part of the Earth School environment. Together these would provide the necessary dynamics that would allow each of us humans to experience all that physical life has to offer.

In the involutionary portion of this designed environment, we students would be able to become continually more totally involved with, and focused upon, all aspects of our outer world earthly environment. Involution would allow for humankind to search for, to experiment with, and to experience personally, lifetime after lifetime, every possible outer world way of finding *lasting* unconditional love, inner joy, fulfillment, and meaning in life here in the Earth School (where it does not exist at our current level of consciousness). Some obvious experimental attempts today may include the seeking of fame, glory, riches, alcohol, drugs, sex, and other time-killing hobbies.

The Earth School environment would allow humankind to move through various degrees of involution searching vainly for a source of unconditional love, lasting joy, and true inner meaning and fulfillment in our outer world activities, but eventually finding instead that all such attempts are in and of themselves quite disillusioning, meaningless, superficial, and empty. After exhausting our search of *outer* world possibilities, we would then be motivated to awaken to the much greater Universal Spiritual Picture and to begin the search in our *inner* world where our soul and our Spark of God reside. After accumulating sufficient personal evidence to the effect that divine life does not exist in the physical world, we would be more amenable to continuing our search Within!

This is the point that would mark the end of our involutionary journey and the *beginning of our evolutionary* spiritual path.

Evolution would consist of our free will refinement of our body's personality to bring it into harmony with our soul and our Divinity Within. Evolution would consist of the search of our inner world to discover for ourselves which of our personality's outer world habit patterns cause disharmony between our personality and our soul. It would continue with our conscious release of attachments and habit patterns that cause our inner disharmony and our replacement of them with new habit patterns that create harmony among our personality, our soul, and the Spark of God Within. Evolution is the part of the path that leads us to our increasing inner harmony, conscious Oneness with God, and to the ultimate goal of Ascension.

See Figure 1-1 on page 28 for a brief synopsis of the Involution/Evolution cycles of our Earth School.

In addition to involution and evolution, several Universal Laws and other educational systems and features were included that were designed to help us evolve ourselves back to conscious Oneness with God. Together these various elements combine to form an educational Earth School environment in which we fallen[5] souls can eventually find our way back to

---

[5] Fallen in consciousness only. Fallen in the sense of losing conscious awareness of being parts of God; in the sense of identifying with our physical bodies and

conscious Oneness with God, while still having a physical body, if and when we chose to do so.

Each of the Universal Laws and other features, which have the greatest daily impact upon all of us Earth School students, will be addressed briefly in chapters 2 through 9, though there will be some overlap.[6] The redundancy is due to the fact that each seemingly separate educational element impacts upon the *one* purpose of the Earth School. Therefore that purpose, the evolution of humankind back to the higher soul consciousness of harmony and Oneness with God, will be repeated frequently in order to show how each of the separate educational elements relates to it.

All the features designed and included in our Earth School were included for the *one* purpose of helping us to discover who we are, what we are doing down here, and how we can get back to the divine life we all once knew.

The Earth School was created only when it was evident that without assistance from the higher realms of God, there was zero probability that any of us could ever find our way back to conscious Oneness with God. Without God's design and creation of such a school there was no way out, and we entrapped souls would have been lost to God for all of eternity.

See appendix C for a reasonably concise overview of the Universal Spiritual Picture of the creation of all souls, the entrapment of some, and the creation of the cycles of Involution and Evolution in the Earth School as our way out. Appendix C omits discussion of the other educational features of the Earth School included in chapters 2 through 9.

---

personalities rather than with our souls; in the sense of feeling separated from God and not knowing how to find our way back to our feelings of true Oneness. Not fallen from the unconditional love of God.

[6] The elements I have included are those that seem to me to have the greatest general impact on our daily human lives and therefore seem to be the most important for the purpose of this book. This is not intended to be an all-inclusive list.

The Earth School Cycles of Involution and Evolution

Higher Dimensions of Divinity
Higher and Finer Frequencies of Vibration

Involution

1. Involution is the path of **increasing** involvement and attachment to physical life on Earth.
2. Entrapped souls identifying with their physical bodies and their personality minds and feeling separated from God.
3. The personalities of entrapped souls following the path of **increasing** involvement with and **increasing** attachment to earthly things, earthly ways, and to all that the outer world physical life has to offer.
4. Personalities seeking and experimenting, for many lifetimes, with all potential ways of finding lasting joy, inner fulfillment, and true meaning in physical life through fame, glory, riches, alcohol, drugs, sex, and other hobbies, but never finding them.
5. When, through many lifetimes of searching in the outer world, the personality of the entrapped soul has tried it **all** and found all outer world activities lacking in unconditional love, joy, and fulfillment, the personality may, in its disappointment and disillusionment, give up the outer world search for a moment. Such a moment allows the soul to make its presence known to the personality.
6. Repeated personal experiences with disillusionment can cause the personality to cease its search for lasting happiness in the outer world and to allow itself, at last, to be influenced by the soul to seek eternal happiness within.
7. When this decision has been made, the student has completed his or her **involution phase** of experience.

Fifth Dimension

Only Positive Energy
Unlimited Light, Unconditional Love, and Divine Will.
Life as a soul with a body of Light in conscious Oneness with God.

Third Dimension

Physical life in a Physical body.
Life as a physical body and its personality.
Life as a personality with habit patterns that create inner disharmony with the soul.
A great deal of negative (self-centered) energy mixed with a little positive energy.

Year 2000

End of Involution

God's creation of all individuated souls with free will. Some souls playing with physical world life and becoming entrapped in it. God's creation of the Earth School's cycles of involution and evolution as the way out for all souls who inadvertently became entrapped in lower consciousness physical bodies in the third dimension.

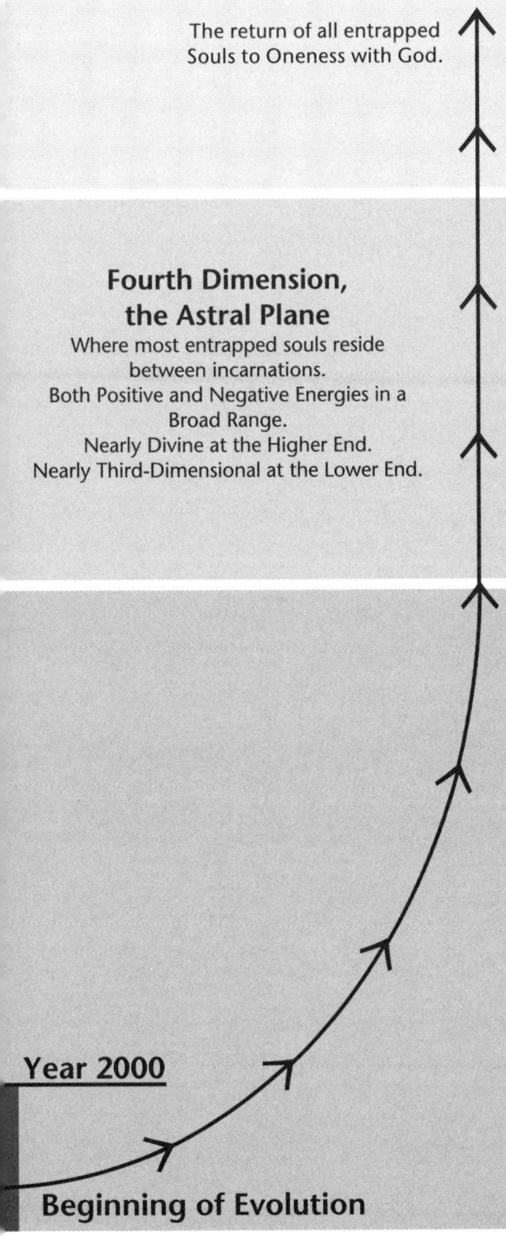

Evolution

Ascension: Spiritual evolution continues after one's ascension.

13. When the soul has refined or spiritualized its personality and itself to a certain degree of harmony with the Divinity Within, it Ascends to a higher dimension (the fifth) and frees itself from the wheel of physical life on Earth, from incarnation, birth, death, and Karma. Such a soul has brought its Godness, Goddessness, and Divinity into the third-dimensional, physical world where it hadn't been before. Ascension is the culmination of an incarnated soul's spiritual path.
12. Increased inner harmony among our personality, our soul, and our Divinity Within automatically moves our consciousness upward from the level of our personality's mind to the level of our soul's mind. This achieves a degree of higher conscious Oneness with our Divinity Within and permits us to receive divine intuitive guidance and higher information from and through our Divinity Within while carrying out our daily activities. It also achieves a higher degree of awareness and Oneness with all other aspects and minions of God everywhere in the Universe.
11. Increased inner harmony is accomplished through the releasing of all negative, third-dimensional habit patterns, which cause **disharmony** with the soul and Divinity Within and the replacement of these with new habit patterns that create increased **harmony** within. Habit patterns here include any feelings, thoughts, attitudes, beliefs, and actions that our personality may have adopted as unconscious habits from its outer world training.
10. The spiritual path is the path of refining the outer world personality to bring it into harmony with the soul and the Goddess/God Within.
9. The soul attempts to awaken its personality to the soul's presence and to influence it to choose the spiritual path back to Oneness with God as the way to find lasting joy, meaning, and purpose while still having a physical body here on Earth.
8. Evolution is the path of **decreasing** attachment to third-dimensional, physical life on Earth.

CHAPTER 2

Understanding the Universal Law of Free Will

Clearing Away the Mystery of Why God Allows Certain Things to Happen

Why We Have Free Will

A recap of the background reasons why free will is an absolute necessity in the Earth School

The Universal Law of Free Will is one of the most basic and important of all the features built into the Earth School system for humans to understand. At the time of the creation of souls, of individuation, God gave all souls free will. God originally created all souls for companionship, but God desires companionship only with souls who of their own free will desire companionship with God.

As souls, we playfully and unintentionally entrapped ourselves in the lower consciousness of physical life long ago. Unintentional or not, we did so using the free will that God gave us at the creation of our individuated souls. God and God's minions, seeing that we entrapped souls had inadvertently moved ourselves into a consciousness so low that there was literally no possibility for us ever to find our way back on our own, designed and created the Earth School to provide us with a path back.

We have free will in the Earth School environment because God desires companionship only with souls who *of their own free will* desire companionship with God. The sole purpose for God's creation of the Earth School was to provide us (the entrapped souls) with a way to return to conscious Oneness, to companionship with God. Therefore, free will was an *absolute requirement* as a feature of the Earth School.

God and God's minions created the Earth School environment with involution and evolution, free will, reincarnation, karma, et cetera, as our soul's way out and way back to conscious Oneness with God. Without these features, we entrapped souls would be lost to God for all of eternity. However, while the Earth School environment provides us with a way back, it also *absolutely requires* that any humans who wish to be conscious companions with God again find our way back *of our own free will*. The Universal Law of Free Will states that entrapped souls may not be forced or coerced in any way by Beings of Light in the Hierarchy of God, to return to conscious Oneness with God against the entrapped soul's free will.

Other Considerations in the Design of the Earth School

Free will being the most basic and primary feature included in the design of the Earth School environment, the other features (i.e., involution, evolution, reincarnation, Karma, and so on) were added to provide the necessary background dynamics for a way back that was understood to enable any who desired to return.

It was known by God and the Hierarchy of God, the creators of the Earth School, that given the free will to try anything and everything in the third-dimensional environment, over a period of many lifetimes, humanity would eventually evolve and expand in consciousness and awareness to the point where we would become disillusioned with our limited, outer world, third-dimensional life. It was known that as we grew naturally through evolution to a more expanded awareness, we would find it easier to understand the concepts of a (divine) life that includes much more than what the physical, third-dimensional Earth School life could ever offer.

It was known by God and God's minions that we humans, after repeatedly failing in our futile search to find lasting meaning and purpose in our physical world life, would be more amenable, *of our own free will,* to seeking it in the world *within,* which is the home of our true identity, our higher conscious soul, and the Spark of God that lies within our soul, connecting us to God, the All That Is.

These are the reasons that God allows things to happen that our personalities may perceive as negative. God, and all God's minions in the Hierarchy of God, know that over time, given the opportunity to personally experience all physical world activities to whatever extent we wish, we humans will eventually decide, of our own free will, that we prefer to seek a more divine life.

The new millennium is the time when all this has come to fruition. We humans are perceived now to be sufficiently evolved in consciousness to be able to comprehend the Universal Spiritual Picture and to use that understanding to guide ourselves back to conscious Oneness with our God

Within. To this end, understanding the importance of some of the effects of the Law of Free Will is critical to our most efficient return.

The first of the three major effects of the Law of Free Will on humankind—we are permitted to search for fulfillment in any way we choose

The first effect of free will, as prematurely described above, is very broad, general, and easy to understand. Everyone has experienced it. The first effect is that in our current state of identifying with our physical body and its personality rather than with our soul, God and God's minions permit us to try anything we wish in our search to find lasting joy, unconditional love, meaning, and fulfillment in our third-dimensional environment (where they do not yet exist).

Due to the Universal Law of Free Will, the Hierarchy of God is not permitted to interfere with our personality's experimentation. Regardless of man-made laws, which are an attempt to control human behavior, we are permitted by the first effect of the Universal Law of Free Will to experiment with anything we wish in our personality's search for divine attributes and qualities in our third-dimensional Earth School lives.[1]

Of course there are Karmic prices to pay for certain types of behavior *against* others, but the fact remains that we humans are permitted to do anything we desire without interference from above.

Background information necessary for a clearer understanding of the second and third effects of the Universal Law of Free Will on humankind's ability to receive divine assistance and information

The second and third effects of the Law of Free Will relate specifically to humankind's ability to ask for and receive general assistance, synchronicity, divine guidance, true information, and other types of divine assistance in our daily activities from the higher realms of God. However, before discussing these two *specific* effects of free will upon humankind, it will be necessary to explain part of the background picture into which they fit. Describing part of the background will take three or four pages, but for a clearer understanding it is necessary to provide at least a partial context into which the second and third effects of free will fit.

---

[1] Have you ever looked at some of the events that take place around the world and asked why God permits such things to happen? The answer is that God created the Earth School with the feature of free will for all humans as a vital part of the way back to companionship with God. All humans have been given free will, and as yet most of us have not harmonized our personality with our soul. Most of us do not yet live lives guided primarily by our Divinity Within. But with the new millennium, the time has come for this to be achieved.

Chapter 1 described very briefly that God and the minions of God in the Hierarchy of God (in the fifth, sixth, and seventh dimensions of consciousness above our physical, third dimension) designed and created the Earth School to include all that was necessary to provide entrapped souls with a way back. Not mentioned however, was that many of God's minions volunteered to make themselves available to assist us humans, individually, on our evolutionary spiritual journey. Also not mentioned was that each and every inhabitant of the planet Earth has the God-given ability to receive divine information. Receiving divine guidance through our natural intuitional path will be the way of the future for all humans who remain on Earth one or two decades into the new millennium.[2]

All Historical Information Is Stored in the Akashic Records

Since the creation of the Earth School for entrapped souls, many types of helpful, true, and divine information have been available from the higher realms of God. This is part of the Earth School's design. To understand how this availability works, one must first understand that all true divine knowledge and all historical information relating to all events, all experiences, all occurrences, and all activities related to *every being on Earth* from the very beginning of time, have been and are continuing to be recorded. All historical information relating to the life of every incarnated entity having an attached individuated soul, has been permanently stored in its eternal soul. This includes all feelings and thoughts related to all incidents and events that have occurred in all the lifetimes of all the personalities to which the eternal soul has been attached. The actual storage space is in the *energy* of the souls of all the beings who were in the vicinity and were personally affected by the activity. This database of information, which has an infinite capacity for details, is sometimes referred to as the Akashic records.

Beings of Light who have permission to assist humans in our spiritual evolution

One must also understand that certain **Angels**, **Archangels**, **Ascended Masters**, and other **Beings of Light** in the higher realms of God have been given permission, within such limitations as adhering to the Universal Law

[2] Chapter 11 in part II has a more complete description of how it is possible for divine information to be made available to all inhabitants of the Earth School and how we can each reactivate the seemingly lost ability to retrieve it. Briefly, this is an innate ability of each of our souls. We have only to create harmony between our personality and our soul for this ability to become a reality in our third-dimensional lives. Creating this harmony is the purpose of the spiritual path for which the Earth School was created.

of Free Will, to provide us (humans) with assistance that may help us on our path back to conscious Oneness with God. In addition to generalized personal assistance, divine guidance and information are available from Beings of Light in the higher, divine dimensions of consciousness above the Earth School.

We Are Not Alone!

One of the neatest parts of the whole Earth School picture is that even though long ago and of our own free will, we inadvertently chose the direction that eventually separated us from conscious Oneness with God, *we are not alone on our inner spiritual journey to return*!

Each of our souls in its disincarnate state, chooses or is assigned at least one **Guardian Angel** and one **Higher Guide** to be with it at all times in its next incarnation on Earth. The mission and purpose of our personal Guardian Angel and Higher Guide is to assist us in every possible way in our spiritual growth back to Oneness with our Spark of God Within. These higher assistants are often old soul companions with whom we have had many previous lifetime experiences and who therefore know us well. We are provided with the assistants who can best help us after we are born into another body and once again lose conscious awareness of who and what we really are and what we're doing down here.

Angels

Briefly, Angels are souls who have never been incarnated in a physical body since creation. They have never been consciously separated nor have they ever felt separated from God, even for an instant. They do not know, as you and I know, just how that feels. They know only the eternal divine feelings of being in harmony and conscious Oneness with God at all times, experiencing, feeling, and transmitting the joy and bliss of unlimited unconditional love as they carry out their soul's missions of assisting humankind in its spiritual evolution back to Oneness with God. Though there are many levels of angelic beings in the vast Angelic Realms of God, those called Angels and Archangels are the two levels most closely connected to the mission of assisting humankind's evolution.

Higher Guides

Higher Guides are souls who *have* previously been incarnated into physical human bodies. These are souls who have already moved along the spiritual path, risen and expanded in consciousness, and evolved to the point of being perfectly competent (as perceived by other Beings of Light in the Hierarchy of God's minions) to help those of us who are still in the unawakened, incarnated state of third-dimensional life, to find our way back to conscious Oneness with God. Because Higher Guides have lived in the third-dimensional experience, they can understand fully how best to help a human who has forgotten his or her true divine nature, character, and direct connection to God. They can remember the experience of living at the human personality level of consciousness focused almost entirely upon outer world things and activities.

The primary mission given to these Guardian Angels and Higher Guides is to assist each of us to find the Spark of God that lies within our individual soul. Their desire is to assist us to the greatest degree possible, in accordance with God's Universal Laws, to grow ourselves back to conscious awareness of our direct, divine connection to God, and of being a part of God. They wish to help us to evolve ourselves bringing our personality into harmony with our soul to the point where we will reawaken our soul's innate abilities to receive any and all information that we ever need or desire, through our feminine intuitional path, from or through our own Spark of God Within.

Higher Guides and Angels (and all other Beings of Light in higher realms of consciousness in the Hierarchy of Godness above) are always consciously connected to God. Therefore, through the Akashic record database, they have divine access to all historical information that has ever existed. In their positions in the Hierarchy of God, in service to God, they are allowed to bring us (the entrapped souls) any information about our spiritual path that would be helpful to our progress on the path or to our daily activities while we are on the path.

However, there are definite rules governing this process. Beings of Light in the heavens above are permitted to bring us higher information *only* in accordance with the Universal Law of Free Will. They are not permitted to force, coerce, or influence us in an unwanted manner to return to conscious Oneness with God. This would be against our entrapped soul's free will. To assure adherence to the Law of Free Will, there are two requirements that we humans must meet if we desire assistance from above.

The second effect of the Law of Free Will on humans who desire heavenly assistance is a requirement for our personal, sincere commitment to the spiritual path

General assistance and higher information are for all humans on Earth, but only *after* we have awakened to the Universal Spiritual Picture and made a conscious commitment to make the spiritual path back to companionship with God *the highest priority in our lives*. If we desire assistance from the higher realms, we must make a personal, sincere, conscious commitment to the spiritual path.

The commitment provides the appropriate beings in the heavens above with our "official" notice that we now sincerely intend to return to Oneness with God. This long-term commitment opens the door of free will to the heavenly realms so that we can then request and receive a higher type of assistance on a moment-to-moment basis as we request it.

This is an excerpt from a reading by Cathy, on free will, received from Saint Germain on 02/12/2000.

✦ Is a commitment required?

Most decidedly a commitment is required. However, it does not necessarily have to occur in the conscious, present lifetime. The commitment might well have been made prior to this incarnation or in a past life experience and be one that carried over.

As the reading indicates, this commitment can last forever. However, when I personally referred to it as a *permanent* commitment I was corrected.

This is an excerpt from a reading by Cathy, on free will, received from Saint Germain on 05/23/2001.

Except that you can always change your mind. You can always un-commit. It rarely happens, but technically it is possible to un-commit. But that too must be a conscious choice.

So, due to the Law of Free Will, if we desire to receive assistance from Beings of Light in the Hierarchy of God we must make a sincere, long-term commitment to the path. But, again due to the ever-present Law of Free Will, we can later, consciously, un-commit.

This commitment to the spiritual path can be made in our own words in our own inner conversation with God in prayer or meditation (if and when we choose to make it). It does not involve any other human being or beings.

At the very moment we make our commitment to the spiritual path, our higher self, our soul, the Spark of God within our soul, our Guardian

Angel(s), and our Higher Guide(s) are immediately aware of it.[3] They also know that they will probably be much busier now than before. All Beings of Light in the higher realms will immediately know of this change in our individual status, and all will be delighted to assist us on our way home (if we ask and then keep the door of free will open to them).

The Guardian Angels and Higher Guides of those who have not yet made a commitment to the spiritual path are limited primarily to bringing us warnings when we put ourselves in dangerous, life-threatening situations (probably to keep us in school if it's not yet our appropriate time to pass over). However, our "official" commitment to the path opens our door of free will to many broader types of divine assistance.

The third effect of the Law of Free Will on humans who desire heavenly assistance is a requirement to ask for it whenever we desire it, as in prayer

The third major effect of free will works in conjunction with our long-term commitment to the path. The commitment must first be in place.

Then, the third effect of the Law of Free Will merely requires us to open the heavenly door of free will, whenever we desire assistance, by requesting it, by asking for it, or by inviting it. This request is very much like prayer. Our request for assistance opens the Universal door of free will *permitting* those in the heavenly realms to respond and help us. Our prayers for help accomplish the same thing. Without such a request, the Law of free Will prohibits the Beings of Light from offering help.

*Why are Beings of Light **not** permitted to bring us information or assistance without our request or invitation*

If Angels, Archangels, Ascended Masters, or Higher Guides were allowed to provide humankind with higher information or general assistance from above without first being invited or asked to do so, our human personalities would, or could, or might take such information or assistance as unwanted influences, directives, commands, coercion, or orders from "God." This would be in direct opposition to and in violation of the Universal Law of Free Will, which makes it clear that if we are to return to conscious Oneness with God, we must choose to do so of our own free will, without even a *hint* of possible coercion or unwanted influence from above.

---

[3] This has been described as a light suddenly coming on in a dark space.

By requiring humans to ask for assistance or information each time we desire it, the Beings of Light in the Hierarchy of God are making it clear to all parties in the heavens above that we humans are *seeking* divine assistance *of our own free will.* The *request itself* opens the door both for *them* to assist us and for *us* to receive their assistance. This condition makes clear to the Universe that these particular Beings of Light are not coercing or unduly influencing us, but rather are only assisting us along our spiritual path *in response to our free will requests,* and in full accordance with the Universal Law of Free Will.

Requesting General Assistance

To ask for general assistance from our own higher self, our soul, or our own Spark of God living within our soul, we may simply and silently invite or call upon them to assist us in our daily activities or along our spiritual path.[4] In addition, if we wish to request general assistance from our Guardian Angel(s) and Higher Guide(s) we have only to ask or invite them to assist us. Still further, if we desire help from specific Archangels, Ascended Masters, or other Beings of Light, we may call upon them by name. On the other hand we may also generalize by daily inviting the "Angelic Realm" to participate in our daily activities. Any and all of these will open the Universal door of free will.

When we silently ask for their generic assistance or invite them to participate in our daily activities, *we are opening our personal door of free will to them.* We are calling them closer to us to assist us in every way. If we ask them for help with a specific situation, project, or emergency, they will immediately focus their assistance on that particular mission.

What kind of help will be offered in response to our request for general assistance? There are three readings in this chapter from Sananda, Saint Germain, and Archangel Michael that should provide the answers.

Requesting Specific Answers to Questions

Asking for specific information to be received through our intuitional path is a bit different from asking for general assistance along the spiritual path.

---

[4] Why is it necessary to address or call upon our own higher self, soul, and our Spark of God Within as though they are higher Beings? Why is it necessary to address and treat them in a manner so similar to the way we would address other Beings of Light when asking for assistance? Because they *are* Beings of Light! Until we have managed to bring our personality into virtual harmony with our soul and our Divinity Within, these higher aspects of ourselves live in bodies of Light at a much higher level of consciousness than the ordinary personality can currently dream of.

To receive information from above, whether from our own soul and Divinity Within or from other aspects of God in the Hierarchy of God, the All That Is, there are certain inner abilities within each of us that must be reawakened.

All such abilities are innate within the souls of *every* human. Our souls have had these abilities since their creation, long before our entrapment in physical bodies. It is only because of our current entrapment and our identification with our lower conscious personality minds that we may not presently have access to our soul's natural intuitive abilities to receive divine guidance. Our soul, at its higher level of consciousness, still has these skills and uses them daily. All we need do, as our personality selves, is to move along the spiritual path. The path itself creates an increasing harmony among our personality, our soul, and our Spark of God Within. When we have created a certain degree of harmony among our personality, our soul, and our Spark of God Within, the information provided to our soul by our request can also be received or known by our now harmonious personality mind. Information specifically requested from other aspects of God, is *always* brought to our Divinity Within. It is then provided to our soul from our Divinity Within. It is our job to harmonize our personality with our soul so that our personality can receive it and put it to good use down here.

To ask for information and understanding relating to a certain area of our lives, we must focus our attention on the area we wish to understand. Of course we must also learn to still our overly busy personality minds and "listen" so that we can receive the answers and information that are given to us. However, that is another issue. There are similar issues relating to what we can do toward becoming excellent receivers of divine guidance and other information, but these will be addressed later, throughout the book.

The point being made in this chapter on free will is that even if we had reawakened and perfected our inner innate soul abilities and were already excellent receivers of divine guidance and higher information, we still would not be able to receive it without opening the door of free will. It is very important to understand that *we* are responsible for opening the door of free will to the higher realms and keeping it open whenever we need help or information.

Asking for General Assistance with a Project That May Involve Other Humans

The spiritual path is a path of soul growth. The entrapped soul is working its way back to Oneness with God by bringing the personality to which it is now attached into harmony with itself and also with the Spark of God that lives within each soul. If we inadvertently ask for assistance in a way that will cause harm to the soul growth of others, we will receive no such help from above. To be most effective to us, our requests for assistance (as in prayer) would include our intention to seek that which is for our own soul's higher good *and* the higher good of all other souls involved (as opposed perhaps to simply asking for something our personality selves might desire).

Our requests are being made to Beings of Light, in service to God, in the Hierarchy of God, whose missions are all related to assisting all of humankind to evolve back to Oneness with God. Such Beings of Light will do *anything* that is in harmony with the Spark of God within their own souls (and therefore also in harmony with God, the All That Is). They will do *nothing* that conflicts with the higher good of the souls of any of the other parties involved. So for the greatest effectiveness, our requests, either for assistance with a specific project or a situation that involves other souls, should make it clear that our desire is for the higher good[5] of the souls of all involved parties.

Angels can bring synchronicity into our lives, but only if we invite them

As Sananda indicates in this next reading, we can receive angelic assistance in the form of synchronicity with various events in our lives simply by inviting the Angelic Realm to participate in our daily activities each morning. In general, this may open the door of free will for the entire day. However, if you have any doubts, invite them again. They won't mind.

What is it that would cause the door we opened in the morning to be closed?

Consider this scenario. We awaken in the morning and invite the Angelic Realm to participate in our daily activities. The door of free will is now open to assistance from the higher realms (i.e., divine intuitive guidance, synchronicity, et cetera). Then we move into our daily activities, whatever they might be.

---

[5] Briefly, the term *higher good* always relates to that which benefits the soul of an entity, as opposed to merely the personality. The personality of an unawakened soul might desire many, many things, which it "personally" believes are very good, but which in truth hinder or block its soul's growth back to Oneness with God. Such personality desires may include more of everything to which the personality has allowed itself to grow attached or addicted. Desires of this kind tend to continue to focus the personality's attention upon the outer world as a source of temporary happiness as opposed to focusing on the inner world. It is in the inner world of the soul where one's Divinity can be found to be the source of true, eternal, unconditional love, joy, meaning, and purpose in life. In this context "lower good" includes personality desires *that hinder soul growth or spiritual growth.* "Higher good" includes personality desires *that are in harmony with the soul and that promote soul growth in self and others.*

If our personality becomes (if we allow our personality to become) *irritated or annoyed* in our outer world interactions, our personality has automatically replaced our decision to open the door of free will to guidance and assistance from above with its new decision to once more take control and be in control. For this reason, opening the door of free will in the morning is not like taking a one-a-day vitamin.

Depending on the way we handle our outer world interactions, we may override our morning invitation and nullify it. In such cases, if we again desire or require assistance, we must open the door of free will with another request or invitation. When in doubt, invite them in again.

This is an excerpt from a reading by Cathy, for validation and editing suggestions, received from Sananda on 10/02/99.

In my editing dialog with Sananda I had just alluded to the point made above that, in general, we are allowed to receive information from the higher realms of God only in response to our questions. This was Sananda's reply.

*And to your **invitation** to them to participate in your life experience.*

✦ And the invitation?

Indeed. You find synchronicity and coincidence, what appears to be coincidence, occurring not always as a result of a question. More often they occur as a result of a commitment to grow and to move along a path guided by the higher self, the Holy Spirit and the Angelic Realm, the Ascended Masters, and other Beings of Light. Synchronicity is available only by invitation. This is why we recommend strongly that all entities who are moving along a spiritual path take the time each morning to invite participation of the Angelic Realms, their Higher Guides, their own higher selves, and their Holy Spirit in their daily activities.

✦ Hmmmmmm.[6]

For through an invitation of that type we are able to participate more freely and more operatively in an entity's life experience. For synchronicity very often does not occur in response to a question, but rather in response to a desire to be a tool, or a channel, or to be guided along a path of highest spiritual development. Do you understand?

---

[6] This was news to me. I was always so happy just to have access to information from the higher realms that I never asked if there were additional forms of assistance available (other than in prayer). Oh well, live and learn.

✦ I certainly do.

And so asking questions is a way to receive information because when a question is asked it certainly invites an answer. But a commitment and a calling upon those in the higher realms are considered to be invitations to us to participate more freely in an entity's life experience.

As an example of how quickly our world is changing in the new millennium, it was only a few years ago (five or six) that it was a requirement to ask questions in a more focused and formal way in order to receive information from one's higher self, soul, Divinity Within, Guardian Angels, Higher Guides, or other Beings of Light in the higher realms of God. Now that situation has been dramatically modified due to the increasing vibratory rate of our planet. It seems to be getting to the point where, having opened the door of free will for the day, we need only to wonder about something and the understanding flows into our consciousness (if we are open to receive it). It is as though our questions, or would-be questions, are picked up earlier now, almost before we have consciously formulated them.

Here is an excerpt from a reading by Cathy from Saint Germain on 02/12/2000 in which the effects of this higher vibrational change are made clear.

✦ Is the invitation to the Angelic Realm to participate in our daily activities more for synchronicity or does it permit angelic help in providing us with information also?

Yes. (An example of higher dimensional humor indicating to me that I asked two questions at one time.)

✦ Both?

Yes. Understand that there are differences due to the increase of the vibratory rate upon the Earth plane at this time. In past times the vibratory rate being less intense, not as high, there was the greater requirement to focus and concentrate and formulate the questions if you will. The answers were more able to move into the consciousness of one who was seeking, and seeking with some focus and intensity.

However, as the vibratory rate of the Earth plane has increased and continues to increase, it becomes easier for that information to be imparted to entities who are perhaps not as focused, who perhaps are not as clear in their formulation of questions. There does need to be a certain focus, but there are times when there will be those entities who suddenly know, or suddenly hear, or perhaps begin to write by hand or with mechanical aid, and information seems to flow through that was not specifically asked. But the openness was there. (The door of free will had previously been opened and remained open.)

✦ Okay. And this is angelic information?

Or information from the higher self, or perhaps from a personal guide.

✦ Oh, okay. Oh, I see. So it's really becoming—.

Much less restrictive. Requiring less rigidity, fewer rules and regulations. It is a much more common occurrence though it is often ignored, passed over, overlooked, not noticed.

So today with the advent of the increased vibrational rate, the optimal way to open the door of free will to the Angelic Realm, to provide us with angelic synchronicity, general types of assistance, and answers to any questions we may have throughout the day, is to invite participation of the Angelic Realms in our daily activities each morning.

It is then our responsibility to keep the door opened by staying attuned. If our personality becomes irritated by its third-dimensional interactions, we lose our attunement and close the door to higher assistance. Then we must open it again if we desire help. This we do merely by extending another invitation to them.

This is an excerpt from a reading by Cathy received from Archangel Michael on 02/20/2000.

Understand that we (of the Angelic Realm) *offer far more than synchronicity into your experience, for we tend to bring you to a consciousness of greater joy and more lightheartedness. It is our way to have flowing harmony and lightheartedness in the consciousness of those with whom we work. It is important perhaps to understand that the increased vibratory rate changes what perhaps appeared to be more formal and structured ways of contacting the higher realms, whoever you choose in the higher realms, to something much less formal. We are far more available. We are closer at hand, shall we say, and there is no need for structure or formality in calling upon us, or upon your higher self, your guides, and those who are in the Hierarchy of the Ascended Masters. Do you understand?*

✦ I'm going to say that I do, because I believe that I do, but that doesn't really mean that that is true.[7]

Let us just say that it is as simple as walking or sitting or driving and saying, "Angels, be with me. Angels, assist me. Angels, help. Angels, be at my side." Anything like this. Even just "Angels," will do in terms of bringing the Angelic Realm more closely into the consciousness, for we are always there, we are always about. And the only reason that we are not always actively present within your consciousness and in your daily activities is because of our respect ***for your free will****. And so any call to us includes us in your free will. Do you understand?*

✦ Okay. Yes.

And we are prepared at any moment to be active in the life experience of any third-dimensional being.

If you ask a question and you have the intent that it be answered by a particular entity, that intent is now sufficient. If you ask a question of your higher self and your intent when you are asking the question is that your higher self will answer it, then that is what will occur. If you call upon the Angelic Realm and you have the intent that you also wish the Ascended Masters that is sufficient. Or you may call directly upon the Ascended Masters. What we are saying here is that it is much freer and more open.

Perhaps for those who are beginning, those who have some questions, it would be well for them to invite all whom they wish. However, keep in mind, and they must know as well, that they may not know whom to invite.

✦ Yes.

And so then they must understand that a general invitation is sufficient.

✦ Okay.

And if they wish to distinguish between the Angelic Realm and Ascended Masters or Higher Guides or higher self or a particular Guardian Angel, then they may do so. It is entirely up to their discretion.

✦ Okay.

---

7 For ten years I had thought the old formal way was just fine. It didn't seem like a hardship to me. I had difficulty adjusting to the idea that we no longer were required to call in specific Beings of Light to assist us. (I personally often call them in because to me they seem like old friends.) Today, once we have opened the door of free will by inviting the generic Angelic Realm and others to help us with our daily activities, our unspoken intentions are sufficient to bring specific Beings of Light to us. And now we receive a broader, more expanded range of help, not just divine information, simply by inviting angelic participation in our daily activities. Neat!

But if they do not perhaps know their Guardian Angel, at the time that they are making the call, then they may call on the entire Angelic Realm or they may just say, "Guardian Angels be with me now." And that will be sufficient.

✦ Okay.

Intent plays a great role. It is not necessary that words be spoken, but often those in the third dimension find that speaking words gives them a greater sense of having acted or having actively invited assistance. You may do so silently; we are quite capable of receiving information in that way. So if you are in a situation where you do not wish to speak out loud, then you may simply think the thought, Angels be with me, or Ascended Masters be with me, or Guardian Angels be with me, or come here, or whatever you wish.

✦ And regardless, the information will come through?

*Correct. So long as the entity has the **belief** that the information will come through, because sometimes the information comes through and it is not heard or experienced by the entity who is calling for it. And often that would be because there is fear or unbelief or something of that order. Not being open, not believing. Not being willing to receive.*

✦ Well, okay. That answers my question. Now I can complete chapter 2.

Excellent. We are delighted to be included in your description of those who are available and helpful and a part of growing along the spiritual path.

✦ I thought it would be helpful for any who still think of receiving divine assistance or information from above as quite a mysterious thing, quite unbelievable, to describe sufficient basics so that they can see, from the higher perspective, some of the elements or dynamics that make it possible. And apparently the dynamics have changed quite a bit in the past few years and will continue to change. I can see how in the new millennium those who still remain here on Earth will find it very easy to be guided by the divinity within their soul.

Correct. And it is our great pleasure to see this occurring. Also it is our great fortune to be among the elements of the higher realms that are more readily accepted and more readily trusted. For even the most structured religions speak of Angels and so many might well be open to beginning their growth, their steps, their search, with Angels.

You can see from these readings that the more formal ways of receiving information that I began with and used for years are no longer necessary. They still work, of course, but they are not essential. The higher vibrational rate now brings those of us still on Earth closer in consciousness to the higher realms. It is no longer required to go into a deep state of meditation, or focus so intently, because the aura of the Earth is now higher in its vibrational rate and therefore has risen closer to that of the higher realms above.

The world is changing quickly and it is becoming much easier now for all of us, *after we have opened the door of free will,* to receive divine guidance, true information, and other types of assistance from the Beings of Light in the Hierarchy of God.

Summary

The three major effects of the Universal Law of Free Will on humankind are a follows:

1. The first effect is merely that we humans have the free will to do or try anything we wish in our search to find lasting joy, unconditional love, meaning, purpose, and fulfillment in our third-dimensional environment (where they do not yet exist). Free will is the reason God allows certain things to happen here on Earth, for these are all lessons that help us or inspire us to find our way back to our divine home.
    a. Because of the Universal Law of Free Will, the Beings of Light in the Hierarchy of God are not permitted to interfere with our personal experimentation.
    b. There are Karmic prices to pay for certain types of behavior *against* others, but the fact remains that we humans are permitted to do anything we desire without interference from above.
2. Assistance from Beings of Light in the Hierarchy of God is available to all humans, but only *after* we have made a sincere, long-term commitment to make the spiritual path back to Oneness with God the highest priority in our lives. Later, if we change our intentions, we can consciously choose to un-commit due to same Law of Free Will that required the commitment in the first place.
3. After making our long-term commitment, we must also request assistance from the Beings of Light in the Hierarchy of God *whenever we desire it.* This is similar to what we do in prayer. Our requests (and prayers) open the door of free will to them, permitting *them* to assist us and allowing *us* to receive assistance.
    a. Beings of Light in the higher realms of God are not permitted to provide assistance or information unless we request it.
    b. We are responsible for opening the door to assistance and for keeping it open.

c. If we inadvertently close the door by allowing our personality to become irritated or annoyed by our third-dimensional interactions, we must open it again by extending another invitation or making another specific request (as in prayer) for assistance.

When we open the door of free will for higher assistance, we are opening ourselves to work with those in the higher realms. We are choosing the quickest, most efficient path back to conscious Oneness with God. In effect, we become team members with those who assist us on the mission of evolving ourselves, creating harmony among our personality, our soul, and our Divinity Within so we can then manifest divinity into the third-dimensional world by fulfilling our soul's purpose, and by helping others to evolve and manifest divinity too.

CHAPTER 3

Reincarnation

The Mortality of the Personality, the Eternal Life of the Soul

A system of many lifetimes was designed and included in the Earth School environment to eliminate the need for time constraints on our evolutionary path. Reincarnation allows each entrapped soul to live as many physical lifetimes as necessary, to experiment with all facets of physical life, and to experience fully any third-dimensional causes and effects it wishes to try until it eventually comes to know that what it really wants is what it already had as a soul—divine Oneness with God. As Earth School students we can flunk as many courses for as many semesters as it takes to awaken finally to the fact that we really want to graduate out of this school into something more divine than is available here. Reincarnation allows a soul the free will to choose when to decide to make the commitment to move along the spiritual path back to Oneness with God.

The Life of an Incarnated Soul

Within this system of many lifetimes a soul can choose to be attached to new baby human bodies as many times as it desires. The soul, eternal and etheric, attaches itself to the body, temporal and physical, at the precise moment when the baby takes its first breath of air and detaches from it when the body stops breathing.

The loss of conscious awareness of being a soul and a part of God usually occurs about four to seven years after the soul attaches to the physical baby body.[1] Prior to age seven, many children are able to see and know things that adults no longer permit themselves to see, such as the child's "invisible" friends. But after just these few years, through the force of external human conditioning and human education, the average human forgets it is a soul, forms what is called a personality or ego, and begins to feel, think, and believe that it is nothing but the mortal body and personality to which it is attached.

As its personality self, it begins to adopt whatever it learns through its outer world teachings and conditionings as truth coming from the highest source it knows, other human personalities. In this state the personality has no understanding that divine truth is available from its own Spark of God Within due to its connection with other Beings of Light in the heavens above. Neither does it understand that what it is learning from its outer world teachings is nothing more than the current, sometimes local, man-made perceptions and beliefs of other human personalities. Few individuals on Earth today have been taught truth as it is perceived from the heavenly dimensions.

During a soul's many lifetimes each new personality creates, adopts, and accepts many personal habit patterns of thinking, feeling and believing, both positive and negative, stemming from and through its outer world learning and conditioning. At the death of the physical body, all such habit patterns (including ways of feeling about certain things, ways of thinking about things, and beliefs and attitudes about the nature of certain things) that were built into the personality in this particular lifetime are stored in the eternal soul.

Simplistically, if the net result of such stored personality habit patterns is positive (more positiveness than negativeness stored), the soul gains ground in its journey back to harmony and Oneness with God; if the net result is negative, it loses.[2] But regardless of net gain or loss, the results, the habit patterns adopted by the personality during each lifetime, are stored in the eternal etheric soul at death.[3]

---

1 This loss of conscious awareness is called by many, the "dropping of the veils of consciousness" between the third and the higher dimensions. We are still connected; we are still souls; we are still part of God, Godness, Goddessness, Goodness and Light. We just don't know it anymore. Our attention has become fixed on physical, third-dimensional, outer world phenomena. We aren't really separated, but we *feel* that way.

2 The terms positive and negative in this context are not intended to be arbitrarily judgmental. By positive I simply mean to indicate any habit patterns that cause greater inner *harmony* among the personality, the soul, and the God/Goddess within the soul. By negative I mean habit patterns that cause greater inner *disharmony* between the three aspects of our beingness.

3 It is because of this that some of us may have phobias that relate to nothing we could possibly have experienced in this lifetime. It is also because of this that we may have

Between incarnations some souls may choose their next type of physical life situation

Knowing this, a somewhat evolved soul that desires to return to Oneness with God is allowed, in its disincarnate state, to design part of its next physical incarnation. It may design into its next life those events or circumstances it perceives to be beneficial to its own eternal higher good. This includes designing experiences it knows will help its next personality to awaken and begin to move into a state of greater harmony with it (the soul) and the Spark of God within the soul.

Upon the death of the body, the soul is first given a review of its activities while on Earth to increase its understanding and awareness of the effects of its latest personality's habit patterns, positive and negative, upon itself and others. After assimilating this review, the soul, depending on its relative position along its path, can then choose or plan the experiences it prefers in its next lifetime. Between physical lives the soul is given classes, schooling, and other experiential forms of education it may need so that it can understand, learn, grow, and expand its conscious awareness more easily in its next incarnation.[4]

The soul learns which third-dimensional lessons it has already experienced, understood, and mastered in physical life, and those which have need of further mastery. The soul is then allowed to choose the kind of life situation it prefers to be born into in its next life on Earth. Many of these choices are made by the soul from its higher perspective between physical lives, and so they might seem quite different from the situations a mortal third-dimensional human personality might choose.

A Soul May Choose Blindness

Here are a couple of simplistic hypothetical examples. A soul, made aware of having a lack of inner vision in the area of introspective skills and/or perhaps a lack of the ability to accept help from others, may choose to experience a lifetime attached to a body that is or becomes blind. If having a blind personality for a semester in the Earth School would bring it a life experience that would create the increased inner vision and trust in the assistance

---

skills and attributes that are seemingly innate, also having nothing to do with our experiences in the current lifetime (i.e., the three-or four-year-old prodigy who plays the piano in a gifted manner without having had lessons).

[4] "Other experiential forms of education" include field trips to other planets, i.e., Venus for love. The point being that when we begin to identify once more as our etheric, spiritual souls we also identify as being extraterrestrial. All Beings of Light are extraterrestrial, which simply means not being limited to the Earth School environment.

of others needed for greater harmony with its Divinity Within, the soul would welcome the experience of blindness.

A Soul May Choose to Be Physically Handicapped

A soul, understanding itself to be overbalanced toward an extroverted focus on external, outer world, physical activities, may choose a lifetime in which it is attached to a body that is born crippled or becomes crippled. If being physically immobilized for part or all of a single lifetime would provide the experience that would create the introspective habit patterns and abilities it knows it needs to grow toward greater balance and harmony with its God Within, the soul would embrace the fact of its body being crippled. So the eternal soul, depending on its evolutionary advancement, is allowed to design its next lifetime in the third dimension in a way that it perceives is best for its own higher good.[5]

The Soul May Choose Its Family

The soul may even choose the family it prefers. It can choose a specific family situation it perceives as most likely to bring the type of experience that it knows it needs, the family situation perceived to best facilitate its growth or progress along the spiritual path.[6] However, after choosing to be born into a certain family situation, if that situation suddenly changes and the soul no longer sees any probability of obtaining the experiences that it knows it needs, it may leave.

If the soul sees the suddenly defunct situation as a lost cause, it may choose to pass over suddenly and wait for a more promising scenario rather than wasting a lifetime in an Earth School class that will bring it no benefit, no progress on the spiritual path it has chosen. Remember that all members of a family have free will. Thus each is able to choose unexpectedly to divorce, to drive recklessly and die suddenly, and to make all sorts of sudden choices which can abruptly change a family situation to one that may no longer be of benefit to the incoming soul. In such cases, the soul of a newborn baby may choose to pass over again and wait for a more beneficial set

---

[5] This information should help many who often ask the generic question, "If there really is a God, how could he allow these things to happen?" God doesn't do these things. God set up the school so that we entrapped souls would be allowed the freedom to evolve our way back. We individual souls *choose* these types of life experiences of our own free will, for our own higher good, or for the higher good of our family members. And we choose all of them, the so-called "accidents" included, I am told.

[6] This information may be put to some good use by those parents who have previously not had an adequate reply to a child's insistence that it didn't ask to be born. The word from above is that as a soul it *did* ask and it just doesn't remember. And *"Just because you don't remember, doesn't make it not true,"* St. Germain 10/10/98.

of circumstances to come along. The same soul may even choose to be born again into the same family at a later time, after the situation has stabilized or changed in a way that it perceives is in harmony with its higher good.

Sudden Infant Death Syndrome

Examples of this sudden passing over may include miscarriage, sudden infant death syndrome (SIDS), or other types of unexpected accidental deaths of very young children. Just remember that such an event (which may seem horrific to an unknowing personality) may have been at the request of the very soul of that infant or child itself, for its own eternal higher good, to avoid a wasted lifetime. Or the soul may have passed over in order to serve the growth needs of family members through their experiencing of the early passing of their child. Because of our limited personality's perspective, we humans may inappropriately blame ourselves for many physical world incidents for which there is no blame from a higher dimensional perspective. Many of these incidents are simply part of the dynamics of a much larger spiritual picture of life of which few of us humans, identifying as only our bodies and our personalities, currently have full conscious awareness.

Obviously it would benefit the mental and emotional state of the personality itself, as well as the personalities of the human relatives and loved ones involved, to awaken and understand these aspects—the dynamics that exist in the higher, larger spiritual life behind and above our physical and material world existence.[7]

Actual progress along the spiritual path can only be accomplished in the third-dimensional physical world

While on the other side, between physical lifetimes, the soul may be more acutely aware of its connection to God and of its true desire to return to conscious Oneness for greater inner peace and happiness, light and love. Its awareness may be higher in nature than that of the average third-dimensional personality mind in today's current state of evolution. However, the fact that the soul is at a higher state of awareness (without the limitation of the personality's brain mind) does not mean it can grow and expand back to Oneness between physical lifetimes. The soul originally chose of its own free will to insert itself into an existing physical animal

[7] These are choices that the *soul* may be permitted to make for its own higher good in order to move more quickly along its path back to Oneness with God. *These soul choices are not related to suicide,* which is *never* beneficial to progress along the path. *"Suicide is a choice of the personality. Suicide cannot be a choice of the soul. It is never a choice of the soul because the soul is fully aware that there is no ending and there is no escaping. Suicide accomplishes nothing!"* An excerpt from Sananda's reading of 10/02/99.

body, which had a non-divine personality. It chose to attach itself to a physical body, which had a much lower level of consciousness, causing its loss of conscious Oneness with God. Therefore, the path back to a conscious awareness of its Oneness with God is through the process of evolving, expanding, and spiritualizing the personality consciousness of its now attached physical third-dimensional body. This process involves bringing its attached personality consciousness into harmony with its soul consciousness and its soul into harmony with the Spark of God Within the soul, all while being in the physical state.

In this way the spiritual path can be seen to be one of simply refining the personality, releasing and clearing the personality of negative habit patterns that hinder its soul's progress, and replacing the released negatives with positive habit patterns, which promote the soul's progress and return. The spiritual path is the process of harmonizing the personality with the soul and the soul with the Spark of God within the soul. However, it is important to note that this must be done while we are incarnated, in the flesh, not between lives.

The soul may certainly learn things while in the disincarnate state, but it must practice the learned behaviors while being attached to its personality in the physical state in order to make real progress on the path. The test for whether a soul has truly learned a lesson is in its ability to manifest, to demonstrate, to practice that lesson through the personality while in the third-dimensional plane. The spiritual path is not merely an intellectual exercise wherein we need only to memorize and repeat "correct" answers in order to pass a course (as is the case in our third-dimensional schools, colleges, and universities). We must be able to show that we have mastered our lessons in the physical world in which we unintentionally entrapped ourselves.

Ascension: The Ultimate Goal

After the soul has refined or spiritualized its personality and itself to a certain degree of harmony with its Divinity Within, upon the death of its body it Ascends to a higher dimension (the fifth) and frees itself from the wheel of physical life on Earth, from incarnation, birth, death, and Karma. This may be called Ascension. Ascension is the culmination of an incarnated soul's evolutionary spiritual path.[8]

---

[8] While Ascension to the *fifth dimension* is the ultimate goal that ends our cycles of reincarnation, birth, and death, there are other intermediate levels in the *fourth dimension* (the astral plane), which a soul can reach. While the fourth dimension is at a higher level than the third, it still supports life that might be called partially disharmonious or negative. The lower reaches of the fourth dimension can have energy that is only slightly higher than what one experiences in the third dimension here on Earth. The

The soul's complete journey of involution and evolution began with the decision to enter a limited physical body in a third-dimensional world. This is true whether we are one of the originally entrapped souls or one of the wayshowers, lightworkers, or starseeds who volunteered to come down to help show the way back. Once here, we are all in the same boat.

The involutionary journey continued with our identification with the physical body and its personality mind, our multiple lifetime experiences, our disillusionments, and inner depression with the meaninglessness of physical world life, all leading finally to our awakening to a larger spiritual picture and our choice to evolve back to conscious Oneness with God.

The evolutionary journey began with the conscious decision to follow the spiritual path. It continues with the discovering, releasing, and replacing of all personality habit patterns that cause inner disharmony with those that create greater harmony among our personality, our soul, and our Divinity Within. With the increase in harmony between our personality and our soul, we soon learn the value of integrating a balance of divine feminine and masculine energy relative to receiving divine guidance through our intuitive path. The releasing and replacing continues until we reach a degree of harmony within ourselves that allows us to carry out our soul's mission of bringing the divine light within us into the outer world in whatever way we can. We are then ready for Ascension.

In this way the soul returns to the divine state of conscious Oneness with God from which it came.[9] In doing so it regains its original freedom, its original conscious Oneness with God, complete with joy, unconditional love, and fulfillment; and it has simultaneously brought Godness, Goddessness, and Divinity into the physical dimension where it hadn't been before.

The Ascended soul is given the opportunity to choose whatever mission it desires as it is restored back to its original spiritual state of harmony and Oneness with God, the All That Is. In its Ascended state the soul is allowed to choose from any number of God's divine missions. The soul may choose a mission that takes it elsewhere in the Cosmos, or it may choose to remain around the Earth School as a Being of Light helping others like us to evolve ourselves back to Oneness with God, just as it was able to do.

---

higher portions of the fourth dimension may have energy that is only slightly lower than that of the divine fifth dimension. After death we go to the precise level that is in harmony with the vibrational level of our particular soul. If we are not yet quite ready to Ascend, we will probably go to the higher portions of the fourth dimension until we reincarnate again.

[9] This is the spiritual truth behind the allegorical biblical story of the Prodigal Son, something I simply could not grasp before I understood the "fall" of man and the return "home" again with "great celebration."

CHAPTER 4

Karma

The Ultimate Educational Tool

Karma, related closely with the Universal Law of Cause and Effect, is very much a part of reincarnation as well as being part of the Earth School itself. Karma was designed into the Earth School as an educational tool that brings us feeling experiences, in each of our many lifetimes, which are object lessons for our continued learning. Karma provides us with firsthand awareness of how it feels to be on the receiving end of certain behaviors that one of our incarnated personalities has previously put out into the world in one lifetime or another. The purpose of Karma is not for punishment, as many believe, but purely for the sake of education, providing the feeling experience from which we may learn and grow spiritually.

Excerpt from a reading by Cathy, on the subject of Karma, from Saint Germain on 10/25/98.

Never has it ever been a punishment! Rather it is the opportunity to grow, to experience.

The Law of Cause and Effect says that one who is kind and helpful to others in one lifetime may, when in need, be given great kindness and help in return. In a similar way, those who have carried out violent aggressive acts such as robbery, rape, or murder, perhaps in a previous lifetime, may be given the experience of just how it feels to be on the receiving end of such activities. These feelings, experienced by the personality, will be stored in the eternal soul at death. Could there be a better way to convey the understanding, the knowing, the feeling experience, the effects of what our personality has put out into the outer world, or what behavioral activities we truly prefer to receive for ourselves?

When we are on the receiving end, such experiences make crystal clear our personal feelings of whether such actions are positive or negative in relation to ourselves. Such understandings at the experience level, the feeling level, the heart level, are stored in the soul at death and therefore last forever. In this way our soul learns more about non-divine third-dimensional behaviors, and the learning carries over into our future lifetimes, eventually helping us to find our way back to conscious Oneness with God.

My personal misunderstanding and its speedy correction from above

My original understanding was that "bad" karma was always the result of our having previously done something similar to another person, perhaps in another lifetime (strictly cause and effect). However, the Ascended Masters, in response to my questions, clarified my misunderstanding of this matter. Karma is not just this type of cause and effect. As addressed in the previous chapter, karma can also include life experiences that are designed into a soul's next lifetime on Earth by the free will choice of the soul itself to speed its progress along its spiritual path.

This means that everyone who has a traumatic event in his or her life, perpetrated by another, has not necessarily carried out a similar deed. Karma is an educational tool and can be used by a soul to accelerate its own educational progress.

In other words, a soul between incarnations may choose to arrange to have a certain type of incident happen in its next physical life for its own higher good or the higher good of family members. Consider a soul, which has no experience, no feelings, and no thoughts about a certain type of third-dimensional behavior that it has never experienced before. It lacks understanding of what such a third-dimensional experience is like. The soul may design and set up such an experience in its next incarnation so that it needn't wait to go through the lengthy process of cause and effect.

In this way a soul need not carry out a certain activity and then wait until the Karmic effect comes around to bring it the feeling experience that it knows it lacks for full understanding. Karma can be a catalyst, speeding up the soul's learning process, removing lifetimes of non-learning and wasted classes, through creating in its own life a single feeling experience that may last forever. Through Karma a soul can quickly gain an experience and understanding that might otherwise have taken many lifetimes to bring around. And this is by the choice of the individual soul itself.

Understanding the Laws of Karma can help humanity increase its desire to release some of its negative habits

A true understanding of Karma can help many to increase their desire to release old habits related to holding onto negative feelings (i.e., thoughts of revenge and a desire for aggressive retaliation). Consider that the basis for Karma is the Universal Law of Cause and Effect. Consider that Karma is always being taken care of with precision by the higher minions of God in the Universe. Remember that all souls have many lifetimes in which to wake up to the larger spiritual picture and move toward Ascension.

Put this all together and you will understand that all aggressive deeds ever done by any human personality have been, are being, and will continue to be handled with perfect divine justice by those appropriate Beings of Light in the higher realms who see all from their higher dimensional perspective. The minions of God who are in charge of the Karma of humankind use higher levels of heart, mind, and will than any human personality could ever dream of. These Beings of Light are connected to all other minions of God and therefore have access to all divine knowledge. To repeat, every third-dimensional aggression acted out by any personality that you see, or read about, or hear of, is already being taken care of quite perfectly without the need for human (personality) assistance. Any aggressive activity in which our personality partakes (including humanly "justified" revenge) will, through Karma, continue to bring to us more aggression until we get tired of it and learn the larger lesson of the Golden Rule.

This was an extremely important lesson for me to learn personally. It helped to bring me to the point of releasing my personality's naturally conditioned desire to bring justice into the world whenever I saw or felt injustice being perpetrated against myself or my loved ones. I now understand completely that all man-made human justice is merely the best that third-dimensional money can buy (it is an illusion), and it has little or nothing to do with divine justice. More importantly, I have learned and know in the heart of my soul that the inequity of the outer world's version of justice does not really matter because all cases are in the hands of the Creative Forces of God and they need no help from us.

I was given several dreams to help bring me the experiential understanding that all actions[1] are always handled perfectly by the Creative Forces of God and are not the responsibility of any human, including me.

In my last dream on the subject a man committed an act of aggression against me and ran away. He got away clean. A little later I found myself on the roof of a tall building in a large city when I happened to see him on the

[1] All actions means *all* actions, including negative feelings, thoughts, attitudes, and beliefs that we might hold against another.

roof of another building. I could see him, but there was nothing I could possibly do to apprehend him or bring him to an accounting. Amazingly, as I watched from my helpless position, a gust of wind came up and blew the culprit off the roof to his sudden death.

In the larger spiritual picture, all is taken care of by the Creative Forces of God

Now these are just words describing the dream content, but in my dream I also had the feeling experience of knowing that all was always taken care of by God. Later I was given an affirmation in an Ascended Master reading to help me to release my personality's habit of desiring to take care of any injustice perpetrated against me (revenge) in my world and to surrender to God's way. The affirmation was, "Everything is in divine order."

This affirmation covered all situations and helped me to cut a few more cords of attachment that had previously tied me to this third-dimensional existence. It helped me to replace my personality's naturally judgmental and vengeful feelings and thoughts with some that were more in harmony with my soul.

This is an excerpt from a reading by Cathy, focused primarily on Karma, received from St. Germain on 09/06/98.

It is important to view one's life from the broadest (and highest) *perspective that one can achieve, and for an entity on the spiritual path this means that it is important to view the life experience above and beyond the third dimension and the physical.*

For all, there is wholeness and there is empowerment. It is not necessary for any entity, in the third dimension or out of the third dimension, to experience something in his or her life that does not serve the highest good. Guilt does not serve the highest good. Blame and judgment do not serve the highest good of any entity.

Oneness with the Creative Force, harmony, peace and joy, these serve and serve well. The negative emotions create a disservice, create a disharmony, and create disease. There needs to be clearing, the complete clearing and releasing of negative relationships. There also needs to be a clarifying in the understanding of entities that there is Grace, and there is empowerment. It is what you choose now, in the moment, that is important to your life experience. It is what you choose that will create and shape your life experience.

There is no Karma that cannot be released and overcome. And to say that one's life experience is shaped by Karma is to give up one's power (to change self). *It is very important to understand here that there needs to be the reclaiming of empowerment for all entities. There needs to be the understanding that the life play can be rewritten precisely as the entity desires. The Universe, God, Spirit, if you will, desires the greatest harmony, the greatest abundance, the greatest joy, and the greatest peace for every entity who is in or out of third-dimensional experience. To believe otherwise is to believe falsely.*

If Holy Spirit, or soul, or higher self were to indicate to an entity that something negative was currently in the path, spirit, soul, and higher self would never state that this is preordained, or that this is beyond the scope of the empowerment of the entity herself to change. Free will. Remember free will. Spirit, God, soul, higher self never override the free will (of the personality) *of any particular entity.*

Is that which we are offering here clear? Is it making sense?

✦ It makes perfect sense, and I believe it will be useful in the book.

Indeed, indeed. We agree that that is a likely and good assessment.

We recommend reclaiming power, returning to the recognition and understanding that there is within self, the power to create the life that is desired. And if that life has not yet manifested itself, then look for blockages (residual negative habit patterns). *Look in the emotional body, look in the physical body, look in the spiritual body, and look in the mind for blockages, for concepts and beliefs that have been accepted that do not serve you. Accept nothing that does not serve you.*

Relationships. Release all negative relationships from this lifetime and previous lifetimes.[2] *Do not allow self to slip into the belief or the acceptance that Karma is creating your life experience.* ***Free will dominates all****. If there are karmic patterns, release them. If there are karmic patterns, use one of our* **spiritual tools** *designed to assist in this release. Your life is a blank slate*

---

2 Negative relationships include negative feelings and thoughts still held toward anyone who has ever brought harm to us, to our personalities. If we retain negative feelings and thoughts about or toward anyone, then we are still karmically tied or attached to them. This is true whether the deeds against us were of a nature that our personality would "judge" to be very serious or even those we perceive to be much less serious (i.e., "Mom always liked my brother best; dad hated the sight of me; my brother wet the bed and I got blamed for it," or any of perhaps a million or so others). Our holding on to such negatives, even if our assessments may be accurate, causes the Universe to bring the same kind of negatives into our life experiences over and over again until we have learned this lesson of forgiveness and release. Karma exists, but our free will release of negative feelings and thoughts is more powerful and releases us from Karma.

at any moment that you decide to focus upon it. Change it, as you will. Release those things that do not serve you. That includes beliefs.

We find that many entities have detoured into a space of victimhood and acceptance of pain and lack of abundance and negativities within the life experience. You have only to change this. You have only to choose harmony and peace and comfort and abundance. Would you have more?

✦ No, but it occurs to me that when you mention experiencing abundance, et cetera, that it means having the true feelings of having abundance and empowerment. From my own experience I know it is easy to rationalize mentally and to conceptualize without having the actual feelings.

Indeed, you are correct and we appreciate that for whenever we say experience and use that word we mean the ***feelings****, not the mind, not the thoughts, but the feelings of being empowered, the feelings of having abundance, the feelings of being positive, and the feelings of the peace and harmony of non-judgment. And we thank you for that addition.*

In general, Karma says that that which our personality puts out into the world around us in our physical lives comes back to us as an educational experience that is stored in our eternal soul to help us in future lifetimes. However, because our soul may design incidents into its next lifetime to speed its experiential education, we humans cannot simply observe a traumatic event that has happened to another and make a judgment that the soul of that individual has previously carried out a similar deed.

If we manifest positives into the outer world, positives are returned to us, through the laws of Karma. But Karma also means that any of our acts of aggression (including actions, words, feelings, thoughts, and attitudes), whether we believe they are justified or not, will continue to bring to us more aggression of the same nature until we get our fill of it all and learn this lesson along our spiritual path.[3]

The lesson would be to awaken to the:

- larger spiritual picture of life.
- laws of Karma, and the other Universal Laws which have always affected us, but which few of the world's population have ever understood.
- power of our very own personal free will to choose to change our life.

---

[3] This may provide a greater understanding of the actual benefits that accrue by following Christ's suggestion that we should all learn to "turn the other cheek."

The lesson would include:

- forgiving all, releasing our negative habit patterns and replacing them with positives. We all have the free will to change our negative feelings, thoughts, attitudes, beliefs, and actions.
- freeing ourselves from any feelings of victimization we may have due to our early education or conditioning (by other humans).
- bringing our personality's consciousness gradually into harmony with our soul and our soul with the Spark of God within the soul.

Karma then brings us peace, harmony, and the Unconditional Love of God.

Our life's theatrical play can be rewritten at any time. We all have the personal power to change what the Universe brings us by changing ourselves. By forgiving all others ("for they know not what they do" [any more than I did]) and by using our free will to release and replace our negatives with positives, we empower ourselves and cause the Universe to bring positives into our life experience. By using our free will, we take charge of ourselves. By changing ourselves, we rewrite our life play to be in accordance with the Spark of God within our soul. Then all the minions of God in the Universe will bring us all that we seek for we will have returned to conscious Oneness with God, the All That Is.

CHAPTER 5

The Universal Law of Manifestation

How We Each Create Our Own Little Worlds

Closely associated with Karma and the Law of Cause and Effect is the ability of any soul to manifest in its world all that it most desires. Sounds great, doesn't it? And it is, but this ability is as a two-edged sword, for it cuts both ways.

> *Through Universal Law, our consistently held inner feelings, thoughts, attitudes, and beliefs cause and create all we see in our own little worlds*

As highly evolved souls with a higher consciousness and a greater degree of self mastery, we would all be guided by our Divinity Within to hold only positive feelings and positive thoughts and to use our higher will (our soul's will) to maintain our focus always on positives. Our soul's positive feelings, thoughts, images, and intentions would immediately be created at the etheric levels. If we continued to hold them in our soul's higher mind, they would eventually become manifested by our Divinity Within, by the Beings of Light in the higher realms of God, and by the Universe, into the third-dimensional world around us.

That's where we humans, who still define ourselves as just our body and its personality, differ from our souls in a very great way. Identifying ourselves only as our personalities, we hold many conditioned thoughts, feelings, attitudes, and beliefs that are unquestionably negative. We hold dozens of fears in our hearts and minds unconsciously all the time. In general, we think that this is a good thing.

By focusing on all the negatives that may or could possibly happen to us, we can believe that we are better able to defend and protect ourselves from these outer world threats. If we are afraid of heights, we can avoid heights. If we are afraid of what others may think, feel, or say about us, we can be offensive toward them to create a distance between us. We may anesthetize our sensitivities and create shells around our hearts to avoid internal emotional pain. Depending on what our particular personal fears may be, we can think of hundreds of ways to protect and defend ourselves that we believe are perfectly appropriate. To a personality it seems very natural and logical to hold fears and other negative thoughts and feelings in our minds and hearts, lest those around us catch us off guard.

*The Universal Law of Manifestation uses **all** our inner feelings, thoughts, and visualizations as blueprints from which to create our own personal worlds*

The problem is that the Universal Law behind the ability to manifest uses all the images, thoughts, feelings, attitudes, and beliefs that we consistently hold in our hearts and minds as a kind of photographic image from which to create these things in our lives. Like attracts like. Feelings of poverty attract more poverty to us. Fears of poverty cause and create poverty in our own little worlds.

If we consistently held only positives in our hearts and in our minds, then those positives would be manifested in our lives. However, as our uncleared personality selves, we undoubtedly hold some negative feelings and thoughts, and the Universe manifests those negatives into our lives over and over again until we release and replace them.

Are these negatives our true, inner desires? Nope. We really desire good things in our lives such as peace, harmony, unconditional love, and abundance. But as long as we hold negatives in our minds and hearts, the specific negatives we hold will continuously be created in our lives. We can simply look at our own little world around us. Any and all negatives we find in our own little worlds are the effects of negative inner feelings and thoughts, attitudes and beliefs we have previously held for some period of time, just as all the positives were created due to our positive feelings and thoughts.

Why does the Law bring us things we don't really desire in our lives? Why does it bring us what we fear? The answer to these questions is another question. If you don't desire it, why do you hold it in your mind and heart?

Positive feelings and positive thoughts cause and create positives in our individual worlds

How do we use the Universal Law of Manifestation to our advantage? The same way that we make progress along the spiritual path: by discovering the negatives we unconsciously hold within us, by releasing them as no longer beneficial for our higher good, and by replacing them with positives that are in harmony with our soul and our higher good. As we continue this releasing and replacing activity, we are setting ourselves up to manifest more and more positive things and events in our lives, and we are simultaneously moving ourselves up toward our soul-state or soul level of consciousness, step-by-step.

Excerpt from a reading by Cathy, on the subject of manifestation, from Saint Germain on 4/10/99.

Well, actually you are going to be manifesting in any case, whether you are conscious of it or not. If you are releasing negativity and replacing it with positive thoughts and feelings, you are going to manifest that which is more positive in your life, because your focus will change.

✦ Whether you are at the soul level or you are still being only your personality?

It is highly unlikely that you will remain at your personality level when you release all of those negatives and move in all of those positives. Do you understand?

✦ Okay.

You simply will shift upward, for indeed, it might well be impossible to release all of the negativity that you are discussing if you are still at your personality level of perception and awareness. It will vary somewhat from one individual to another, but on the whole that kind of clearing, releasing, and replacing will take one to a higher state of consciousness and bring one into attunement, alignment with the soul state, as opposed to the personality state, the ego, the lower mind, the lower will.

By releasing our negatives and replacing them with positives, we are evolving ourselves up to our soul level. At our soul level we are able to receive direct divine guidance from the Goddess/God within our soul, whenever we ask for it. By moving ourselves to our soul level we are moving into a state of consciously manifesting more positives in our lives. We are also moving ourselves to the level of our higher will, for our higher will is the will of our soul, as distinguished from the will of our personality or ego.

At our soul level we can use our higher will to hold our immediate focus on positive feelings, thoughts, and images, instantly creating them at the etheric levels. We can also use our higher will to focus upon remaining at the soul level in order to hold positive feelings and thoughts for a long enough period of time to cause them to be manifested in our third-dimensional world. For if we allow ourselves to drop back down to our personality's negative habit patterns of conditioned feelings and thoughts, we will negate what we have only partially manifested.

Manifestation Is a Motivational Tool in the Earth School

The Law of Manifestation can be seen as another motivator for the students of the Earth School. From a higher perspective it can be seen as a way to encourage us to change what we hold in our personality's heart and mind. It can be seen as a way to encourage us to evolve ourselves to our soul level where we can learn to use our higher will to master our thoughts and emotions. It is a motivator to encourage us to grow and expand our vision of life and to expand our ability to function at a higher level of conscious awareness in our life, to function at our soul level. Then we can begin to hold, in our higher minds and hearts, that which our true selves (our soul selves) really desire in our lives rather than what our personalities fear in our outer world environment at our personality level of consciousness. Then we can create our heaven on Earth.[1]

Christ's Manifestations

This is how Christ was able to manifest healing. This is how He was able to manifest bread and fish for the multitudes (and wine for a few others). He had cleared His personality of negatives and had become His soul self, always attuned to His Divinity Within, the Spark of God which He called "Father." He was a master of His feelings, thoughts, and visualizations and could focus His higher will so sharply and clearly on the results He desired that the Creative Forces of God could manifest what He visualized immediately. If He had allowed himself to feel, or think, or believe that there was not enough food for the thousands who came to hear His words, they would all have gone hungry.

---

[1] Of course the Law of Manifestation acts as a motivator only to those who awaken to, know of, and understand the larger spiritual picture. We can benefit from these Earth School systems only if we know that a cause and effect relationship exists between what we choose to feel and think and what the Universe creates around us. However, learning this too is part of our own spiritual awakening and evolution.

CHAPTER 6

Prayer

A Tool for Intimate and Unfailing Communication with God

After most of part I of this book had been completed, Sananda mentioned in an unrelated reading something to the effect that prayer is a very powerful tool. This was enough of a nudge to cause me to realize that I had not yet included anything on prayer in and of itself. Why had I overlooked something as basic as prayer? Because I saw and felt prayer and the Universal Law of Manifestation as one and the same. This reading was conducted to take care of my omission.

This is an excerpt from a reading by Cathy, on the subject of prayer, received from Sananda on 08/08/99.

Greetings beloved and blessings be with you this day. This is Sananda.

✦ Good morning Sananda. I am asking for information on the subject of prayer that you believe would be beneficial to all the readers of the book.

Very well, we shall be pleased to do this.

Prayer is a tool for communication

Prayer is probably the method or tool most commonly used by beings in the third dimension to ***communicate*** *with those in the higher dimensions, most specifically with God, but occasionally with others as well. Sometimes even with those who have departed the Earth plane and are in the fourth dimension. As widely used as it is, it is not clearly or fully understood as a tool, as to that for which it is intended.*

Prayer that is effective, and indeed most prayer, comes from the ***heart*** *of the entity who is praying. This is because, generally speaking, prayer is offered up because there is some situation or some occurrence in the life experience which makes it so that the entity feels overwhelmed or incapable of handling this from the ego level and the mental level. In such a case there is, to some degree at least, a letting go* (of a solution by the personality) *and a seeking of divine or other intervention. This in fact is a result of the soul of the entity working toward, or moving the entity toward,* ***awakening to itself, itself being the soul, and to the Divinity Within the soul****. And that would be the reason that the situation has occurred or been brought to the individual.*[1]

Prayer can move us to a deeper, higher level of consciousness

Now other prayer, particularly that which is taught in certain religions, is prayer that is more like a mantra, and often actually leads the person, the individual, the entity, into something of a trance state. Frequently for those who repeat what is known as the rosary in the Catholic religion, if the focus is indeed on the repetition, then there is the movement toward the trance state. And in many of your Eastern religions, prayers are chants of a sort which again bring the entity into a different state of consciousness, moving from the beta to the alpha and of occasion, deeper. Do you understand?

✦ Yes.

Even when the entity is praying because he or she is overwhelmed by some occurrence, there is the shifting from the beta to the alpha. All prayers, even those which are memorized and repeated, actually come from the heart and not from the mind. At least once the prayer is learned. Do you understand?

✦ No, I do not. When you say prayer is learned, that would be—

We are talking now about the prayers that are said repetitiously or those that are chanted, for there is the period of learning for each individual in the third dimension, a time of learning these prayers. And in those times there is something of the mental involved in that process.

---

[1] In essence, the "troubles" occurring in our third-dimensional life experience are brought to us to bring us eventually to this feeling of being overwhelmed by something we know our personality alone cannot control. When we make that admission and invoke prayer as a way of communicating with a higher power, we are awakening our personality or ego to the existence of a higher power in our lives. This can lead us to the desire to begin to harmonize our personality with our soul, and with the Spark of God within our soul, which is the gateway back to harmony and conscious Oneness with God, the All That Is.

✦ Okay, I understand.

Prayer from the heart, the vast majority of the time, will touch the Divine Within because the soul seat, the seat of the soul of an entity in the third dimension, is in the area behind the heart **chakra**. *It may be a little above or a little below or directly behind. And as the entity moves deeper into the alpha state or into the induced trance state then there is the connecting with the Divine Within. Often this goes unnoticed by the entity because there is the belief system which says that God, the Divine, is external. Usually external and above. But it really does not matter if there is the conscious awareness because the connection is made in any case. Is that clear?*

✦ Yes.

Prayer follows the Universal Laws of Manifestation

Prayer is a very powerful tool and one of the reasons that it is, is because it is a combination of words or thoughts and emotions. It is extremely rare that prayer does not include emotions, the emotional body if you will. And it is particularly powerful because that combination of thought and feeling, or words and feeling, ***is precisely the same as the combination used in the Laws of Manifestation****.*

The emotion may well be fear and if the emotion is fear then there is the possibility, even the probability, that that which is manifested will be that which is feared. If the emotion or devotion is positive, then that which is manifested is often the positive, often that which is desired. That form of prayer often brings about what you may call in the third dimension a miracle. Is that clear?

✦ Yes.

And so it is important for your readers to know that praying ***believing****, which will always mean prayer with a positive emotion, a positive feeling, is an excellent way to both manifest and to become One with the Divine Within, even though there may not be the awareness that the Divine is Within.*

✦ Okay.

And this is because of the state of consciousness that is attained. The state of consciousness that is attained in prayer is very similar, if the prayer is sincere and the prayer is intense or repetitious, to that which is achieved in meditation, though in meditation the consciousness can go deeper. The verbalization of prayer sometimes, though not always, keeps the third-dimensional entity from recognizing, hearing, feeling, or knowing that the response has come. This is not always the case because often those who are in sincere and deep prayer are aware of a shifting when to their consciousness it appears that the prayer has been answered. Then if they go and check, indeed that which is being sought has occurred or will occur in the very near future. It works very much as manifestation does in the sense that that which is sought occurs first in the etheric (realm) *and then appears in the physical.*

Maintaining positive feelings and thoughts after prayer is crucial

Now again it must be understood that even when prayer is intense and sincere, and there is the shift in consciousness, and there is the occurrence in the etheric of that which is sought, if the entity then leaves the prayer state and begins to function in the beta consciousness (personality or ego level) *again, and in that state begins to experience fear, then you see the dilemma. In this case the fear is manifesting often the opposite of what the prayer intended. And that which appears in the third dimension depends entirely on the strength of the emotions.*

Is the negativeness of the fear stronger than the positiveness of the prayer? Is it held more intensely? Is it held for a longer period of time than the believing?

✦ I understand.

This is an important point because there is always the question, why does God not answer prayer? And the answer is that no prayer is ever uttered that is not answered. No prayer is ever thought that is not answered. Whether or not the entity permits the manifestation of the answer in the third dimension (by continuing to hold the positive feelings, thoughts, and words) *is an entirely separate issue.*

Sananda's summary on prayer

There are several aspects on the subject of prayer that may be important for your readers to understand.

Prayer is powerful and entities should always be aware of what they are praying for.

Prayer is also a method of connecting to the Divine Within. It allows for the shifting of the consciousness to a higher state.

Prayers are not always answered in specifically the manner that the entity believes that they will or should be. Prayers are sometimes misguided, in the sense that if you are praying for an entity who is ready to leave the Earth plane and you are praying that that entity will not depart, that that soul will not leave, you can very well delay the departure of that soul but you cannot stop it because the soul has free will (and is ready).

In such cases the more appropriate prayers may include a request for ***the highest good*** *of the entity or entities being included in the prayer and the one who is praying because this is more in keeping, more in harmony with the Universe and the concept of free will. Understand that the entity who is* *praying may truly believe that he or she is praying for that which is best, but they are not allowing for the free will of the soul that is being prayed for.*[2]

It may also be well to include in your book the concept that because everyone is One and because everyone is One with God, and One with all entities in the higher dimensions, all things are available to bring each entity into a state of Peace. And so the truest prayer is the prayer to remove fear, fear of change, fear of seeing clearly, fear of knowing the future, and all of the ego's fear, because once fear is removed then there is only love and inner peace and Oneness and understanding. Without fear there can be an experiencing, or a recognition at least, of Oneness.

The truest prayer is to remove all fear and to bring about a change in understanding, a change in perception, a change in knowing. The truest prayer is to pray for that which is for the highest good. The truest prayer is to pray that whatever the perspective may be that is bringing negative emotions to the person who is praying, that that perspective will be shifted to a true perspective and a true understanding.

Sananda's reading on the power of prayer needs no further summary. I will only say that it should now be clear to all readers why I saw and felt prayer to be the same as the Universal Laws of Manifestation.

In a deeper state of prayer, we can pray and pray for all types of beautiful things for self and others, but afterward, if we regress to the more superficial level of personality consciousness, the Universal Laws of Manifestation will create what we are feeling and thinking then, overriding the beautiful feelings and thoughts we were holding while in the deeper consciousness state.

Beta and Alpha States of Consciousness

In this reading on prayer, Sananda mentioned two terms, beta and alpha, that I had not yet included in the book, and it seemed a little odd to me that he would do so. Because it felt or seemed unusual in some way, I asked my highest self about it in my own journaling session.

Question: Was this done so that I would see that I have not included these terms before and perhaps be motivated to do so?

---

[2] By praying for the *higher or highest good* of others we remove the chance of asking for that which may not be in harmony with their higher good. By praying for the generic higher good of others we place the situation clearly into the hands of God. The Creative Forces of God truly know that which is the highest good for the soul of each party included in the prayer.

Response: Yes. By creating another table you can relate the various states of consciousness that you mention in part II in terms of personality, soul, and divine Spark of God Within to these terms used by certain elements of the world's cultures. This information will fill out the ideas already presented.

So, here it is. This information is also covered in part II (with a few graphics). These terms and a couple more are used to name various states of consciousness we humans may achieve. These terms were more in vogue in the sixties and seventies than they seem to be now. For those who know the Greek alphabet, please don't hold me responsible for the strange way in which these states of consciousness happen to be named. It makes no sense at all. However, the naming conventions are not important. What is important is that the existence of the various states of consciousness I have been calling the personality or ego state, the soul state, and the state of the Divinity Within, can be related to specific numbers of EEG (electroencephalographic) brainwave cycles per second as measured by third-dimensional, outer world, scientific instruments.

For those learning to still their personality's mind (as in meditation), an electronic device with earphones, hooked around the forehead, can give instant feedback as to which state of consciousness they are in at the moment. In the early seventies the idea was that one could learn to still, to quiet the busy personality mind much more quickly by receiving instantaneous feedback. I have no doubt that such a device would have been enormously helpful to me, but I simply could not afford one at the time and I have no idea what the cost would be today.

By receiving a signal when an entity had successfully stilled the personality mind and moved into the peaceful alpha state of the soul, or conversely moved out of it, the concept was that one could learn more quickly just what was required to maintain that state. By knowing when he or she was in the soul state, the seeker could more readily experience and know how the soul state felt. After a while in this experience, the instrument would no longer be necessary because eventually the experience would become a feeling habit to which one could return simply by remembering it. Like reminiscing.

Sananda stated that the activity of repeating the rosary, or praying in a chanting way could, "bring the entity into a different state of consciousness, moving from the beta to the alpha and of occasion deeper." He could just as easily have said that it could, "bring the entity into a different state of consciousness, moving from the personality state to the soul state, and of occasion to the deeper state of the Divinity Within." But of course, he wanted me to wake up and make this point.

The Beta State

The *beta state* is the same as our *personality state* of consciousness. This is the state of consciousness of most ordinary human mental activity at the current stage of human evolution. This is our ordinary everyday walking-around mental state. It is the busiest we can be mentally and the lowest state of consciousness we can attain. Most humans believe that having a busy, left-brained, personality mind is good, but the truth is that this busyness prevents and precludes any reception of higher knowledge from the higher realms of God. The personality consciousness (beta state) processes only the man-made knowledge that we have adopted from our outer world teachings, which includes only human perceptions, opinions, and hypotheses of the truth of things made from other human's study and observations of the physical world. This is not necessarily spiritual truth from above.

The Alpha State

The *alpha state* is the same as our higher *soul state* of consciousness. Stillness of the personality mind allows us to move our consciousness up to our soul level, which is a quantum leap higher than our personality's physical brain mind can ever attain. This is where reception of higher truth from our Divinity Within and the realms of the Angels, Archangels, and Ascended Masters begins. This is where the higher perception and awareness of our soul begins to become available.

The Theta State

The *theta state* is the same state of consciousness as that of conscious *Oneness with our Spark of God Within.* This again is a whole step higher, broader, more expansive, more impersonal, more divine, and more unconditionally loving than our alpha or soul state of consciousness. This is the state of consciousness of our Divinity Within, the Spark of God that lies untainted within our individuated soul (our "Christ consciousness"), connecting us with and to all other minions of God in our Universe.

The Delta State

The *delta state* is the same state of consciousness as that of conscious *Oneness with God, the All That Is.* This is the state of conscious Oneness, with all the Sparks of God that lie within the souls of all minions of God in the Hierarchy of God and within the aggregate of all individuated souls comprising God, the All That Is, in the Cosmos.

Sananda only mentioned the first two, beta and alpha. For the scope of this book, the latter two, theta and delta, can both be considered as the state of consciousness of the Divinity Within, the God or Goddess Within. If you can go to that level at will, you can receive all the knowledge from above that you wish. I can understand a slight difference between the theta and the delta, but the best I can do to describe the difference in words is already included in the list immediately above.

The important point here is simply that the terms I use throughout the book relating to our three levels of beingness (personality or ego, soul, and Spark of God Within) can be related to and identified with physical evidence that can be obtained from a third-dimensional EEG device. If you can reach a reading of eleven on the EEG, you will know that you are at your soul level of consciousness at that moment in time. See Table 6-1 for a summary of states of consciousness measured, moment-to-moment, on an EEG.

One of the important things to grasp from Table 6-1 is the negative correlation between the number of brainwave cycles per second registered in our personality's (left brain) mind and the higher levels of consciousness we can attain. At twenty cycles per second we are merely at our ordinary personality state. At eleven we are well into our soul state. At six we are at a state of Oneness with our Divinity Within.

The higher the registered number of cycles per second, the more superficial and shallow is our state of consciousness (the more outer world is our

TABLE 6-1 States of Consciousness Related to EEG cycles per second (cps).

State of Consciousness	*Corresponding Aspect of Our Beingness*	*EEG Brain Wave (cycles per second)*	*Related Aspects of Heart, Mind, and Will*
Beta	Personality or Ego	40–14 cps	Our Personality's mind Our Personality's heart Our Personality's will
Alpha	Soul	14–7 cps	Our Soul's mind Our Soul's heart Our Soul's will
Theta	Oneness with our Divinity Within, our Spark of God Within, our God or Goddess Within, our Holy Spirit Within	7–4 cps	Our Divine mind Our Divine heart Our Divine will
Delta	Oneness with God, the All That Is	4–0 cps	The Divine mind, heart, and will of God, the All That Is

focus). The busier we allow our personality's mind to become (focused on outer world activities), the less we can know and understand of the higher things in life in which our soul and our Divinity Within are most interested.

If we wish to reach and communicate with the higher states of consciousness of our soul and of our Divinity Within, we must learn to still our personality's mind, to slow it down, so that our soul can get in a word or two now and then. The degree to which we learn to relax and to still our personality's mind determines the upper limit of our higher mind's consciousness, perception, and reception that we can reach.

Communication with our own higher aspects of beingness (our soul and our Spark of God Within the soul) depends upon our learning to quiet our personality's hyperactive mind at will. When we can do this we can receive information from our soul self and our Divine Self whenever we choose. By learning to still our personality's mind we open our inner line of communication to receive calls from above, otherwise the line is always busy.

Messages and information from the Angels, Archangels, Ascended Masters, and other Beings of Light in the higher realms are always passed to our Divinity Within. Our Divinity Within passes the information to our soul. Therefore, we cannot know, or hear, or understand at our personality level, anything that was given to our higher aspects unless we are able to raise our personality's level of consciousness to the higher level of our soul so that they are in harmony. This is accomplished only by stilling the personality's mind.

Anyone can do this! This is for everyone on Earth once we understand the dynamics, the hierarchy of consciousness within us, and the benefits involved. Just as we were earlier conditioned and taught by our outer world environment to keep our personality mind busy, so now we can teach ourselves to Be Still and Know the Heart and Mind of our God/Goddess Within.

CHAPTER 7

Meditation

A Tool for Learning to Listen to God's Answers

Meditation is one of the most important tools for those who choose the spiritual path. It is one of the absolute basics of the path and as such it has no substitutes.

While prayer is talking to God, meditation is listening to God

This is an excerpt from a reading by Cathy, on the subject of meditation, received from Saint Germain on 03/11/01.

Truly, meditation is considered listening to God whereas prayer is considered talking to God. But it has more far-reaching effects or efficacies, for meditation is, as you say, a stilling of the mind. It is a stilling particularly of the personality mind, which tends in third-dimensional incarnation to be rather active and often rather dominating. And so there is the stilling of the mind together with the purpose or intention of going within.

In meditation one attunes oneself to that which is within. And so it serves the purpose of bringing one into a greater attunement and even into a state of communication with the Divinity Within. It also serves to give one the learning experience, through regular communication with the higher self, with the individual's soul, with God, and with the higher dimensions, as it is done in meditation, that God and All That There Is lies within.

*This is an important point. It is important for the seeker to know that God and the higher dimensions are **not external** to him or herself but rather are **internal**. It is important to know that there is, at the core of the seeker,* *the **connection** to the God force, the **connection** to All That Is. Do you understand?*

✦ Oh, yes.

And this is not always pointed out or brought to light in treatises on meditation. This is because of the fact that a very important and well accepted purpose for meditation is to gain connection to higher wisdom, to facilitate a greater flow of the intuitive, and to bring to the being who is practicing meditation an experience of a state of peace and love and harmony that cannot occur in the beta state of the active conscious personality mind.

And this is of great importance. It is valuable to the entity and it is attractive to the entity. This causes a desire to practice meditation, which is not always easy in the beginning. Stilling the personality mind can take focused concentration and for some can be rather a frustrating experience. But having moved past that experience there is the promise of the inner guidance, of the greater flow of intuition, of the tapping into the broader, much more expansive state of consciousness where information as well as guidance can be sought and attained with relative ease once the practice of meditation is mastered. And so this is usually the focus of any information written regarding meditation.

*It is interesting that even entities who enter into meditation **successfully**, who gain a greater expanse of consciousness, and who are able to achieve or attain greater information and clear guidance can still believe that this information is coming from realms that are above and external to them, from God external to them, and from the Angelic Realm also external to them. And it is well worth mentioning in your book that God and the expanded consciousness **are in the core essence of the being, of the entity her- or himself.** Do you not agree?*

✦ Oh, yes.

And so meditation is the entering into a different state of consciousness, which can be empirically measured by brain wave activity, should that be desired, and which is an experience of the greater truth of who one truly is. In meditation the illusions of the third dimension can be released, can fade or fall away. The entity can become very aware that who and what he or she is, is something quite broadly expansive, much more beautiful, and supremely intensified if you will. For in the state of meditation the intensity of the awareness of the entity is greatly heightened. And given sufficient intent and desire, an entity can experience and explore all that he or she truly is and all of the higher dimensions of consciousness.

Practicing meditation also brings an entity more smoothly to a consistently expanded conscious awareness. Because as intuition begins to flow and answers and information come in during the meditative state, the entity who practices meditation with discipline and focus will find that he or she is able to have the same intuitive guidance flowing ***even in the conscious state.*** *Given regular meditation an entity will eventually come to realize, or at least it could be measured, that the entity most often, even in the conscious state,* ***resides*** *in the alpha wave length* (of the soul) *as opposed to the beta* (wave length of the personality).

✦ Yes.

And so the practice of meditation has practical application in the third-dimensional living, conscious, experience, and it also has very practical application in assisting the entity, the seeker on the path to become more aware and to have the experiential evidence of the truth, the reality of his or her own being. When that attunement becomes a part of the conscious awareness, then is the seeker truly expanding his consciousness and moving upward on the spiral at a steady pace.

And so while meditation is listening to God, meditation is also exploring expanded reality, exploring truth, experiencing one's totality of Beingness, one's expanse of Beingness.

Is that sufficient?

✦ Yes, it's great. Thank you.

Prayer Is Talking to God

In prayer we can talk and talk and talk to God. Like letters to a loving Santa we can describe what we want and what we desire to have happen in our lives. However, as already given, the Universal Laws of Cause and Effect and the Laws of Manifestation use all the images, feelings, thoughts, attitudes, and beliefs that we consistently hold in our hearts and minds, when we are not in prayer, as a blueprint to create these things in our lives. Therefore, as given in the previous chapter, anything we ask in our deepest prayer can be and will be overridden by any negatives we consistently hold in our hearts and minds. In prayer we may ask for only good things in our lives, but outside of prayer if we continually have feelings and thoughts that include fears, anger, hostility, or animosity inside us, then we ourselves are creating those very types of disharmony and disease in our own little worlds.

Meditation Is Listening to God

Meditation is listening to God. In meditation, as in prayer, we can raise our consciousness from the level of our personality (beta state) to the level of our soul (alpha state) and even higher to the level of our Divinity Within (theta state). By learning to still our personality's conscious mind, reducing its brainwave activity, we raise the level of our consciousness to that of our soul and even higher.

At our soul level we can listen and know what our God/Goddess Within prefers in our lives. In meditation we can listen for the "still small voice," the divine guidance and information that comes from and through the divine Spark of God that lives within our soul. In meditation we can learn from our higher self, our soul, or our Divine Self, what these higher aspects of our beingness would prefer us to do in and with our lives.

In meditation it is the stillness of our personality's mind that allows us to receive higher guidance from the higher aspects of ourselves. We may pose a question, focus our attention on a subject, or just "wonder" about a specific subject area. Then in the stillness of meditation, we may receive, first in our heart (our feeling realm) and then in our mind (our higher soul mind as opposed to our personality's mind), a complete understanding of the area of our focus.

In the silence of meditation, we can know which way to go when making decisions. We can shift our consciousness higher, experience our soul, and know how our soul feels about each of the various possibilities we set before it.

In the peace of meditation, we can shift our consciousness still higher, up to the level of our Goddess or God Within, and know the feelings of this divine aspect of our own beingness. We can experience both the divine feelings and the divine knowing of anything we desire to understand in our own lives, from the fifth-dimensional perspective of our Divinity Within. These are some of the benefits of bringing our personality into harmony with our soul and our Divinity Within.

In the quietness of meditation, we can open our natural path of intuition to receive both divine guidance and divine love from within and above. In opening ourselves to receive unconditional love, we can resonate with that divine love, experience the feelings of divine love, and transmit those feelings, the love resonance, to our surroundings wherever we may be.

In opening ourselves to receive knowledge and truth, we can feel as well as know the truth of any situation. It is not merely the personality mind's intellectual type of understanding being received; it is also the experiencing, the true knowing, of the very dynamics of a situation. It includes the feelings and the experience of the soul's understanding.

Meditation Is Practice in Stilling Our Personality Mind

How can and does all this happen? Because in meditation *we still the personality mind!* It happens *only* when we still the personality mind. We practice and practice and learn to quiet, to still, the personality mind. We learn to stop thinking and start feeling. When we are successful in silencing the limited personality mind, we simultaneously and automatically open the door to the higher, finer, deeper, and more expanded reaches of our soul mind, and perhaps even to the mind of the Spark of God within our soul if we are very still. The stilling of the personality mind causes the shift of our consciousness, or allows us to shift our consciousness, to our soul level. It allows us to experience ourselves as our soul in those moments, if that is our intention.

This is the nature of meditation. We still the personality's left brain, logical mind and in doing so we free the right side of our brain to receive guidance from our higher self, our soul self, or even our Divinity Within. The waking state consciousness of humanity today is largely filled with the hyperactive static of our personality's "logical" outer world mind. In general, humankind has the belief that constant lower mind activity such as thinking, using logic and reasoning, is the highest, most valuable achievement possible to mankind.

Man-Made Information Is Not the Highest Available

However, using only the personality mind limits the information used by humans, in their logic-and-reasoning decision-making activity, to man-made information. Man-made information is largely quite temporal, transient, and inferior to that received from the higher perspective of our eternal soul, from the Divinity Within our soul, and/or from other Beings of Light in the Angelic Realms above. However, generally speaking, humankind today is not yet aware that there is a better and higher alternative to using only man-made information.

Man-made information consists mainly of the personal perceptions, concepts, and opinions of the personalities of other humans who perhaps know no more about a larger spiritual picture than anyone else on Earth. Humans simply study the outer world, weigh and measure, make calculations, create hypotheses, and attempt to derive or contrive convincing arguments, so that they are believed by the masses and receive the esteem of other humans as experts in their fields. It is a case of the blind leading the blind. For example, it was once both thought and taught that the Earth was flat, and thus it was believed (by all but a few).

Our personality mind's thinking precludes reception of divine inner guidance

In general, humankind does not yet understand that keeping our personality mind constantly busy precludes and prevents our ability to receive intuitional guidance from and through our Divinity Within. It is somewhat analogous to using a telephone. If we are constantly keeping our own phone line busy, we cannot receive incoming calls. In our personality mind there is no "call waiting" device to help us handle this dilemma.

The point being made here is that if we desire to receive divine information from above, meditation is the doorway to the soul's natural, intuitional ability to do so. It is also the doorway to making smooth progress along the spiritual path. Meditation is beneficial to all aspects of the evolutionary spiritual path back to conscious attunement and Oneness with God.

There are many different types of meditation, but all are similar in one way. All are designed to help us still our personality minds and thus provide us with experiences, guidance, and knowledge from our soul level. For example, there are guided meditations as well as personal meditations. Guided meditations are often used in group spiritual activities. Their purpose is to take the individuals in the group on a consciousness journey, a shift upward in consciousness that is peaceful, harmonious, joyful, and inspiring. This is effected through the stilling of the personality mind and the resulting automatic shifting upward to the soul level of consciousness and experience.

So the basic purpose of all meditation (methods and techniques aside) is to give us the practice we need to become adept at stilling our superficial, conscious, personality mind allowing us to move into the higher mind regions of our soul and our Divinity Within. Our eternal soul mind is older and wiser and has a much higher viewpoint and perspective than our little, temporal, externally taught, personality minds can even imagine.

At our higher soul level of consciousness we can remember what our soul already knows

In one of our early sessions with the Ascended Masters, I was speaking of our human need to learn or relearn how to be divine again, and I was gently corrected. They said that it wasn't really learning, it was more a remembering. They said it was a remembering of our true nature and character as etheric souls and as Beings of Light. At the time I couldn't quite understand how we could remember what we hadn't yet experienced; but that was before I understood our original creation as spiritual souls and our subsequent choice to insert ourselves into existing physical bodies, which caused the lowering of our consciousness to that of the personality of the body and the ensuing need for the evolutionary spiritual path of the Earth School.

What the Ascended Masters were telling me was that as my eternal soul, I already know all the things that my mortal and short-lived personality self feels I would be required to learn. Generically, as our soul selves, at our higher soul level of consciousness, we already know all the things that our personality selves may feel we will have to learn.

When we learn to still our hyperactive personality mind, we automatically shift our consciousness upward to our soul level. At our soul level we experience how it feels to be our soul again. We experience how it feels to use our higher mind, our soul's mind, again. We can shift our consciousness upward and see our world from the higher viewpoint, from the higher perspective of our soul's vision.

This is like remembering. It is not so much like learning something new. It is like being there, experiencing, and remembering. Then, if our personality is in harmony with our soul and our personality mind is still, we can bring the knowing of the soul down to our personality.

Most of humankind today does not know how to return to being our soul selves or our Divine Selves again. A very large part of that challenge is to acquire the skill, the ability, and the habit of stilling the conscious mind, the hyperactive personality mind.

Intuitional divine guidance is the optimum for those seeking truth and light on their way back to Oneness, and it is available to everyone, to ALL inhabitants of Earth, not just a few "special" cases

For obtaining divine truth and guidance related to any subject area, nothing can exceed the latent natural ability of our soul to receive truth and light from above. We can all re-awaken and remember this innate ability by making progress along the spiritual path, through creating increased harmony among our personality, our soul, and our Divinity Within. It is part of the spiritual path of evolution for each soul to be able to receive divine guidance from within, to manifest that guidance, and to live in harmony with that guidance in the third-dimensional world. Regaining the ability to receive divine guidance is part of the Earth School's design. It is part of the design for our evolution and graduation from the Earth School and part of the prediction for the Golden Age.

When we can still our personality mind at will, as a new habit pattern, we are giving ourselves the opportunity to experience the lovelier, more divine, unconditionally loving feelings, and higher vibratory rate of our soul and our Goddess/God Within. In this way we are giving ourselves the opportunity to experience, to feel, and to remember our true nature and character as divine souls and heavenly Beings of Light. We make it possible to *know* ourselves. We also make it possible to obtain divine guidance and information from Beings of Light in the higher dimensions of God (above the Earth plane). With access to that divine guidance we ensure ourselves a smoother, more rapid movement back to conscious Oneness with God, whenever we choose of our own free will to do so.

The Ultimate Awareness

In addition to what I have written on the subject of meditation, Saint Germain has added these truths, which are "not always pointed out or brought to light in treatises on meditation" and which I know to be of critical importance to any who are on the path.

Meditation, done on a regular basis, provides an entity with the actual experience of the ability to attune to, and to communicate with, her or his higher self, soul self, and Divinity Within. It is the recurring experience of communicating this way with these higher aspects of our own Beingness that provides us with the *personal evidence* that allows us to learn, to feel, and to know that God and All That There Is lies within us. This habitual experience that provides us with the personal evidence of the truth that our *connection* to all the Beings of Light, to all of God's minions, to all the Angels and Archangels, to all the Ascended Masters, and to all of our own Guardian Angels and Higher Guides, is the Spark of God that lies *within us*!

As we still our personality mind and receive intuitive guidance and answers to our internal questions about various aspects of our life on a regular basis, we gradually experience the reality that access to God, access to all we wish to know and understand, lies within. Our experience teaches us that our access to all this is internal, not external as we may have been taught.

Saint Germain further makes clear that one's Spark of God and one's expanded consciousness are in the core essence of our Being, at the very center of our beingness. He points out that if we wish to explore, to experience, and to know our true inner beauty and divinity, we can do so while in the higher consciousness of our soul in meditation.

Finally, Saint Germain states that the habitual experience of seeking and receiving guidance and information in regular meditative states moves one upward into a consistently expanded state of awareness or consciousness. He makes the point that one who practices meditation with "discipline and focus will find that he or she is able to have the same intuitive guidance flowing even in the conscious state." He makes clear that what he calls the conscious state in this case is truly the alpha or soul state of consciousness. (See Table 6-1 showing states of consciousness in Chapter 6, Prayer. See also Chapter 12, Phase 5).

Such an individual is one who has successfully made the transition from identifying with just the body and personality to becoming, to being the soul again, able to remain in the soul state of consciousness while conducting outer world activities. This individual has been successful in bringing his or her personality into such harmony with the soul that the soul state of consciousness can now be maintained without aggressive or disharmonious reactions (of the personality) to outer world circumstances.

In other words, through practicing regular meditation an entity will come to find, to experience, to realize, and to know that he or she can remain in the soul state of consciousness even while carrying out daily activities. This is the experience of being in this world, but not of it. It is also the experience of what is sometimes called enlightenment. One poses an internal question or perhaps merely wonders about something, and the understanding of that situation flows into his or her consciousness from within.

It is through the *evidence* of one's own such experiences in receiving divine inner guidance and truth through the intuitional path that one begins to realize the truth and reality of the divine nature of her or his inner Being. It is at this point along the path that one truly begins to *feel* and to *know* Self as a soul that is actually a part of God.

Meditation and the resulting ability to receive divine intuitive guidance from and through our God/Goddess Within, help us all to come to this evidential knowing.

CHAPTER 8

The Universal Law of Grace

The Ultimate Shortcut to Conscious Oneness with God

Grace is the voluntary alignment of an entity with God. It is the alignment of the personality and the soul with the Divinity Within. Grace is the potential for an immediate, instantaneous transition from being one's personality to being the soul in alignment with and guided by the Divinity Within.

Relating to an entity who is moving along the spiritual path, processing is a word that describes the clearing of the personality of discordant habit patterns one by one as each is discovered, released, and replaced with new harmonious habits. Time is required to go through this "processing."

In contrast, Grace is the more or less instantaneous transition or transmutation of an entity who learns of God's ways within the larger spiritual picture and suddenly chooses to follow them with no further ado. Grace requires only the belief that such magic is possible (through the Creative Forces of God) and that the entity herself or himself is worthy of such a gift.

The following are excerpts from a reading by Cathy from Saint Germain on 1/18/99.

✦ My question is, what is the Law of Grace?

Grace is the way that the soul has of bypassing everything. The Law of Grace is really that which allows, in its ultimate form, an instantaneous return of the soul to an experience of Oneness while in third-dimensional consciousness.

✦ Is that what we simulate or experience glimpses of in meditation?

True, yes. Yes, there can be the experience of Grace in meditation, but Grace is connected emotionally to unlimited forgiveness, unlimited acceptance, and unlimited experience of being in the flow, the Universal Flow. Grace, for that entity who is still incarnated in the third dimension, is that point at which he or she is guided by the Divine Within and allows intuition to show the way, to light the path for the next step, without question. Grace is a ***willingness to respond to higher guidance****. Grace is an* ***experience of truly letting go and letting the God Force guide the way and not grasping the reins back again****. And Grace can be experienced intermittently. It can be experienced what you would call periodically or it can be a permanent experience. In other words, an entity in consciousness can move in and out of Grace, any time it so desires.*

As an example look at the story of Saul of Tarsus who became enlightened by the side of the road. By all third-dimensional accounts a wicked man. One who manipulated and took advantage of others. One who did great harm to other human beings and yet in an instant became enlightened and who never looked back, never went back. He only moved forward in his expanded consciousness to serve God, to serve the divine within himself with unconditional love and acceptance. He became a clear channel in an instant. And Grace is not a fairy tale. It is true and it is available to any and all who are in the third dimension at this time if you seek it, if you call out to God, to the higher force, and if your commitment is true and steady.

Grace Is Available to All

The Law of Grace is also part of the Earth School's design. It allows any who suddenly awaken and understand consciously that they are still connected to God from within and are parts of God themselves, to bypass all other processes, procedures, and laws and reach Oneness instantly. In a different reading, Saint Germain mentioned that Saul of Tarsus went on to become Saint Paul.

This example means that anyone, "if your commitment is true and steady," has the potential to leave the past behind, to choose to follow the guidance from the Divinity Within and to become a clear channel of the divine, following divine guidance, and manifesting divinity into the world around them, instantly.

The Law of Grace makes it clear that for Oneness to occur, we need only to become aware of our Spark of God Within and to remain in harmony with that Goddess/God Within. All that is necessary is to follow God's ways now, regardless of the past.

Eventually we will all experience Grace. I personally had too many beliefs, thoughts, feelings, and attitudes that were unconscious hindrances to my taking the path of Grace at the beginning of my journey; but I know I am getting closer now, and it is very comforting to know that Grace is there. What hindered my spiritual progress most (carried from thirty or more years ago) was my belief that I had to know, understand, and process each of the negatives in my past life, one at a time. In this way I was very much attached to my past life as a focus of attention. Years went by until I finally asked about this and learned otherwise.

Hopefully, you will not have similar attachments, or perhaps having read this you will be aware that you can ask about such things, change such limiting beliefs, begin believing that the new ways are better, and take the quicker and smoother road that is now available. Using spiritual tools, created by the Archangels and Ascended Masters and designed for the generic dissolving and removal of our negatives, together with our personal efforts at replacing them with positives, with unconditional love and other divine attributes, can save us decades.

And of course to save the most time, try Grace. Grace is available at any time. For Grace we need no special training. We can simply choose to align self with the Divinity Within, follow our divine guidance, be our Divine Selves, and let the past go. For those who do not believe they are worthy of Grace, Saint Germain has also stated that, "All who commit are worthy of Grace."

The Law of Grace makes it clear that behaviors committed before we awaken to the fact that we are parts of God are literally of no importance and are instantly forgiven, if we ask for forgiveness. All that is necessary is to surrender to God's Way, to follow our divine guidance within, and to allow our intuition to show us the way.

This will be the way of the future in the Golden Age.

CHAPTER 9

Evolution

God's Creation of Our Way Out, Our Way Back

All mortal animal habit patterns that our human personalities have learned or adopted from our outer world environment, which cause disharmony with our soul and Divinity Within, are as attachments that hold us like a magnet to the limited, physical, third-dimensional, human life on Earth.

Involution Revisited

In the beginning of involution we took our individuated, divine, etheric souls and chose to put them into existing non-divine, physical bodies so that we could experience the feelings of physical life. We began to identify with our physical bodies and their connected personalities as opposed to our souls with their bodies of light as we had previously. However, the level of consciousness of the physical bodies we chose to play with was much lower than that of our divine soul minds, and in time we lost all awareness of ever having been souls in conscious Oneness with God. We truly identified ourselves as being merely our physical bodies and the personalities of those bodies.

In this limited state of awareness, our personalities began to learn habit patterns from the other beings in their physical, outer world environment. This method of learning was also in sharp contrast to our previous ability to receive divine guidance from the Spark of God placed within our souls at creation.

Identifying with our physical bodies and personalities, with no remaining conscious awareness of our connection to God, our personalities learned and adopted virtually everything from the outer world environment. Many of these new learned habitual ways of feeling, thinking, and believing about things were totally out of harmony with the divine ways of our now attached, entrapped souls.

The remainder of the involution phase of physical life in the Earth School simply continues the story of our increasing involvement with, experience with, and attachment to, all that we feel or think physical, human life might have to offer. Throughout the designed involution phase in our search for lasting joy, we have become increasingly involved in our personal experiments and experience with our outer world physical life until we have reached the point where we have, practically speaking, "done it all" and found it lacking.

Eventually, through our experiences, lifetime after lifetime, we may come to feel that the physical, material life we lead today in our worldwide human culture is superficial and without true, lasting meaning. When we have done it all we tend to discover (whenever we are alone, quiet, and still) that inside we feel depressed, unhappy, and unfulfilled, even though we may have attained what is commonly defined by other humans as material outer world success. When we have tried everything in the transient, mortal, material, outer world and still have not found lasting inner peace, joy, unconditional love, meaning, purpose, and fulfillment in our lives, we may find that there is nowhere else to look but within.

So the probability is that only when we have tried everything in the outer world that has ever interested us and still have failed to find lasting joy and meaning, will we then be ready to expand our horizons and seek within and above for that which we vaguely remember having once enjoyed in our original heavenly soul state. This change in our desires, our goals, and the very direction of our search (from the outer world to the inner world) is for each of us the point where our spiritual path changes from the involution phase to the evolution phase.

Evolution Is the Opposite of Involution

Evolution is the path of decreasing attachment to, and involvement with, everything in the external world that we once thought and felt was the best that physical life had to offer. It is the growth toward the increasing remembrance of the inner harmony and peace that the soul experienced in its original, divine, nonattached, spiritual form, and the increasing desire to return to the blissful and fulfilling state of conscious Oneness with God that it once knew.

Individual Evolution

Habit patterns include the unconscious, habitual ways (of feeling and thinking about certain things) that we, as our personality selves, have acquired, as well as the habitual attitudes and beliefs that we express in our daily activities. These we have learned and adopted from our personality's external world education and conditioning. Habit patterns that create, maintain, or increase disharmony between our personality, our soul, and our Spark of God Within obviously hinder or block our progress along the path toward Oneness.

Our individual spiritual evolution consists of *discovering* personality habit patterns that cause disharmony with our soul and our Spark of God Within. It includes the *releasing* of personality habit patterns that cause disharmony with our soul and Divinity Within. Our evolution also includes our *replacing* disharmonious habit patterns with new habits, which create and maintain increased harmony among our personality, our soul, and our Divinity Within.

In this way we are spiritualizing the physical body we chose to inhabit.[1] We are automatically expanding and raising the consciousness of our personality to that of our soul. We are becoming our soul again and returning to conscious Oneness with our Spark of God Within while still in our physical body experiencing physical life.

By divesting ourselves of disharmonious habit patterns, we are returning to the condition our souls once knew in our original heavenly state, where we can once more experience eternal unconditional love, meaning, purpose, and fulfillment. These are the things we have missed and found lacking in our physical life experiences. These are the things we have searched for but could never find in our physical outer world existence.

Why is it not possible to find them in the physical world? Briefly, it is because the source of all divine, unconditional love, meaning, and purpose in life is God, the All That Is and the Creator of All. It is also because the many minions of God, who are attuned to God and therefore are capable of

---

[1] As given, our *souls* were originally created by God in God's etheric or spiritual image as perfect and divine. However, after we chose to try out physical life and inserted our souls into existing physical bodies, *thus creating our own personalities,* all the habit patterns we have adopted, positive and negative, have been stored in our souls at the time of death of our mortal body in each of our many lifetime experiences. This is how our soul may have accumulated a few negative habit patterns that need a little clearing and replacing too, to create harmony with our loving Spark of God Within, which still remains untainted and divine. Most noticeable of these are *phobias* carried over from previous lifetimes in which we experienced severe trauma. Thus we may find in many humans, extreme fears of situations they did not and could not have experienced or learned in their current lifetime (i.e., fears of needles, heights, closed places, drowning, etc). But also important to note are those seemingly *"supernatural" gifts* manifested by children, such as the three- or four-year-old child who skillfully plays the piano without ever having had a lesson. Fears or gifts, these are influences from previous life experiences that were stored in the soul and are now manifesting themselves through the new baby human.

being channels of God's divine unconditional love (i.e., Angels, Archangels, Ascended Masters, and other assorted Beings of Light), all live at higher states of consciousness (fifth dimension and above). If we are looking for divine love we must first find the path to the higher states of consciousness where divine love exists, for divine love does not exist at the un-cleared personality level of humankind.

The path to higher consciousness lies within us, not outside us. To find divine love we must first seek and find the Spark of God that lies within our soul for it is truly part of God, the All That Is, and as such it is our path, our connection to the source of all divine love in the entire Cosmos.

> *Evolution is the part of the Earth School that was designed and created by God to allow us to have a way in which we, of our own free will, could grow and evolve ourselves back to conscious Oneness with God*

This is an excerpt from a reading by Cathy, on the subject of evolution, received from Saint Germain on 10/10/98.

The evolution here is from a consciousness that is or feels itself to be separate from God, all the way back to Absolute Oneness with the Creator.

What do we or can we actually do after we make the decision to move along the spiritual path of evolution? As already given, it is a matter of clearing disharmony from our personality, which aligns and attunes us with our soul and the Divinity that lives within our soul.

> *Releasing attachments to negative habit patterns that we have learned from our outer world physical life helps us to find true purpose, meaning, and fulfillment in an inner life of higher consciousness, in the realms above the physical, even while still having a physical body*

It is our attachments and addictions to outer world Earthly things, formed over our many lifetimes, which hold us like magnets to the lower consciousness of our outer physical world. We adopted and created our attachments because we knew of no other life. After the veils of consciousness dropped at age five to seven, we learned about life only from other humans who themselves knew little other than the physical and material. Humankind had not yet evolved far enough toward harmony among the personality, the soul, and the Spark of God Within, to be able to receive divine guidance and truth from above. But now, with the coming of the higher vibrational rate of the new millennium, humanity is ready.

As the world culture awakens to the larger spiritual picture, to the truth of life presented from above, humankind will begin to move in the direction of letting go and releasing attachments to any habit patterns, which we as individuals grow to understand no longer serve us well, no longer serve our higher good. We will simultaneously replace them with harmonious habit patterns that expand our awareness and understanding and move us higher in consciousness toward greater harmony and joy among our personality, our soul, and our God/Goddess Within. We will be bringing our inner heaven into the Earth School and transmitting it to those around us.

Rather than ignoring or denying certain disharmonious or negative habit patterns in our lives, we will happily identify them and acknowledge their presence so we can begin to release them and change our lives by replacing them with positives. Each negative habit or attachment that we replace with a positive brings us closer to the higher dimensional level of our soul and to the increasingly greater harmony, joy, love, and peace with our God/Goddess Within. We will no longer hide negatives from ourselves for we will understand that to do so will only prolong our Earthbound, lower-dimensional limitations and unhappiness.

This is how evolution has always been since the Earth School was created. But today something new has been added. In the context of the new millennium, we are now living in a unique time frame that provides any of us who wish to evolve back to Oneness with God with a tremendous advantage.

The spiritual meaning behind the new millennium—the third since the life of Christ, one of the early wayshowers

---

This is an excerpt from a reading by Cathy, on the subject of evolution, received from Saint Germain on 10/10/98. We were speaking of various aspects of evolution relating to the new millennium. I was verifying several concepts that had been given previously.

✦ For a thousand years evolution will take place probably with greater and greater speed during the thousand years, taking a while to get going?

From the perspective of the third dimension and time that is correct.

✦ And then those who are of a lower vibratory rate, who were excluded from incarnating during this millennium, will be allowed back in? The planet isn't going to go downhill again (in consciousness), is it?

No. Do you not recall that spiritual development is a spiral (in the shape of an upward spiral) *and even in the higher dimensions beings come back* (around) *to the same point again and again, meeting similar challenges but always from a higher point on the spiral? Evolution for the planet is the same* (as for any soul). *It is a spiral.*

✦ I find that hard to get my arms around. A parallel between being a planet and being just me.

There is no difference whatsoever. Understand that the mission of your planet is to be the school. And not forever, not forever. Planets change as the focus of incarnation.

✦ Okay, but will there always be a place for the school?

For as long as it is necessary. Souls evolve in many places. As long as there is the need for the kind of school environment that the Earth plane offers, it will be available. But the Planetary Logos moves on from its use of the planet as a body in the same way that you do.

Planetary Evolution

The planet Earth itself is a great conscious being with a soul just like ours. It is called, by those in the higher realms, the Planetary Logos. The soul of planet Earth is now in the midst of making a quantum leap in its own evolutionary path toward its divine state by moving upward to a higher state of consciousness. In fact, the effects of the higher vibrational rate caused by its movement into a higher dimension have been noticeable to many of its inhabitants since 1986. This is why it is now so much easier for many of us to learn to receive and speak or journal information from the higher realms of Godness. The planet is moving naturally from the third-dimensional vibrational rate (that we have been familiar with) to a fourth-dimensional rate that is the next step closer to its divine state of consciousness.

The fact that the planet is in the midst of this evolutionary step at this time affects all inhabitants of Earth dramatically and beautifully. Because the Earth planet has been increasing in its own vibrational rate, we inhabitants also are now living in the atmosphere of that increased rate. The increased frequencies of spiritual vibration exist within, through, and around the Earth planet and its inhabitants. Calling this an increased vibrational rate is synonymous with calling it a higher frequency of light in the aura of the Earth. Though the "light" is not yet visible to most of us, the effects of the increased frequency of the vibrational rate are noticeable to all, either consciously or unconsciously.

What does it do for us? It lifts us higher in consciousness! It makes it easier to receive helpful information from our soul, our Goddess/God Within, our Guardian Angels, our Higher Guides, and others in the Angelic Realms through our natural feminine intuitional paths. The increased vibrational rate affects our minds and facilitates our ability to understand larger, more abstract philosophical concepts and relationships. The higher rate also makes it easier to remember our nightly dreams and to understand their meanings relating to our spiritual path. It narrows the distance between Earth consciousness and the higher consciousness of the heavens above.

Worldwide Spiritual Evolution

This rate of vibration of the Earth planet will continue to increase until the planetary Logos has moved completely into its new higher vibrational rate of consciousness in a decade or two. Up to the present time, all existing entrapped souls have been permitted to reincarnate into this Earth life, this school, regardless of their personal vibrational rate. All souls have been permitted to mingle together in school, whether they were in the beginning, middle, or end of their involutionary or evolutionary phase. This is similar to the way our old one-room schoolhouses merged all students from different grade levels or age levels into the one room available.

However, when the Earth has moved more completely into its higher vibrational rate, souls that still exist at a lower rate of consciousness, a more aggressive rate of consciousness, will find the new vibrational rate of the planet Earth no longer compatible to them.[2]

Then, for one thousand years, only those souls whose vibrational rates are compatible with the higher fourth-dimensional frequencies and who live at those frequencies or higher (fifth and upward) will be able to incarnate in the Earth School environment. The lower vibrational, more aggressive students (those souls who are still in their involution phase) will automatically be separated from students who have chosen the spiritual path and made some progress along it.

This will be a self-imposed separation. They will be separated by their own freewill choice to remain at their lower vibrational rate. Because the planet itself is moving to a higher rate, these souls will no longer be able to support physical life on Earth at their lower rates of consciousness. The two rates will be incompatible.

---

[2] This is truly why the meek shall inherit the Earth. Those students still having lower vibrational, *aggressive* tendencies will not be able to sustain life in the new higher vibrational rates that the soul of the Earth planet is taking on in its evolutionary growth. "Higher vibrational rates" mean more divine love and fewer aggressive tendencies. Higher vibrational rates facilitate our approach to the higher dimensions of heaven above.

Souls of a disharmonious rate of consciousness will be given another place in which to continue their schooling until they also finally learn that they desire something more divine than mere physical life has to offer. There they will remain in school until eventually they make their own freewill choice to return to wholeness and completion, joy and love, in conscious Oneness with God.

This is an excerpt from a reading by Cathy received from Athenarious on 10/12/96. This reading was requested for the purpose of receiving information on the value of intuition for the future evolution of humankind and the requirement for a balance between divine feminine and divine masculine energy in any who desire the ability to receive intuitional guidance.

There is never a time, there is never an activity in the third dimension where intuition would not be an incredibly valuable tool, an incredibly valuable activity in daily living. In survival, but more importantly in spiritual development in the evolution aspect of this designed Earth experience. ***For the involution process will soon be completely eliminated from the experience of the planet itself.*** *Currently there are still those entities that incarnate into the Earth plane who are in the involution cycle. With the coming of the new millennium this will cease entirely. Only those who are in the evolution cycle and only those who have made good progress, who are in the upper portions of the evolution cycle, will find themselves able to manifest bodies, to create bodies which are compatible with the vibratory rate, the ambiance, the environment of the new millennium. And so you see that it is absolutely required that the feminine be integrated and balanced with the masculine.*

The next thousand years will provide an environment that allows humankind to make tremendous gains on the evolutionary spiritual path and to bring into life on Earth greater harmony, peace, fulfillment, and unconditional love than has ever existed on this planet before. It will bring to all inhabitants of Earth a complete understanding of the larger picture of all life throughout the Cosmos. This will be the Golden Age often alluded to in the Ancient Wisdom teachings.

Arrangements for those who do not yet wish to move back to harmony and Oneness with God are already designed into the plan. As they pass over, they will be provided places with other souls of the same vibrational rate as their own. They just won't have the opportunity to reincarnate on Earth for the next thousand years.

This is an excerpt from a reading by Cathy received from St. Germain on 10/25/98.

✦ Will you, can you, are you permitted to describe the sort of life humankind on Earth will be living toward the beginning, middle, and end of the coming millennium?

In terms of the culture then, in terms of humanity?

✦ Yes. I'm sorry (for my ambiguity).

Very well. As you know, as you experience yourself, and as you perceive in your experiences, the awakening of many souls, the awakening of many consciousnesses, to their higher selves, to their soul selves, to their true purpose, or, at a minimal their awakening to the existence of a higher self and a true purpose, a life mission, if you will, is becoming much more commonplace in the world today compared to that say ten or even five years in the past.

Seeking is becoming a way of life for many, and in that seeking frustration is becoming a way of life for many because of the differences between the true spiritual reality and that which the culture teaches, that which is fairly ingrained in most entities who have not spent some time being awakened to an expanded consciousness. There is the frustration for there is the finding of self living the life experience that has been primarily created with the understanding, the awareness, the perspective of ego (personality), *and cultural guidelines, often religious guidelines, as well as political guidelines.*

And so now particularly there is a time of discomfort that may or may not lead to a time of disease for each individual. For as the soul gains access to the consciousness (the time being what it is, and the vibratory rate, and the level of light of the Earth plane being what they are and increasing as rapidly as they are) there is in truth not great time and space for adjustment, for moving along at a slow pace. The awakenings, the turnarounds are quicker and they are more or less complete. Some awaken and instantly turn their direction to the path and never look back. This is not the norm, but it does occur. Others awaken and find themselves greatly torn between the life that they now lead, which they find most unacceptable, and a life which they find they are drawn to, but which is quite unknown. And fear of the unknown is one of the greatest fears in the Earth plane that humanity has to experience. And so there is the great need for teachers and guides and lightworkers and those who are willing to encourage, to support, and to show the way.

As the millennium takes hold, as we move more toward the middle time of the millennium, we find the time of great inner peace. We find the time of connectiveness, of Oneness, of expanded consciousness and awareness on the part of each entity as to who he or she is, what he or she is, and a clear understanding of his or her purpose in this life experience, of the mission that they are to lead, to pursue, the life they are to lead.

In this time you will find that entities will primarily be guided from within. *They will be very much aware of their intuition, of their inner guidance, and they will seek consciously and actively the harmony and the peace that comes with following this inner guidance without question. This will continue on throughout the entire millennium, perhaps becoming stronger, perhaps becoming more prevalent toward the end, but in any case this is really the description of the being who will be able to be incarnated on this planet, in the third dimension, and be in harmony with the vibratory rate, the aura shall we say, of the planet itself.*

New spiritual tools are available to speed up spiritual progress for those who choose the spiritual path

Because there is no longer an unlimited amount of time for those who wish to make themselves available for classes during the millennium times, new spiritual tools have been created by the Archangels and Ascended Masters and made available to anyone who desires to use them. These spiritual tools can help anyone on the path to reduce the time and effort required for her or his journey to a fraction of what it would take using the old "processing" methods.

In part this is possible because the Ascended Masters advocate handling the release of our negative attachments en masse and have designed spiritual tools to do just that. Now, for example, by using the new spiritual tools, we may if we choose, release all our fears in general, without going through the agonizing detail of dealing with every fear inside us one by one by one. It is also the same with other types of negative attachments.

Because of the increased availability of information from above, there is a much clearer path in these times. Previously, very few knew that there existed a Universal Spiritual Path behind physical life, much less of what it consisted, its nature, its purpose, and its end goal. Treading any path without knowing one's purpose or goal provides little motivation, and doing so without a clear direction can waste a lot of time.

Previously, due to our education and conditioning from "the perspective of ego and cultural guidelines" (man-made information), very few humans even knew that they were all assigned a Guardian Angel and a Higher Guide to assist them to find their God Within, much less how best to use their help. Very few understood the context of how life on Earth related to the true Spiritual Life behind it as offered from the higher realms. Few understood the true meaning and purpose of life on Earth, the fall in consciousness of humankind, or of the Earth as a school to help us get back to

Oneness (when and if we choose). Lastly, very few knew that the highest purpose of all humans on Earth is to return to their own natural state of Oneness with God and to manifest their Divinity into the world around them in whatever way they find is most appropriate.

There is now an increased awareness of the availability of assistance from above[3]

The information you are reading in this book was provided by the Angels, Archangels, Higher Guides, Masters, Ascended Masters, and other members of the Hierarchy of God, those "extraterrestrial" parts of God whose primary mission is to watch over the Earth School and to assist us humans in our evolution.[4] All of these same entities, these Beings of Light, have helped many others to create many other books, each intended to help humankind on its path of evolution.

This all means that due to today's extraordinary circumstances one can now take a very direct route back to Oneness with God, as compared to using the trial-and-error methods related to man-made concepts about God and the Spiritual Path. Now we can use knowledge received directly from the heavens above to hasten our progress.

See Appendix C for a reasonably concise overview of the Universal Spiritual Picture of the creation of all souls, the entrapment of some, and the creation of the cycles of Involution and Evolution in the Earth School as our way out.

---

[3] Chapter 13 has more detail on the Beings of Light who are available to provide all of humankind with the assistance needed for spiritual growth back to conscious Oneness with God.

[4] The quotation marks here are meant as sort of an inside joke. As mentioned briefly, all *souls* are extraterrestrial. We all were created as etheric souls with Bodies of Light having no attachments to any planet. And ever since we chose to attach ourselves to physical life on Earth, we still spend a great deal of time on other planets during our soul's life between incarnations, while taking part in our classes and field trips.

PART II

An Overview of the Spiritual Realms

The view of human evolution as seen from above

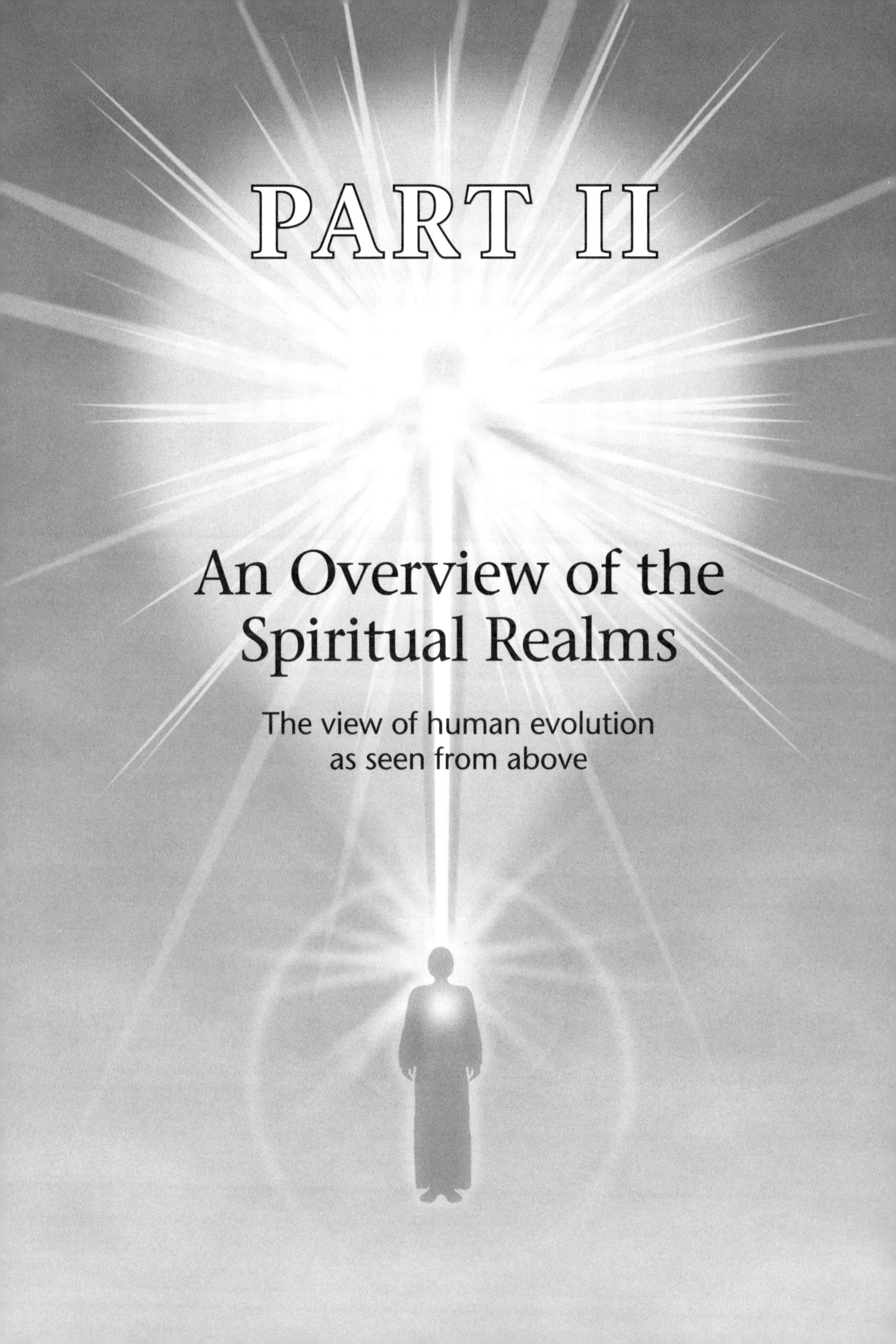

CHAPTER 10

The Three Parts of Our Beingness

The Trinity Within

All humans have three distinct aspects or parts to our Beingness. Each aspect lives at a different level of consciousness and in a different dimension. The relationship between them is hierarchical, as shown in Figure 10-1. The soul is reached through the personality (from within the personality), and the Divinity Within is reached through the soul. (See Table 10-1 for a condensed guide to the aspects of human beingness.)

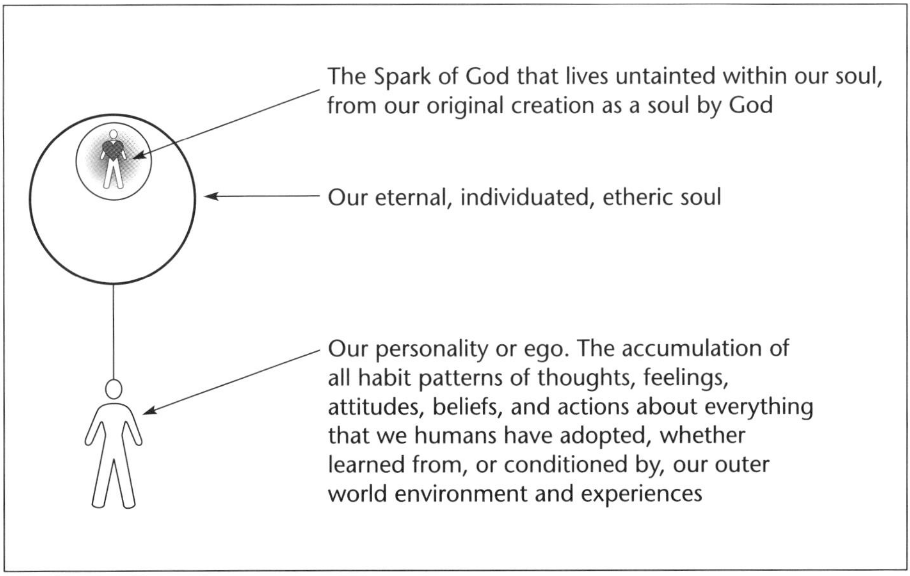

Figure 10-1 The three aspects of our beingness

The Personality

The personality is the consciousness of our physical body. The mind of the personality is the lowest level of consciousness available to all the students of the Earth School. Our personality includes all the accumulated habitual ways we have of feeling and thinking about everything we have experienced. Our personality also includes all the beliefs and attitudes that we have adopted and accepted as true through our "education" and/or our conditioning by our external, outer world environment.

In general, in humankind's current state of evolution, our personality learns only from its outer world environment. It therefore learns and adopts only man-made outer world knowledge, beliefs, perceptions, and understandings.

The personality of the physical body, the ego, is the aspect of beingness with which most people on Earth identify in today's world. We have been cut off from being consciously aware of our soul, and the Spark of God that lives within our soul, for so long that most humans now identify only with the physical body and the personality that is tied to that body, the consciousness of the physical body.

Since birth we have learned, or have been taught and conditioned by the external world, to believe, to think, and to feel that we are only our physical body and its personality. We have been taught to feel and think in very *personal*,[1] egocentric ways about all aspects of life on Earth because we have learned about that life from other human personalities having only their own limited perspectives to guide them. We have, at various times, in various lifetimes, been taught and conditioned to believe such things as that the Earth is flat. Entire populations were taught to believe that we could fall off the edge of the Earth if we voyaged too far, that heavier than air machines could never fly, and millions of other transient, limited, man-made beliefs.[2]

---

[1] This may foster a question something like, "What other way is there to see, to feel, or to think?" And the answer is, *impersonally*, from above, with the wonderful, beautiful, and loving feelings and the higher perspective of our higher dimensional soul self. Once you experience this on your path, you will probably remember having felt this way at other times in your life, perhaps when you were unable to identify the experience as that of being at your soul level (as you being your soul). It is a very light feeling, a very expansive feeling. It is almost like being weightless and floating or flying above yourself while walking around in a physical body. It is joyous, and it was once our natural state of being as a soul before we decided to become involved in physical life.

[2] For a more graphic example of mankind's concept of truth, notice how frequently the FDA changes its opinions about which drugs are safe for human consumption. It often declares a product as safe and then overrules its own man-made judgments after the body count exceeds a prescribed number of deaths attributed to drug interactions or incompatibility.

We accept these concepts as truth from the "highest" source, the human mind. In large measure we have learned to live our lives only in accordance with the guidance offered by other human personalities and their personal outer world perceptions. We have based our concept of truth only upon the physical world perspectives of other human personalities. Until now we have never even dreamt of the potential for all of humanity to evolve itself to a higher level of consciousness that would enable it to receive divine truth and understanding directly from the higher realms of God above. However, with the added light present in the environment of the planet Earth today, at this beginning of the Golden Age, the time has come for all of humanity to naturally raise its level of consciousness to its next higher level, the soul level.

One of the most limiting of the man-made beliefs, which humanity has accepted, was/is that we humans are separated from God. This belief seems valid because many feel separated from God and the feeling translates to the belief. The awesome effect of such a belief is obvious. If you believe that you are indeed only a physical being, completely separated from God and anything divine, you are far more likely to behave like an animal. If you learn that you are a part of God with a spark of Divinity within you, you are likely to act in more divine ways until you become divine once more. When you begin to taste the effects of inner harmony with this divinity, you will find that you will never consciously wish to do anything that you know will diminish that inner feeling of divine inner harmony.

In truth, as given from above, we are still connected to God. We are each still a part of God. We simply have lost our conscious awareness of the divine part within us that is our "connection."[3] This is the how and why of our entrapment in physical life.

Until now we have been taught from birth by nearly everyone in our outer world environment that we are merely our mortal bodies and our outer world conditioned personality minds. Few understand that we were created by God as etheric eternal souls with a Spark of God within our soul. Few understand that at our soul level of consciousness, we all (already) have the innate ability to communicate with our Divinity Within on a

---

[3] The Ascended Masters have frequently taken exception to my use of the word "connect" (i.e., the Spark of God within our soul connects us all to God, The All That Is). From their perspective the word connect still connotes the unreality of a kind of separation and then a subsequent 're-connection' to that which was once separated. From their perspective there never has been a true separation *except in our level of consciousness*. You can see their point. There exists in each of our souls an actual part of God from our creation. That part of ourselves, at the level of our soul, *is* God, *is* a part of God. Their point is that that part is not merely a "connection" to God, the All That Is; it is truly *God* within us. It is truly *God* within our soul. This is a problem I have with our human semantics whenever I wish to convey the concept of our relationship, our connectedness, to God and to each other in Oneness.

moment-to-moment basis and can thereby receive the type of divine guidance that would allow us to stay in complete harmony with God at all times and in all circumstances.

With the added light or higher vibratory rate (which is part of the new millennium's environment) many are learning to receive information from the higher realms through their natural intuitive paths. As this continues and this information, this truth from above, becomes more widespread, more and more of the world population will be taught the higher knowledge that comprises the Universal Spiritual Picture.

Growing numbers of ordinary people will be provided with information coming from the higher realms of God, which indicates that they are, in truth, souls created by God still having a divine part of God within them. More ordinary humans will be given the perception from above that they are all truly parts of God.

As the higher knowledge becomes more commonly available, all humanity will better understand the possibility of discovering their true identity and their true potential for the future. Humankind will test this higher knowledge through personal experience and begin to know that God has indeed created a way out of this personality mind dilemma. Thousands and thousands will soon be making the personal choice to commit to the spiritual path.

As these first few grow along the path they will be evolving themselves and bringing divine light and love, a natural by-product of spiritual growth, into themselves and into the Earth School environment around them. Their success along the path will motivate others who will begin to see the personal benefits of the journey in terms of greater inner harmony, peace, joy, understanding, meaning, purpose, fulfillment, and unconditional love in those who undertake it. These blissful inner feelings all occur naturally in all entities who have made the changes to themselves that harmonize their personalities with their souls, and their souls with the divine Sparks of God Within their souls.

The Soul

The soul is our original, eternal, and etheric beingness as created by God. Our soul is our real self, our true identity.[4] It lives at a much higher level of consciousness than that of our personality. Our soul has a much higher

---

[4] Our personality is a kind of false self, created *not* by God, but in one of two ways. It was created either by our soul's naïve, unintentional, playful activity of inserting itself into the physical bodies of existing animals and becoming one of the original entrapped souls, or by our soul"s volunteering to become human in order to be a

perspective (the higher realms) from which to observe life than does our personality. Our soul has a more impersonal view of life on Earth. It also has a much more loving heart, a higher mind, and a higher will (i.e., desiring that which is for the higher good of all humankind) than does our personality.

Our soul knows itself to be eternal. It has been around for dozens, hundreds, and perhaps even thousands of its various personality's lifetimes. Our soul has learned from all its experiences far more than our personality can in only one lifetime (for each personality).

Though etheric, our soul does have a vehicle called a light body. With practice we can learn (relearn or remember) how to experience our light body at will (part III has a meditation exercise to help us do just that and part IV has more). In the Light Body **State of Being**, we *are* our souls, living at our soul level and feeling what it is like to be a soul, while still having a physical body. We move our consciousness (from our personality state) to the higher conscious plane of our soul. In the Light Body State of Being we are multidimensional, transcendental, and have a direct communication with our Goddess/God Within. It is a natural state, which occurs as a result of progress along our path of spiritual evolution.

As our soul selves we can open to receive, experience, and resonate with the unconditional love of our Divinity Within. We can also receive light and love from all other appropriate minions of God, the All That Is. We can receive both light (in the form of information and understanding) and unconditional love through our soul's natural inner intuitional path, from our own Goddess/God Within and/or from other divine Beings of Light, in accordance with God's Universal Laws.

Our soul is in a state of evolution just as is all of life. Before it became entrapped in this physical world life, our soul's evolution and advancement in the hierarchy of Godness were under its own control. Now however, our soul's evolution is dependent upon our individual ability to bring harmony among our personality (which our soul inadvertently created in its playing with physical life), our soul, and the Spark of God that still lives untainted within our soul. This is the way out of our entrapment, as designed by the minions of God in the higher realms of God, when they first observed the catch-22 dilemma in which we had entrapped ourselves. Inner harmony is the way to graduation from our physical, limited consciousness, Earth School environment.

---

wayshower to others. There are many of these lightworkers, starseeds, or wayshowers here on Earth today who have not yet awakened from what the Beings of Light call their slumber. That is to say, there are many volunteers here who do not yet remember or realize their mission or purpose for being here.

The Spark of God Within

The Spark of God Within is one name for the divine part of God that God placed within all souls at our original creation. It remains pure, untouched, and untainted by our soul's immersion into physical life forms. It is our God/Goddess Within. It is our Holy Spirit Within. It is an actual part of God and our connection to God, the All That Is (i.e., all other minions of God in the Hierarchy of God including the Angels, Archangels, Ascended Masters, and others). There is no limit to the number of synonyms that can be used to refer to the Divinity Within. Our Divinity Within is the highest possible level of consciousness in our beingness. In some circles it is called our Superconscious mind.

All divine knowledge is brought to the personality level of our beingness *from or through* our Divinity Within. Higher knowledge that we desire and request may come directly from our Divinity Within if that information is already in its repertoire of experience. However, if we seek information that is not already within the breadth of experience of our individuated Divinity Within (individuated since the moment it was placed in our soul at creation), then higher knowledge may come from other appropriate minions of God who are in the higher realms of other reaches of the Universe. In this case these minions of God may bring our requested information to our own Divinity Within, which passes it down to our soul where our personality can receive it (but only if our personality is in harmony with our soul). Regardless, relative to our souls, all higher information and knowledge comes to us from the divine Spark of God within our soul, whether that information comes directly from our Divinity Within or through it passed to us from other minions of God, the All That Is.

This is an example of part of the Oneness of God to which we all may be able to relate. If our intentions[5] are for the higher good of all life everywhere, we will receive the information we request. To know the specific source of such knowledge, we would have to ask. Even then, unless knowledge of the precise source serves a valid, beneficial purpose for other humans, it may not be provided. Remember, we are speaking of the higher realms of God here and entities at that level of consciousness do not require or desire personal acknowledgment or thanks. They know the will of God because they live in full conscious Oneness with God, and they carry out their missions in blissful harmony with full conscious awareness of God's will.

Our Divinity Within is the highest level of consciousness in our beingness. It is our divine mind. It is also our highest vibrational level of feelings, our divine heart, and our highest level of will, our divine will. Our

---

[5] Our true intentions are all always known by those in the higher realms of God.

Divinity Within is always in conscious Oneness with God, the All That Is, and therefore with all the many minions of God comprising the All That Is. It is the source for all divine guidance to our soul on its evolutionary path back to conscious Oneness.

Table 10-1 The Three Aspects of Our Human Beingness

Dimension	*Common Names of the Aspects of Our Beingness*	*Related Aspects of Heart, Mind, and Will*	*Definition or Description*
The Third Dimension The Physical Plane Our physical 'Earth world'	Personality or Ego	The conscious mind, heart, and will of our physical body's personality.	The consciousness of the personality of our physical, third-dimensional body. The entirety of all habit patterns (including feelings, thoughts, attitudes, beliefs, and actions) that our human personality has adopted or learned from all our outer, physical world environmental conditioning and experiences.
The Fourth Dimension The Astral Plane	Soul	Our Soul's Higher mind, Higher heart, and Higher will	Our eternal, individuated, etheric, spiritual soul. Our real self created by God in God's etheric or spiritual image in a body of light.
The Fifth Dimension (and higher) The Divine Etheric, Spiritual Planes	The Spark of God that lives within our soul The Divinity Within The Goddess/God Within The Holy Spirit The Christ Spirit The Monad	The Divine mind, Divine heart, and Divine will of our Spark of God Within	The Spark of God, which was placed in our soul at our original creation as a perfect soul. A part of God existing within our soul, that remains divine, perfect, and untainted by our physical world activities. The part of our Beingness, which is the cause of our Oneness with the Divinity of all other souls or minions of God everywhere in the Universe.

The awakening of all students in the Earth School to the three aspects of the beingness of all humans

Each soul is an individuated part of God because of its Divinity Within. All souls are part of God through their Divinity Within. All souls are thus part of the Oneness of God. As our souls, we are really all parts of God, all parts of the One God.

God, the All That Is, comprises all Life throughout the entire Cosmos (not just that of our Earth School). God comprises all the Sparks of God that were placed within the souls of all beings everywhere at creation. This includes the souls of those beings who are now Angels, Archangels, other members of the entire Angelic Realm, Higher Guides, Masters, Ascended Masters, the **Great White Brotherhood**, and on and on. God, the All That Is, includes the souls of humans who were among those who originally became entrapped in physical life and the souls of those who volunteered to become wayshowers. It includes the souls of all who are now incarnated and attending classes in the Earth School.

Awakening to the larger spiritual picture behind our physical life includes awakening to the very real existence of these three aspects of our own beingness. When we awaken to the possibility that we are not just our physical bodies, nor merely our outer world fashioned and shaped personalities, we also begin to awaken to the possibility of evolving ourselves back to our original higher state of blissful and fulfilling conscious Oneness with God, from whence we came.

Our current belief that our personality is our true identity causes us to place our main focus of attention on outer world activities (somewhere around 100%). This prevents our learning or remembering how to experience and enjoy the higher, more refined levels of ourselves. Our extreme focus on the outer world prevents us from seeking within and growing to know and experience our true divine nature and character (which lies within). It therefore prevents us from Being and manifesting our true selves in peace, in joy, and in our love of God, of self, and of all others. This is why personalities lack lasting inner feelings of true fulfillment. When we are being only our personalities, *we are not all there*! To find what is missing in our lives we must seek within.

When we have progressed along the spiritual path to the point where we are able to achieve a certain degree of harmony and balance among our personality, our soul, and the Divinity within our soul, we can each receive divine guidance and divine love through our soul's natural intuitional path (from and through our own Goddess/God Within). That will be when and where we find the inner feelings of true joy, unconditional love, wholeness, completion, and fulfillment, which we have long felt to be missing from the lives we lead as only our personality selves.

CHAPTER 11

Divine Dynamics

Receiving Higher Information from the Higher Realms of God

In the beginning there was only God. Because there was only God, God created all souls from God's Beingness so all souls have a divine Spark of God within them.

The Spark of God within our soul is an actual individuated part of God, and as such it connects each of us to the center of God, the All That Is.

We are each a part of God. We are each connected to God. Because all souls are connected to God, we are also connected to each other. Together we all comprise the One God, our Creator. We are all One. See Figure 11-1 on page 116 to better visualize these concepts.

Because of our soul's involvement with physical life on Earth, we humans have simply lost conscious awareness of our connection to our soul and to the Spark of God within it. We once knew our soul and its body of light to be our true identity, and we once received divine guidance and other information from and through our divine Spark of God within our soul; but now, in our entrapped state of lower consciousness, we are largely quite unaware of our higher aspects. They are still a part of our beingness, but we have lost our moment-to-moment awareness of them due to our extreme focus on our outer world environment. In general we now believe our body and its personality to be our true identity.

> *All information in the Universe is stored and available to us and to all other minions of God*

During each of a soul's many lifetimes or incarnations, the new personality learns, accepts, and adopts many personal habit patterns of thinking, feeling, and believing, all coming from the outer world. *All these personality*

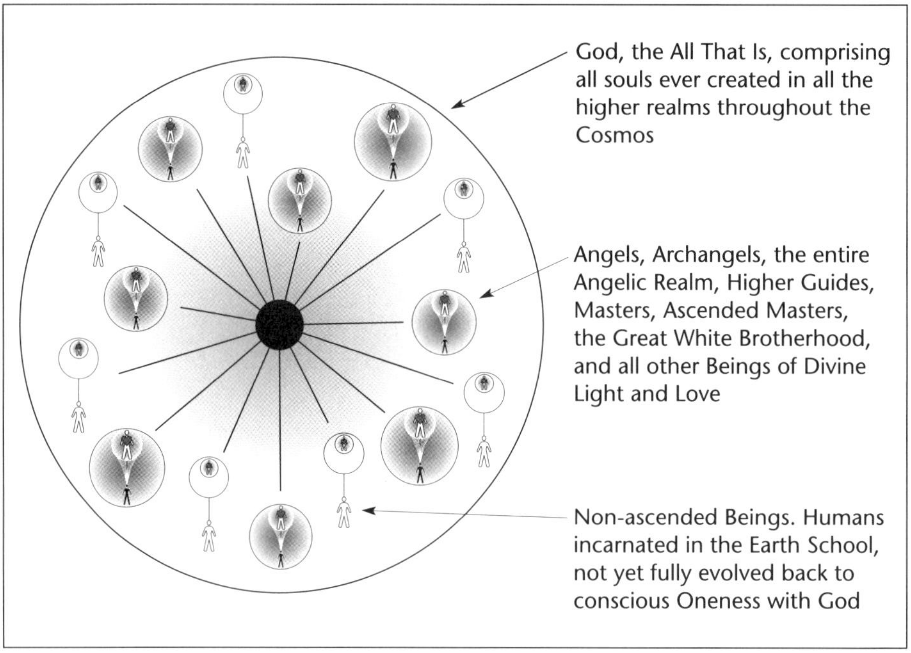

Figure 11-1 We are all One, we are each a part of God, and together we all comprise God, the All That Is

habit patterns, including the habitual ways we feel about certain things, the habitual ways we have of thinking about things, and all the man-made beliefs we have accepted as truths due to our outer world learning and conditioning, *are stored in our eternal soul at the death of our mortal physical body.* All our personality's habit patterns are stored in our soul whether they are positive or negative, whether their effect is to increase our inner harmony or decrease it.

In addition to the personality's habit patterns, *all information related to anything and everything that has ever happened to a soul, and all information related to all events that have occurred in the mere presence of a soul, in all its many lifetimes, is also stored (as it occurs) in the energy of that eternal soul.* So if your soul witnessed a huge volcano at some time in the distant past, and another soul desires to know about that event now, the information stored in your soul may be provided.

Receiving Higher Information

It is very much like using the keyword volcano to retrieve information stored in a large database. Using the database keyword analogy, all that is needed by a soul to find the correct information on a particular event or person is a unique key. To find information on a specific volcano, the unique key may only require its name, global location, and a date. For a person (as in the case where someone writes questions in a letter and mails them to one who can receive such information) the unique key may require their name, and the location, date, and time of their birth. Name, location, and the date and time of birth usually will uniquely identify the *personality* involved, and the appropriate Beings of Light in the heavens above will know which *soul* is or was connected to that personality. There is very little mystery involved.[1]

What if information is desired about someone for whom the location, date, and time of birth are not known? There are other methods of uniquely identifying a soul. Two such methods include using a photograph in which their body appears or obtaining an original signature. The reading is then conducted and information is requested for the soul of the person "who appears in this photograph" or "who signed this letter." Either of these methods will precisely identify the soul for whom the information is desired. Obviously, there are dozens of other methods of uniquely identifying a soul, including simple dialog. For the divine connections to be made to the appropriate eternal soul (to retrieve the correct stored information), it is necessary merely to uniquely identify the person to whom the soul is or was attached.

The following is an excerpt from a reading by Cathy provided by Saint Germain on 09/11/99.

✦ In the book I have written that everything that happens to an individual and everything that happens around an individual or in the presence of an individual, is stored in the aura of the soul, and I am looking for verification of the accuracy of that information.

You may actually say that it is stored in its soul. However, the soul itself does not have what equates to the aura in the third dimension.

✦ Oh, it does not?

[1] If the individual receiving the information is doing so consciously, any possible conflicts or confusion (as in the case of the birth of identical twins whose names you may have forgotten) will be taken care of by means of a little dialog with the higher dimensional source of the information. For example, "I mean the twin who now lives in Heafford Junction, Wisconsin in the big white house next to the guy who sells minnows for bait." The dialog would continue until there is sufficient understanding on both sides.

The auric fields about the physical body are not the same. ***The soul itself is energy.*** *It has no physical component.* ***And the information is stored within that energy.***

✦ Oh, so the concept is correct but the use of word aura is not appropriate?

Correct.

✦ And so the Akashic records are the composite of all the information stored in all souls?

That is sufficiently accurate, yes.

All this is being divinely managed from above. Heaven is highly organized. All Beings of Light are competent in their positions. (This is why it is called Heaven.)

All these types of communications are divinely monitored. Information is provided from above only in accordance with the three major effects of the Universal Law of Free Will. The purpose of these higher means of communication is to help those of us who are entrapped in our personality consciousness to find our way back to conscious Oneness with God and there are Karmic prices to pay for those who use higher information against others. Perhaps merely understanding how all this can and does happen, will help some to see that there is a much larger life to be lived than what our personalities have been taught down here.

Obtaining divine guidance is and always has been an innate ability of all souls

Because all souls are connected to each other and all information even faintly related to a soul is stored in the soul, all information about anything can be obtained by those who have reclaimed their soul's ability to do so. All souls are eternal. This is what makes it possible to obtain information about anything (even in the distant past) deemed helpful toward the mission of assisting humankind to evolve back to Oneness with God.

Our eternal souls have always had this ability. Each soul in all of humanity has the potential to obtain information about itself or anything else in the Universe that is appropriate. Regaining this ability is now part of the spiritual path, like a milestone. It is like an enlightenment milestone or an intuitional divine guidance milestone.

How do we get to the intuitional milestone? Merely by choosing the spiritual path and making progress along the path by creating increased harmony between our man-made personality, our God-created soul, and our Divinity Within. As we discover and release some of our personality's disharmonious habit patterns and replace them with habits that increase harmony among our higher aspects, there is an automatic upward movement in consciousness toward our soul level. When we have created a certain degree of harmony among our three aspects of beingness, our personality will begin to receive the divine guidance and other helpful information presented to our soul from the higher realms of God (which include our own Divinity Within) through our natural intuitive path.

> *All information received from above comes either directly **from** the higher aspects of our own beingness or **through** them from other Beings of Light in the heavens above (whichever we choose)*

We may pose silent inner questions to our higher self, our soul, or even to our Goddess or God Within, still our personality mind, and receive the answers directly through our soul's higher heart and higher mind. Such answers may come directly *from* the higher aspects of our own self (for they are parts of God).

Or we may call upon specific Beings of Light whom we know have a specialty area that coincides with the information we are seeking. In this case the information may come *through* our Divinity Within, from our Guardian Angels, our Higher Guides, or other Angels and Beings of Light whom we specifically request.

All the information we request that is provided by other Creative Forces of God must come to us through the Divine Spark of God within our soul. Other Beings of Light may retrieve the requested information from somewhere in the Universe and pass it to our Divinity Within. See Figure 11-2 on page 120. Regardless, if we wish to receive information at our personality level, we are required to create and maintain a certain degree of harmony among our personality, our soul, and our Divinity Within.

Basic Requirements for Receiving Divine Guidance

There is no generic sequence or order which could be termed "better" or "best" to get us back to conscious Oneness with our God Within, and with God, the All That Is. Other than the first two items, there is no particular sequence to the order in which these are to be attained.

- Awakening to the Universal Spiritual Picture.
- Committing to the spiritual path back to Oneness with God.
- Creating an inner harmony among the personality, the soul, and the God/Goddess Within.

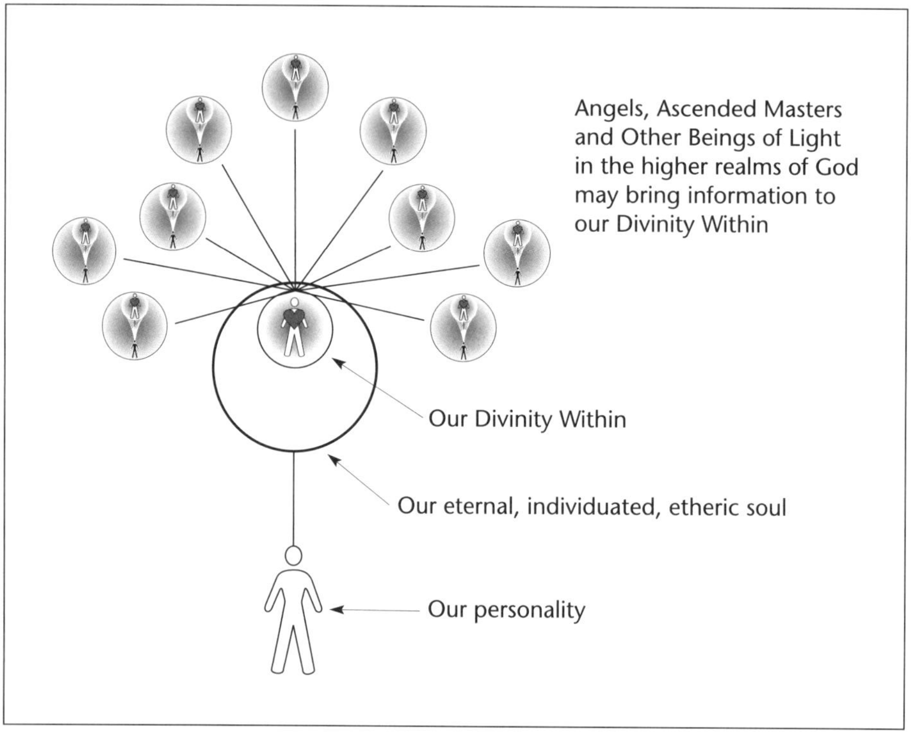

Figure 11-2 All information comes to us directly from or through our Divinity Within

- Creating a balance between our divine feminine and our divine masculine energies within.
- Developing the ability to still the personality's mind (the conscious, logical, reasoning mind), thus opening the door for intuitional information and messages to come to us through the higher mind of the soul.
- Requesting the information or other assistance we desire from the higher realms. To open the door of free will for the Creative Forces of God to assist us, we must request the information, and/or invite their assistance in our daily activities.

Some readers may already have all of these in their personal repertoire. Others may have most of them. Still others may have none. It doesn't really matter relative to the final results.

There is no competition in heaven, only peace, harmony, cooperation with all other minions of God in various missions, and unconditional love. The best sequence for attaining these requirements is the order that we choose (of our own free will) as unique souls. The best way is our way.

As we each move along our unique path, the guidance we receive from our soul and our Spark of God Within will indicate our best way at the moment. When that inner guidance shows us one of these requirements that needs additional work, that is the best time to focus on it. Sooner or later all requirements will need to be met to one degree or another to take us back home to conscious Oneness with God again.

The following is an excerpt from a reading by Cathy provided by Saint Germain on 3/27/99. I had asked about the validity of material that I had journaled for inclusion in part II of the book.

✦ I have described God, the All That Is. (Friendly spiritual chuckles from the other side). In doing so I describe each of us as having been created by God when there was nothing but God, and that therefore each of our souls still has that original Spark of God Within, and it is conscious Oneness with that Spark that we're trying to get back to now. I also describe the reason, or the way it is possible to receive information from within and above, about anything that has ever transpired, is because all souls are connected to God through that inner Spark of God. For if we are all connected to God, we are therefore all connected to each other. I write that souls were created all over the Cosmos, not just here on Earth, and that God, the All That Is, includes all souls everywhere, within what we call the Universe or the Cosmos or "All That Is." Am I misleading in any way?

You are entirely correct. And it is very important in the time to come, in the next decade as you measure time on your planet, that there comes to the consciousness, to the awareness of those who are incarnated in the Earth plane, that they are in fact all One.

✦ And the One, when we speak of the One God, is as I have described the One that includes everything, the One of which we are all a part? That together we are all One, or make the One, or comprise the One? Is that the same thing or am I off the track?

No, that is correct. You have done a wonderful, complete job of describing what it is so imperative for those souls who are lightworkers and starseeds to remember. And for those souls who are incarnated in the third dimension who are not starseeds and lightworkers, to begin to awaken to. They must awaken, you see, in what is really a very short amount of time as you know it. They must come to recognize and experience this Oneness.

✦ Will that be the differentiation between those who are enabled to reincarnate in the next millennium and those who are not?

A major part of the differentiation if you will.

✦ Well, I thank you for all this.

Indeed, it has been our pleasure.

Lightworkers and Starseeds

Because Saint Germain happened to mention lightworkers and starseeds in this excerpt, I will offer a short definition of those terms. Lightworkers and starseeds are former Beings of Light in the Hierarchy of God who volunteered to become human in order to assist in the evolution of humankind back to Oneness with God.

When the first souls became entrapped in physical life forms and attracted the attention of the Beings of Light in the hierarchy of God's Creative Forces, a call was sent out in the Cosmos for volunteers. The mission called for souls who were adept in the ways of the higher realms to volunteer to become human, to join those souls already entrapped in physical life and to evolve, thus showing the way out of the physical entrapment dilemma.

Precisely, the mission was not just for these volunteers to become like humans; *it was for them to become human.* No disguises allowed in this mission, just the real thing. If they did not become truly human, their influence would have been considered in conflict with the Law of Free Will and therefore could not be part of the Earth School's design. But if the volunteers actually became human and experienced the veils of consciousness being dropped exactly like all non-volunteer humans, then the examples they set would be true, good, and valid in every way. The major difficulty would be that the volunteers themselves would have no conscious awareness of their connection to God, of their true nature and character, or of their mission to help others. *They would be in precisely the same position as all of entrapped humanity.*

At present, many of these volunteers, these lightworkers and starseeds, have not yet awakened to the Universal Spiritual Picture. This is the situation to which Saint Germain alluded in the reading above.

The question may arise within you, "Could I possibly be a lightworker or a starseed?" I know of no litmus test that could answer that question! However, I do know that if you are interested enough to ask the question you probably are. And if you have already been interested in the spiritual path for some time, you probably are.

But I also know that it doesn't really matter, for once we are down here we are all in the same boat. Some of those who are not volunteers may awaken and become lightworkers before some who are volunteers. There is no difference between the two situations.

Remember what Saint Germain said in this reading. We are, "in fact all One." Whenever we awaken to the larger spiritual picture of life we are ready to begin to move along our own spiritual path. Whenever we choose to begin to move along our path we are as ready to help any and all who are one step behind us as we are to accept help from those who are a step ahead. We are all One and we are all on our way home again.

CHAPTER 12

Milestones Along the Spiritual Path

Back to Conscious Oneness with God

In this chapter I describe five phases along the spiritual path. Please do not take this number seriously. I certainly don't! In truth there are probably somewhere between one and one thousand stages or phases. It is similar to the situation with insights. There are not just a few insights that are gained along the path, there is the potential for thousands of insights, and one can have the same insight many times—as many times as he or she forgets it.

Phases Along the Spiritual Path

The phases that I describe are just crude milestones that provide a simple way to indicate some of the changes in our inner experiences and/or abilities that we may be able to notice as we move along and grow. This growth is unlike the personality's idea of "intellectual growth" accomplished in our man-made educational institutions where one may memorize things, recite them at test time, and be considered somehow superior to others achieving lesser scores. Rather this is the stepwise growth of human inner beingness from the personality's level of consciousness and awareness to the higher consciousness and expanded awareness of the individual's soul.

On my own journey, monitored from above by various Beings of Light and described to me in response to my questions, I was consistently told of progress I was making of which I, as my personality, was totally unaware. I expected to be able consciously to notice all progress as it occurred, but I could not. In one sense it was good to hear from above that progress was being made but in another I was disappointed that I was not sensitive enough to experience the changes as they occurred.

Whenever I would ask about progress, because I couldn't notice any for a while, I would be told encouraging things. Whenever I felt like I wasn't getting anywhere and asked if that were truly the case, I would be told that I was progressing on the inner planes and that I was on the brink of a new level of consciousness. I was always on a new brink. I was told this so often by the various minions of God in our readings that finally, in frustration because I still couldn't notice any great differences in awareness, I told them that they were brinking me to death and asked them to brink me no more brinks. After that they never used that term again unless it was as a joke (which happened a few times).

If during any of these incremental brinks, or increases in conscious awareness, we were able to compare our new current state with our original beginning state, we would easily experience a dramatic difference. The difficulty arises only because we cannot (or do not wish to) go back to our very beginning state of consciousness for a comparison once we have experienced growth. For me the stepwise changes were so subtle that I couldn't detect a noticeable difference between them. Hopefully you will be able to notice more than I, but in case you don't, the generic information in these descriptions of phases may provide a helpful glimpse down the road to any not yet familiar with the spiritual path.

If you are one who chooses the spiritual path, it is possible that you too at times will be making inner progress of which you have little or no conscious awareness. For you, these so-called phases contain information that my Divinity Within believes will be helpful in a generic way to assist all of humankind to better understand the nature of the stepwise growth from human (personality) consciousness and awareness up to the higher more expanded (impersonal) state of the soul. Nothing else is intended. Keep the following concepts in mind as you read about these milestones.

- Free will is the Universal Law.
- Inner guidance is the way.
- Finding our way back to conscious Oneness with God is the challenge.
- When and how we choose to accomplish that is up to our own free will.

As a reader, be certain that you always feel free to do or not do anything you read about in this book. Know that God designed the Earth School to be this way, to include your free will.

With all this in mind here are some things you may be able to notice along the evolutionary spiritual path of expanded consciousness.

Phase 1. Feeling Consciously Separated from God

Figure 12-1 is a graphic portrayal of a personality that has no conscious awareness of its connection to its soul or to the Spark of God within the soul. This personality may have read or heard of souls but it has no clear perception of its connection to or its relationship with its own soul, nor of its soul's true nature and character. The personality truly feels, thinks, and believes that it and its body are all there is (to its beingness).

All human bodies have souls, but not all souls in the Universe have human bodies (nor do they want them). When the personality is completely unaware of its soul, the soul lives above the physical body and its personality. This is due largely to the natural disharmony between the two levels of consciousness in the Earth School. It would be nearly impossible for a personality to be in harmony with a soul of which it was not aware. The level of conscious life of humankind is in general so much lower than that of souls in their natural etheric state that it would be very uncomfortable for the soul to come down to that level of disharmony.

However, the situation changes when we awaken, begin to focus our attention on our inner life, and begin making changes that increase the harmony among the three levels of our beingness. Our soul comes nearer as we create harmony among our three aspects of beingness until ultimately it surrounds our personality. At that point we have made the transition from being only our physical body's personality to consciously becoming our

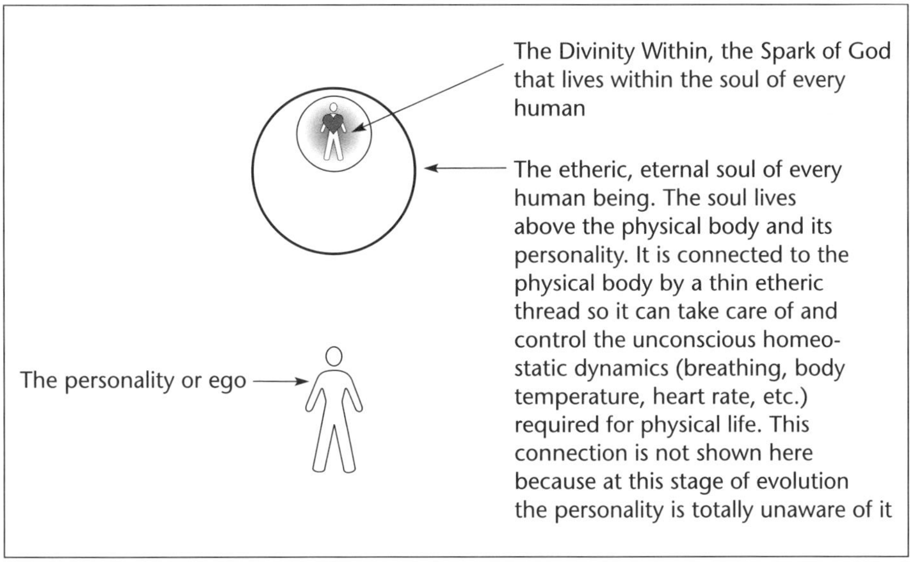

Figure 12-1 Phase 1. Humankind in its present state of feeling consciously separated from God—not in conscious Oneness with God

soul again, while still having our physical body. As we make progress toward this end, we regain the appropriate innate skills that our soul has had from before our entrapment.

The connection of the soul to the body is made *at the moment the baby human draws its first breath. The connection is severed the moment the body stops breathing.* It is through this connection that the soul causes the body to breathe when the personality is asleep. It is the soul that monitors and regulates the body temperature, rate of heartbeat, blood flow, and all that sort of thing. The soul handles all the homeostatic dynamics of the body that we are told are unconscious. The soul also designs and creates our nightly dreams specifically for the education of the mortal and temporal personality to assist in creating a greater awareness and harmony between the two and to assist in its awakening to a larger picture of the spiritual life.

Regardless of all this, from the perspective of the personality at this phase of its spiritual evolution, there is *no awareness of such a soul connection.*

Phase 2. Beginning on the Spiritual Path

Figure 12-2 portrays a personality just beginning on the path. A personality in this beginning phase may be able to feel connected to God in prayer or meditation but probably is unable to sustain this feeling or awareness when confronted with daily outer world activities (i.e., being cut off by someone in heavy traffic, etc.).

This personality has most likely become aware that, in general, in quiet moments alone, it has been feeling unloved, unfulfilled, unhappy, and depressed. At quiet times it probably feels, or knows, that there must be

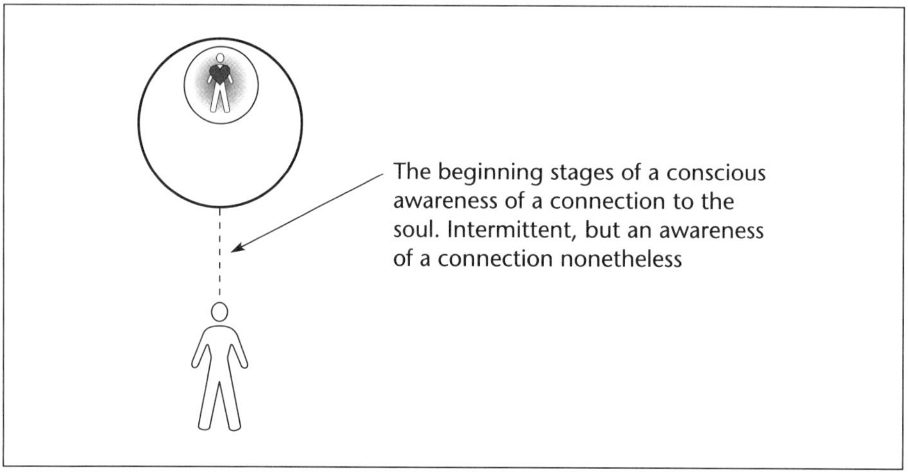

Figure 12-2 Phase 2. Humankind just beginning on the spiritual path

something better than physical, material life as it is being experienced today, which seems meaningless. It may have tried everything in the outer world in its attempt to find unconditional love, lasting joy, and fulfillment, but has found all such attempts to be illusions and temporary at best.

According to the Ascended Masters this feeling of a generalized depression is a result of, and a true natural symptom of, the human condition of feeling consciously separated from God. According to them, an inner depression is the feeling experience caused naturally by conscious separation from God.

As the millennium moves along, the increased light, the added divine light in the Earth's atmosphere is making communication between the soul and the personality easier. Humankind's generalized depression, felt in quiet moments, is an effect of the soul's feelings about its disharmony with the personality of the body to which it is attached. In other words, the soul may have been unhappy about the personality's disharmony with it for some time, but now, due to the added light and better communication between dimensions, the personality is probably becoming more aware of its soul's depressed feelings and is starting to feel them too.

So take heart. If, in your quiet moments, you too are feeling depressed and unhappy inside about the meaninglessness of life lived only as a body and its personality in a material world, then ironically *you have cause to rejoice and be happy!*

The depression felt by your personality may mean you are no longer content to follow the rest of humankind's superficial, material ways. It may mean you are ready to end your path of involution, to awaken to the larger spiritual life that lies behind our physical world, and consciously to begin your path of inner spiritual evolution. It may mean you are ready to choose to set out upon the spiritual path back to the experience of conscious Oneness with God (complete with its eternal inner feelings of bliss, joy, wholeness, completion, fulfillment, and unconditional love, just for being your own true soul self).

But in God's eyes this is your free will choice to make or not.

Phase 3. Progressing Along the Spiritual Path

A personality which has been clearing and releasing some of its habit patterns of negative thinking, feeling, and believing (in human man-made beliefs) is shown in Figure 12-3. This personality has learned that these negatives hinder its return to wholeness and Oneness. It has replaced them with new habits that are in harmony with the soul and its Spark of God Within.

This individual has begun discovering for itself which of its current habits are creating greater inner harmony in its life and which are creating inner disharmony. Here we are speaking of all kinds of personality habits,

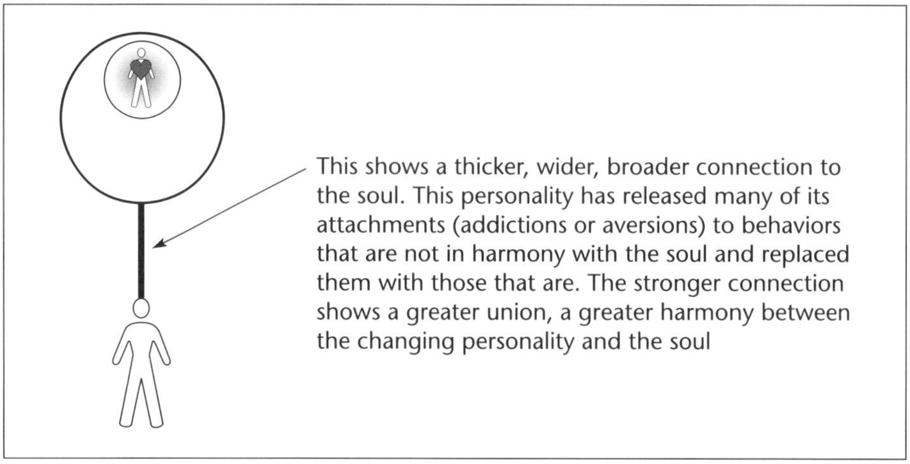

Figure 12-3 Phase 3. Humankind progressing along the spiritual path

such as our ways of feeling about certain things, our ways of thinking about specific things, and the beliefs we may have adopted long ago that we now learn have a severely negative impact upon our progress toward inner peace and harmony. One way we can make this determination is by experiencing just how that activity "feels" in soul level meditation as we focus upon new spiritual concepts, ideas, and information relative to our old habitual activities. For example, as you read this book (written for your soul, not your personality), you (as your personality) may come across an outrageous concept that is quite new to you, such as that there is a divine Spark of God within you now. If, while you are reading or when contemplating that concept in stillness, you feel within your heart region a harmonious resonation or other blissful inner experience, it is probably your soul communicating its harmonious feelings with this concept to you (even though the concept may still seem strange to your personality's mind).

A different way of testing the validity of such new spiritual concepts is to tell your soul or higher self, just before dropping off to sleep, that you would like a more complete understanding of the truth of that new spiritual concept. Your soul will give you a dream, or a dream experience, that may bring you the understanding you ask for, in a powerful feeling way that it knows you can grasp (if you make the effort to remember your dreams).

Another way to learn and then know for ourselves is simply for us to test the concept in our everyday activities. We can tentatively accept the new idea and try it out in our own life experience. If in the long run it brings us greater inner harmony and peace, we can know it is true for us. The first way our soul has of communicating with our body and its personality is through our feeling heart. Our soul can send to our heart region its own harmonious resonance with a truth, a concept, or an idea we may have while reading, watching a movie, or enjoying a silent moment. Long before we may be able to receive intuitional downloads of higher information, we can begin to feel and know how our own soul feels about the things in our life that we may focus upon.

When I was still a school boy, I would sometimes get chills up and down my spine while I was watching a wonderful movie or reading a beautiful book and was somehow moved by something the leading man or woman did on screen or on the printed page. It might have been the incredible grace and ease with which Fred and Ginger danced to an inspiring tune, or perhaps some act of unselfishness that a character acted out which seemed to me to be of a divine nature, above this world. Whenever my personality's inner emotions felt inspired by something I perceived to be of a divine nature, I would often get these ecstatic feelings up and down my spine.

It wasn't until much later in my life that I recognized that these chills were actually reflections of harmony between my personality and my soul at that moment in time. If my soul felt the same way that it knew I was feeling, it used the divine chills to tell me so. Even without my intellectual understanding of the experience it was an ecstatic kind of encouragement for me to continue to seek and take notice of the divine whenever I saw it, heard it, or felt it.

By testing the words of others through our own personal inner connection to our soul and our Divinity within our soul, we grow ourselves spiritually; we evolve ourselves back to harmony and Oneness with God.

Regardless of how information comes to you or is provided to you, as through this book for example, you are the one who must determine whether the words you hear or read are truth *to your soul*. In these ways you may begin to know your soul as the closest (future) friend your personality will ever know. You will be expanding your awareness of your soul, discovering and learning more about its nature and character and also the nature and character of your Divinity Within (now and then). You will also probably be beginning to get the feel of following inner guidance due to your increased communication with these higher aspects of your beingness.

In this phase, you will probably be gaining interest in the possibility of receiving more information from the higher aspects of yourself and from the higher realms above. Due to the better, stronger, and broader connection to the soul, you may even be experiencing the beginning glimpses of enlightenment, of receiving direct inner answers to internal questions you pose to your soul or Divinity Within. You might possibly be actively working on the integration of more divine feminine energy into your daily activities to create a more equal balance between your inner divine feminine and divine masculine energy, which is a requirement for the ability to receive information more efficiently and effectively. You would also probably be getting more comfortable with the idea of calling upon your Guardian Angel(s) and your Higher Guide(s) for assistance in whatever you are doing in your daily activities.

In the longer run, you would also be determining whether you will follow your newfound spiritual truths or continue in your old ways. When you find that the new ways bring greater inner peace, joy, unconditional love, and meaning to your life, you will know you are on the right path for you.

While working on the phase 3 text, I wasn't quite certain that I had included all that was appropriate for someone in this hypothetical phase of the journey. So in a journaling session, I asked if there were more information that would be beneficial for this part of the book. This is what I received from my soul, my Divinity Within, my Guardian Angels, my Higher Guides, others in the Angelic Realm, and from the Ascended Masters who were interested in co-creating this book.

Journaling session April 2, 2000, for Chapter 12.

Each soul is unique. No two souls have traveled precisely the same route in their experiences since their original creation by God as individuated free will souls. As souls we are all unique in terms of our differing experiences and our positions on our spiritual path.

Therefore what is true for one may not be considered true for another, for we are not all in relatively the same place on our individual soul's evolutionary path. Consider the evolutionary path of all life as a climb up the spiritual mountain. Take two souls. One is on one side of the mountain and the other is on the opposite side of the same mountain (as shown in Figure 12-4).

Figure 12-4 Two souls climbing opposite sides of a mountain

Each soul is adept at receiving divine knowledge from its Spark of God Within. Each asks its God Within, "In which direction shall I go in order to find my most direct route to the top, to Ascension?"

For one soul the personal answer is to go west. For the other the personal answer is to go east. Each has received the correct information, the truth for each as a unique individual. If they had asked the question together in a group reading, perhaps with other souls, the answer would have been, go toward the top of the mountain in the way that is best for you each as individual souls. That answer would be truth for all and would in turn suggest that for the most precise personal information and divine guidance, all should seek the truth for themselves, from their own intuitive path to their Divinity Within.

At this hypothetical point on the journey you will probably be getting interested in seeking your own truth from your Spark of God Within. We recommend that you do so. You may have doubts about your ability to do this. Ignore those doubts and begin to receive and to speak or journal such information from your higher self, your soul, or your Spark of God Within.

You may choose, in your initial attempts, to seek your truth from your personal Higher Guides, or your Guardian Angels. If you choose the latter method, their information to you will still be passed through your Spark of God Within and your soul. This is because the mission of your Guardian Angels and Higher Guides is to assist you in discovering and in becoming your soul, at One with your Divinity Within, once more.

Your personal choice may be modified at any time.

The point here is that in the near future all humanity will come to realize the potential for everyone remaining on Earth to do this, to receive divine guidance from within. It is the way of the future in this, the beginning of the Golden Age. This is the difference in humanity that can and will bring about the vast positive changes in the Earth life predicted to occur during the Golden Age.

Humans have evolved sufficiently now to experience this ability. It may take a little practice or it may take none. Any difficulty encountered will occur within the personality, and this can always be changed and corrected. Your soul already has this ability. Your task would be only to move your (personality's) consciousness upward to the level of harmony with your soul and your Spark of God Within. Then remember how this still small voice benefited you as a soul before your current entrapment.

Each soul is unique. Each may be at a different place on the mountain. Each personality that has made the personal choice to commit to and to follow the spiritual path back to Oneness with God may be at a different place from all other personalities. It matters not a bit.

You now know that you have higher aspects within your personality (your higher self, your soul, and your Divinity Within), which are all parts of God that live above the dimension of your personality to help you. You know you have personal Guardian Angels and Higher Guides to assist you in any and every way to find your Spark of God within your soul.

You may call upon all of them to assist you and they will all work together in a divine fashion to help you to bring harmony between your personality and the next higher level. At the beginning of your spiritual journey, your next higher aspect may be your higher self (which is above your personality, but not quite your entire soul as yet). Later on in your journey, your next higher aspect may be your vast eternal and etheric soul. When you have moved up to become your soul, your next higher aspect would be your very own Spark of God Within.

Regardless of where you are on this journey, you will always have assistance available from all these Beings of Light and more, if you invite the Angelic Realm to participate in your daily activities. You may have still more assistance if you also call upon those Beings of Light who comprise the Great White Brotherhood, which has the mission of watching over the Earth School.

You are not alone on your journey. You are never alone on your journey, even if you are miles away from any other human personality. Wherever you are, wherever you may be, you will always have your soul and your God/Goddess Within inside, and your true, knowing, spiritual friends in the divine realms of God, the All That Is, with you to assist you in every way to take your next step, if you only ask.

Obviously the Beings of Light who were offering me this information believed that it was appropriate fare for my hypothetical phase 3 student on the path, but they told me to place it either in the phase 3 portion or at the end of the chapter, whichever seemed most beneficial. So I put it here.

Regardless, the gist of this message from above is, don't wait! Get started on this as soon as you become aware of its possibility in your life. It is important now for all who are on the path to have the ability to receive divine truth from above. Don't wait until you have become adept at certain skills that you may believe to be prerequisites! Remember, all souls are unique in their previous life experiences. You may pick up a book on channeling or journaling and succeed on your first attempt with the exercises. This ability will change your life!

To a *personality* such abilities may seem strange, but they are innate in every *soul*. This is the way all souls communicate. (At least until they foolishly entrap themselves in physical life and are forced to reduce their communication to a limited man-made vocabulary and syntax.)

Phase 4. Growing in Inner Harmony with the Soul and the Divinity Within

The individual in Figure 12-5 has continued to discover and release more and more of its personality's negative beliefs, feelings, and thoughts, and has replaced them with those that foster greater inner harmony. She or he has probably established regular meditation periods in which to experience the higher vibrational feelings of harmony and Oneness among the personality, the soul, and the Divinity Within the soul. This person can probably maintain these higher states of feeling and being most of the time during his or her daily outer world activities.

Because the ability to receive consistent enlightenment, divine guidance, and other information through the soul's intuitional path is proportional to the degree of one's inner balance of divine feminine/masculine energy, this personality possibly has achieved or is actively working on the further integration of divine feminine energy for a better balance. It has probably become quite aware of its ability to receive enlightenment and guidance through its intuitional path and knows it would like more.

Our nightly dreams (created and provided by our soul) can point out areas of the personality's negative habit patterns of which our personality's conscious mind is quite totally unaware. For this reason it is likely that this personality now places a higher value on its dreams, recording and interpreting them on a regular basis and using the resulting information to

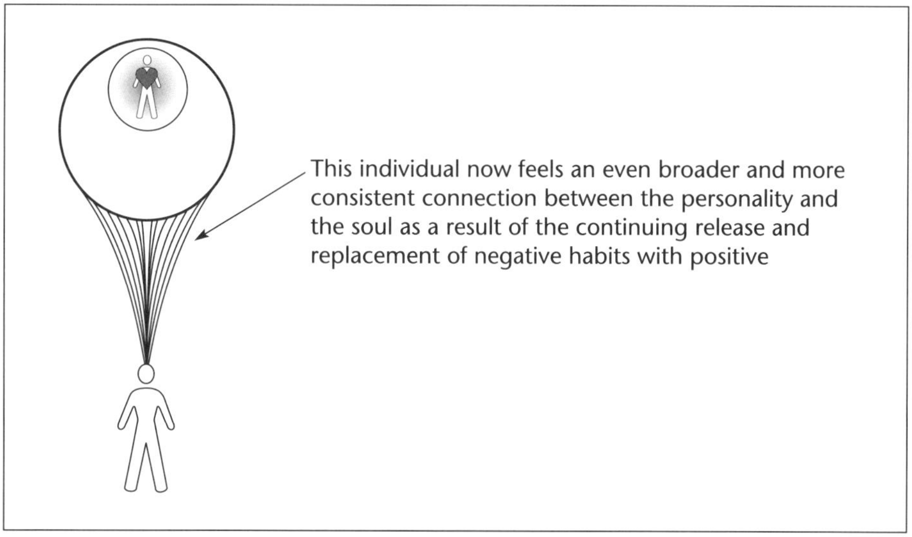

Figure 12-5 Phase 4. Humankind progressing well along the spiritual path, growing more steadily in inner harmony among the personality, the soul and the Divinity Within the soul

bring about changes that continue to increase his or her feelings of inner harmony.

Phase 5. Making the Transition to Being the Soul

This entity (see Figure 12-6) is cleared of most of its attachments, which once held its focus of attention like a magnet on the outer world physical life activities of the Earth School (nearly one hundred percent of the time). It now lives as a soul in harmony with its Divinity Within. After the death of the physical body it may ascend in its body of light, if it chooses, into the divine life of the higher dimensions where it will be released from the evolutionary Earth School cycles of reincarnation, birth, and death.

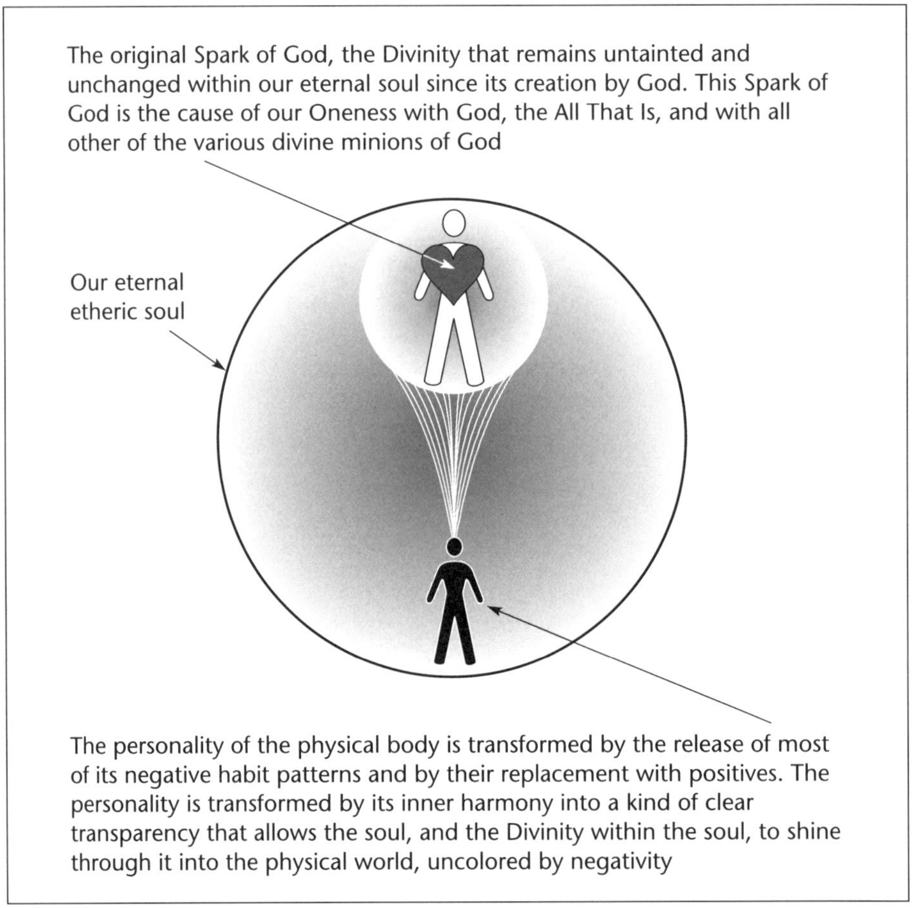

Figure 12-6 Phase 5. Humankind having completed the transition from feeling, thinking, and believing itself to be only the body and its personality to being the soul once more, guided by the Divinity Within, all while retaining its physical body

> *Because of the increased inner harmony, the soul no longer remains above the personality. Rather it moves down, encompassing the body and its personality*

This individual is now living in the harmony it has created (with assistance from above) among its personality, its soul, and its divine Spark of God Within. It is now living as a soul, consciously aware of itself as being a soul, and is guided by its Divinity Within in all that it does. This entity now carries out all its outer world activities, whatever they may be, in ways that are in harmony with its Divinity Within. Her or his highest priority is to retain the inner blissful feelings of mutual unconditional love that resonate from that harmony.

By now its personality has become quite transparent (relative to the soul) due to the releasing, clearing, and replacing of negatives with positives. The transparency of the personality allows this individual, now living as a soul, to manifest the true higher nature and character of its soul and of the Divinity Within its soul into the outer world, without the divinity being colored by the personality's original limited, negative, man-made, human beliefs. This entity is well balanced in its integration of both the divine feminine energy and the divine masculine energy of God and thus is able to receive clear divine guidance from above at all times, through its feminine intuition.[1] It is also able actively to carry out that divine guidance with gentleness and love, in its daily life through its divine masculine energy.

This being has made the transition from identifying only with its personality to becoming its soul, its true self, attuned always to the divine Spark of God Within, once more. It is now a multidimensional being who may be "in" this world, but not "of" this world. This entity no longer needs any of the old third-dimensional psychological defense mechanisms it learned from its outer world conditioning because it has now learned higher-dimensional ways to place protection around itself. In addition to the etheric and spiritual protection it can place around itself, it can always seek the additional assistance of other parts of God, such as the Angels, Archangels, and other appropriate Beings of Light in the heavens above, who are always available.

This being has taken the same situation we are all in as humans on Earth (that of having no conscious awareness of our connection to God), released its attachments to its adopted negative, man-made, outer world

---

[1] This is such an important aspect of the spiritual path that it will be addressed in a separate part of this book. Part III will deal entirely with the Universal requirement for, and the benefits of, developing a balance between the divine feminine and the divine masculine energy within the souls of any who are on the spiritual path.

ways, and created inner harmony among its personality, its soul, and its Divinity Within. This soul no longer needs to return to the life and death cycles—the reincarnation cycles—of the Earth School. It has graduated and, after passing over, is free to make its own choices as to where it wishes to go in the Cosmos in its body of light and which available mission in the Hierarchy of God, the All That Is, that it prefers to accomplish next, for heaven is not inactive. In accordance with its life purpose or soul purpose, this soul has now brought the Divinity of God into the physical Earth plane. It has spiritualized its body and personality. It has achieved its soul's primary purpose (to return to Oneness with God) and now is probably busy completing its secondary mission and purpose (to manifest its Divinity Within into its outer world by helping others to know the way).

This is what all the true Saints and Ascended Masters have been doing for thousands of years. Now, however, due to the advent of the increasing light and the higher vibrational levels of the new millennium, hundreds of thousands of us will be accomplishing this transition soon, and millions in the next few decades. It brings with it great promise for the future.

CHAPTER 13

God's Minions

The Beings of Light in the Higher Realms Whose Missions Are to Assist with Humankind's Evolution

I have already presented bits and pieces about various Beings of Light wherever it was pertinent to the subject at hand. Now I would like to expand a bit more on the help available from the divine realms of heaven above in a chapter by itself. I would like to present a glimpse of a larger picture of the loving assistance that is available from the divine Beings of Light in the heavenly realms of God. Some of this may be a bit repetitious. However, I would now like to go a little further with it so that all may understand the magnitude of the various divine forces of God that have volunteered to assist all students of the Earth School and to assist the soul of our living planet Earth itself to evolve to a higher, more divine level of consciousness.

Limitless, invaluable, divine assistance is available to all students of the Earth School from the divine Beings of Light in the Hierarchy of God in the divine dimensions above us

Unknown to many humans, perhaps most of humankind today, is the fact that there exists a vast heavenly collection of divine Beings of Light comprised of many groups (i.e., Angels, Archangels, Ascended Masters, etc.) whose combined mission is to assist humanity on its path of spiritual evolution back to conscious Oneness with God.

All these are divine parts of God, minions of God, in the divine Hierarchy of God. All these Beings of Light comprise the divine Creative Forces of God though they may come from other locations in the Universe and in the Cosmos. All are souls created by God who have evolved themselves to levels of *divine consciousness, divine love, and divine will,* which are uncountable levels higher in nature than the personality level of most of us incarnated in the Earth School today. In these beginning times of the new millennium, many Beings of Light in seemingly distant places have a great interest in assisting the freewill evolution of the Earth planet and its inhabitants to higher positions in the Hierarchy of Godness in the Universe and/or Cosmos.

Our living planet's evolution to a higher dimension and a higher level of consciousness is of tremendous importance to all divine life in the body of God, the All That Is, in the entire Cosmos. These Beings of Light all have a divine perspective, a divine nature, and a vastly greater ability and capacity to transmit God's unconditional love. They all know of God's plan for the Earth School. From their higher perspectives, our Earth School planet has always been seen as having a disharmonious nature due to our loss of conscious awareness of our connection to God, even threatening at times to destroy itself (through our destructive pollution of air, water, and soil and our ignorant misuse of nuclear energy). Our living planet's growth and evolution to a higher level of consciousness, harmony, and divine love will be a blessing not only to those of us inhabitants who are ready to move on but also to all the Beings of Light throughout our entire Universe.

In general we humans do not yet recognize ourselves as parts of God who are truly connected to each other. Therefore we are always in competition with one another in an attempt to prove to ourselves that we (as our personality selves) have value and worth. If we already knew and felt ourselves to be parts of God following the guidance from our divine part of God within us, we would also know and feel our true value and worth to God, with no competitive need to prove anything to anyone outside ourselves.

From the higher perspective and awareness of the divine Beings of Light in the heavens above, we humans have generally been seen in the past to be capable of using only the consciousness of our personality mind (which we inadvertently brought to ourselves). They know that without the ability to seek, receive, and follow the divine guidance of the Spark of God that lies within the souls of all inhabitants of the Earth School, we humans will continue to manifest disharmony, competitiveness, and aggression.

They know (as all on Earth will soon know, in the context of eternity) that peace, love, and harmony are a natural result of a soul's conscious harmony and Oneness with its God/Goddess Within. So all the many Beings of Light in the heavens above have a deep interest in assisting the evolution of the inhabitants of the Earth School to a higher level of consciousness that will allow us all to know ourselves as souls, as divine parts of God.

The loving intent of the Beings of Light in the heavens above is to do all they can to help us out of our predicament. See Figure 13-1. Their

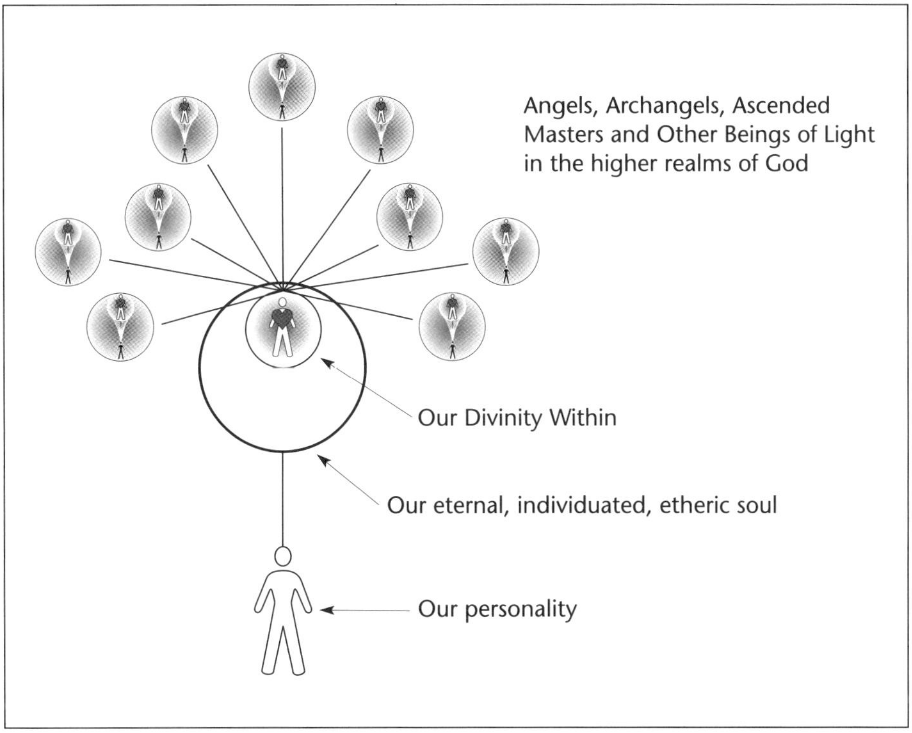

Figure 13-1 These Beings of Light are eager to bring us the information and encouragement we need to assist our evolution back to conscious Oneness with God

desire is to help us find our way back to our God Within and to the peaceful, heavenly, blissful home we once knew in the mansion of God, the All That Is, where they live now.

They know that when we humans begin to understand that we are already parts of God, when we each grow or evolve our personality into harmony with our soul and with our Divinity Within, we will also know and feel ourselves to be One with each other and One with all other parts of God everywhere. They know that when this occurs, when we begin to feel (and know) ourselves to be valuable and worthy parts of God, we will no longer have the inner desire or need to compete with others to prove our value. They know that when we create sufficient harmony within us to move to the higher level of consciousness of our soul, we will release our current personality's habit patterns of *competition and aggression.* They know we will replace these with our soul's desire for *sharing and cooperation* with any and all other parts of God, in whatever of God's missions for which we may then volunteer. They all know the nature and purpose of the Earth School and how to assist its inhabitants.

Angels and Archangels

All souls were given free will at their creation. Some chose to remain in their heavenly, blissful, and fulfilling state of conscious Oneness with God. These entities have never lost their conscious awareness of being part of God. They have never known the experience of being or feeling consciously separated from God. For this reason they have always acted in ways that are in harmony with God's Will to which they are always attuned.

Some of these are the Angels and Archangels who have never been incarnated in a physical body (and therefore have never felt separated in consciousness from God). There are many levels of Beings of Light in the Angelic Realm besides those called Angels and Archangels, but the missions of the others provide them with little direct contact with humans. The major, generic, long-term mission of the Angels and Archangels is to assist all of humankind in its evolutionary path back to Oneness with God. They live in the divine light and love of conscious Oneness with God as they carry out the various minor missions that occur within their long-term purpose or goal. In this environment they continue to evolve themselves to higher and higher positions in the angelic portion of the Hierarchy of God.

Ascended Masters

Other souls were given free will and like all students in the Earth School chose to experience life in an existing physical body instead of remaining in their spiritual etheric body, attuned to God. Whether they volunteered to do this as lightworkers, starseeds, or wayshowers after the entrapment occurred or were part of the original entrapped group, some of these souls have already completed their involution and evolution cycles in the Earth School. They have evolved themselves by harmonizing their personalities with their souls and their souls with their Divine Self within. They have thus spiritualized the personalities of the bodies to which their souls were connected and have returned themselves to conscious Oneness with God. They have evolved themselves back to their original soul state of consciousness, attuned to their Divinity Within. They have ascended. Though there are various degrees of self-mastery, the highest of these souls are called Ascended Masters.

Upon Ascension each soul may choose from various current missions that need attention throughout all of God, throughout the entire Cosmos, all Universes and all Galaxies comprising All That Is. Some (many) of these Ascended souls volunteer to stay involved with the Earth School in their divine Ascended etheric state to assist those of us who are still in our personality state of consciousness to move back to conscious Oneness with God.

Because they have undergone the experience of evolving themselves, they know how it feels to be human. They know (remember) the limitations of the personality's consciousness and how it causes us to see and value only the outer physical world around us. They know how the limited conscious mind believes that the physical-body state is the only, and therefore natural state of all life. They remember how it was when they too identified with their own physical body and its personality rather than with their soul. They know how to help others to evolve through that condition back into the totally free and truly natural soul state of consciousness, where we can once again commune with our Divinity that lives within our soul.

Other Beings of Light

Are these Beings of Light really so advanced? You bet! But so is our very own Divinity, the Spark of God within us! So is our higher self and our soul in its original state (without a lot of parochial, negative, limiting, Earth baggage to haul around)! All the higher aspects of our beingness are extremely advanced when we get to know them.

Is it that the Angels, Archangels, Higher Guides, and Ascended Masters are so advanced? Or is it that when we humans chose to enter existing physical bodies in play, we didn't know what we were letting ourselves in for and the path we chose led to our diminished (physical mind) conscious capacity? Two guesses and the first one doesn't count!

These are *divine* Beings of Light. All of these Beings of Light have volunteered for the mission of assisting humanity as a group or assisting any of us as individuals (if and when we choose to move along the spiritual path to find the Spark of God that lives within our soul). All information in this book comes from just such heavenly Beings of Light.

Spiritual Evolution Is Both Eternal and Cosmic

All Beings or entities everywhere in the Cosmos are on an evolutionary spiritual path. The path of evolution for Angels will certainly differ from the path of Ascended Masters, but all beings everywhere are always evolving to higher planes and a higher, more expanded consciousness. Those who have ascended from our Earth plane life are still on an evolutionary spiritual path of some sort. Theirs may be a more advanced path from ours as Earth School students, with different steps and goals; but it is nonetheless an evolutionary spiritual path. All souls are evolving. All life everywhere in the Cosmos is always evolving.

The point here is this: There are many groups of souls, who are all divine Beings of Light, who have volunteered for the mission of helping entrapped humanity to evolve, and few of us humans know of their availability to assist those of us who choose to make the spiritual path the highest priority in their lives.

They are available to assist us. They are eager to assist us. All appropriate information is available from them. When they assist *us,* they are fulfilling *their* missions, and thus they are further evolving. They can help us only if and when we ask for it because of the Universal Law of Free Will. Within the constraints and limitations of the Universal Laws, they joyfully, gently, kindly, and lovingly do all they can to assist us in finding our Goddess or God Within and in returning to conscious attunement and Oneness with God, the All That Is.

From their higher perspectives, their positions of conscious Oneness with God, these Beings of Light are in perfect situations to help all of humankind on our spiritual paths of evolution. They can provide us with information about our selves, our path, or any subject we are interested in knowing more about so long as it is in harmony with the Universal Laws. They can help, as Archangel Michael says, to lift the level of joy and inspiration in an individual's consciousness.

The Archangels and Ascended Masters also create spiritual "tools" that allow us to speed up our spiritual progress by releasing our negative habit patterns en masse rather than processing them one at a time. There are many other such spiritual tools used for other purposes that also speed us on our way back to God. Melchizedek has provided one of these in a reading I requested to validate and expand upon that which I had already journaled for this chapter. (I will include this tool in an excerpt from that reading in part IV, The Spiritual Path.)

The spiritual path consists mainly of releasing old negative habit patterns and replacing them with positives. The word negative in this context includes those things we discover along the path that diminish our personality's harmony with our soul and Divinity Within. Positive means those things that increase our inner harmony with our higher aspects. After we have released any negative habits, we must immediately replace them with new ones that are in harmony with our souls or we are likely to regress.

To help us reinforce and maintain the new habits, these divine Beings of Light can help us to hold a "space," perhaps a new feeling that we are working on, such as practicing the Presence of God, or a feeling of value and worth as a part of God, or anything else we choose. If asked to help, they can make it easier for us to feel, and to be consciously aware of, the Presence of our Spark of God that lives within our soul *while* we are carrying out our daily activities. They can help us to maintain our new, more harmonious habit patterns until we feel secure in them, until we have changed ourselves permanently.

Our Awakening Is Instantly Known

Our personal Guardian Angels and Higher Guides know the moment one of us awakens to the existence of the Larger Spiritual Picture. They take immediate notice. They understand that with our awakening they may be much busier than before. They will be overjoyed to be able to help us more!

If we take the next step and make a conscious commitment to the spiritual path, it is as though a light is turned on that can be seen from the heavens above. It has been described as a bright light appearing in the darkness of the Earth's atmosphere. Our personal commitment is known everywhere above, at even higher levels than that of our personal Guardian Angels and Higher Guides. The commitment consists simply of our personal inner decision and promise to make our spiritual path the highest priority in our lives. The commitment may take any form, often it is in the form of a silent prayer to God.

At the moment one commits to the path, additional help becomes available on a case-by-case basis depending on what may best serve her or his individual higher good. Perhaps additional Guardian Angels or Higher Guides will be assigned by God. Perhaps spiritual experiences will be provided in our nightly dream states by our soul. All the appropriate Beings of Light in the heavens above the Earth School know instantly of all our inner choices and sincere personal intentions. Knowing of our inner commitment, they will work in complete cooperation with our soul and our Divinity Within to do everything permitted within Universal Law to help us along the path if we request their assistance.

As we wake up and begin to know enough to ask for assistance, information, emotional support, or healing, we can travel a straighter path with less trial and error (than if we were using man-made knowledge). As we ask for and receive help from these divine Beings of Light, they are at the same time joyfully fulfilling their own missions and further evolving themselves.

By asking for their assistance we discover that we are developing new friends. These are not just the types of physical 'friends' we have been involved with in our third-dimensional experience, but rather are highly evolved, divine, spiritual friends who know and understand our inner lives perfectly and who at the same time love us unconditionally.[1]

Eventually we humans will grow to find that all Beings of Light in the Universe are our friends and co-workers. You might say we will grow to find that we have again become Beings of Light who are friends and co-workers with all other Beings of Light in the Universe. From their positions above the physical dimension, they can assist us to find and create heaven, first

---

1 For they know the purpose of the Earth School and understand the dilemma of its inhabitants.

within ourselves, and then in the Earth world around us. We will find that together we are all One, and God, the All That Is, is the One.

What I am attempting to depict is a divinely beautiful process that mere Earth words cannot come close to describing. This divine assistance is a spiritual blessing, a gift from God, available to everyone on Earth. It is a blessing that is to everyone's advantage to use, and it is all part of the Earth School's ongoing design for the evolution of all humankind back to conscious Oneness with our Divinity Within and therefore with God, the All That Is.

This is an excerpt from a reading by Cathy, on the subject of validating and expanding upon what I had already journaled for Chapter 13, received from Archangel Melchizedek on 03/11/2000.

Greetings and blessings and much good will from all who are gathered here today. For there are many gathered about seeking a voice on this morning. I am Melchizedek.

✦ We are honored. (Melchizedek is the Archangel who is currently presiding over all of the Archangels and Angels.)

As are we.

✦ Shall I go ahead? (Sometimes Beings of Light have special messages that they wish to impart before they deal with our questions.)

Indeed we shall deal with that which you desire.

✦ Thank you. In Chapter 13 my desire is to present a larger description of those who watch over the Earth School. My aim or goal here is to describe a more expanded, more generic picture of the higher realms, who comprises them, their purpose related to us, plus some little things such as whether the term "Angelic Realm" is a generic term which also includes other Beings of Light who are at the same vibrational rate as the Angels.

I want to make it clear that this massive assistance is part of the larger spiritual picture, part of the great design to help us out of this Earthbound dilemma that many of us do not yet recognize, have not awakened to. I describe starseeds and lightworkers as volunteers, those who answered a call from the Hierarchy of God, who volunteered to become human and to go through incarnation and separation in consciousness from God, to help show the way. I state that they are volunteers not merely to become "like" humans, but actually to *become human.* Otherwise their example would not be a true example. I would like to know if I have omitted anything important from that description and/or anything else that you believe would be helpful.

This information on the higher realms will be a chapter by itself. I would like to convey the idea that there is a lot of God's attention being placed upon the Earth School these days (due to the new millennium), that there is a lot of assistance available from perfectly qualified divine minions of God, and that this is all part of the plan for the Earth School. Now I will cease and desist so you may go on from here.

So what you are really offering here is that you are putting into a chapter in your book that which would be contained in volumes. Is that correct?

✦ Yes. I am trying to present a condensed, nutshell version of the whole picture.

Make it clear that you are not covering the entire scope, that it is not possible to cover the entire scope in the confines of your work. *It is important that you do that for indeed it is truth. You will wish to convey the awareness that this is indeed a broad area, a broad topic and that you will be able to touch upon various or different areas, but* ***that this will in no way be a complete or detailed description****.*

✦ I will. Thank you.

Indeed, that will be required if you are to impart to your reader that which is truth, that they are only touching truth and not embracing the whole of the truth, that you are not able to convey the whole in such a small area, such a small compartment.

In answer to your question (about the term "Angelic Realm") *keep in mind that semantics are yours, definitions of terms are yours, those in the third dimension. They are not ours. We merely fit ourselves into the definitions that you give in order to make available information with the greatest clarity. For third-dimensional words are not large enough. They are not capable of conveying that which would be* (and is) *available telepathically, clairvoyantly. Do you understand?*

✦ Yes.

It is important to bring this too to the perspective of your reader, for those who journey into this in consciousness, into this area, may find that they touch upon a different portion of the elephant if you will.[2]

---

[2] Referring to the story of the two blind men who are each touching a different part of an elephant's anatomy and describing to each other what they perceive through their touch. Each may provide an "accurate" description from his perspective, but the descriptions may be different because each is referring to a different part of the entire picture.

✦ Okay.

It is well for them to know that, for otherwise if they did not find precisely what you describe, they might feel that they were incorrect, that they were in fact not at the level of consciousness that they had truly attained.

✦ I understand.

The term Angelic Realm encompasses only those who are in fact Angels. Angels have a great hierarchy, and there are many different skill levels, many different taskings (missions) *among Angels, but the Angelic Realm does* ***not*** *include others. It does not include those who are personal guides. It does not include those who are the Ascended Masters. It does not include those who are indeed what you would call members or inhabitants of the greater Cosmic environment.*

There are many who have come at this time, as you know, due to the position that the Earth is in (relating to the new millennium) *with regard to both a quantum leap in consciousness and its rather surprising position for the quantum leap. Indeed in your time frame of perhaps twenty or thirty years ago, this leap in consciousness would not have been deemed as a likelihood. This current* (higher) *level of consciousness was never considered to be an impossibility but neither was it seen as a likelihood. For in fact the consciousness of those who are incarnated on this planet has changed quickly, abruptly, and dramatically in direction and has followed that direction over the past several of your decades. You understand.*

✦ Yes.

And so we have gathered about the Ascended Masters, the Great White Brotherhood, who are those caretakers who have ever been a part of the Earth's environment, a part of the Earth's evolution. They are here now as they have always been, in their role as caretakers of this particular planet. And you understand the composition of this group, do you not?

✦ I don't know whether I understand fully or not.

The Great White Brotherhood is the group comprised of those who have experienced life in the Earth plane and who have, through their own choice, volunteered to move through and to become Ascended. And these are the groups that include those with whom you are frequently in contact.

✦ Then I do understand.

Very well.

✦ I have one question about Ascension. When individuals Ascend do they have the choice of their next mission? A mission they prefer to perform? (I had to ask this question to validate what I had journaled and understood intuitively.)

All souls who reach the level of Ascension are given that choice, but the primary participants in the hierarchy of the Great White Brotherhood made that choice prior to their incarnations, long prior to their Ascension if you will.

✦ Thank you.

And there are those who have moved on as well. Those who are no longer involved in that activity (with the Earth School). *For there is evolution everywhere and always, and there are other assignments. There are other areas of work. And so you might consider it, if you were to look at it in terms of a military organization, you might consider it a promotion that takes them away from that particular group. But those would be the ones who have served for a very long time. Do you understand?*

✦ Absolutely.

In other words, it is not a permanent and static arrangement, a permanent and static grouping. And many souls who Ascend, even today, choose to remain and to work with that group while others choose to move on. An example that we might give is that Sananda is now what you would call in your terminology the head of the Great White Brotherhood. Prior to Sananda's movement into that position it was occupied by the Lord Maitreya. Lord Maitreya has now moved on and up into other areas of work. This is the clearest example of that which we offer here.

✦ What you have given is in perfect harmony with what I understood and I thank you.

Very well. There are of course others of the scope of guides; some who are ***personal****, and some that are more* ***planetary*** *in their nature. You are familiar with your own personal guides and the personal guides of this channel. The guides who are somewhat planetary include Kryon, for he is a guide who is interested in working with the gridwork of the planet itself and there are others who fall into that category of helpers.*[3]

There are those who are from different areas of your Galaxy, of your Universe. And indeed we have with us today representatives from the star Solaris and from Arcturus in particular, but others as well. And you are familiar with your channel's guide Arthruss who is a member of the Intergalactic Council, a representative thereof.

And there are many, many who are members of the Cosmic Galaxies who are watching, lending their vibrations and standing ready should they be called upon to be of service as the Earth plane moves, as the Earth itself moves, into the next higher dimension.

---

[3] Kryon calls the increasing light that has moved into the Earth School environment a Photon Belt.

✦ Yes.

What else is there that you would wish to know?

✦ Starseeds and lightworkers. Readers will wonder, am I one of these volunteers? Is there any way to distinguish lightworkers or starseeds from anyone else? I have indicated that there is none, except perhaps from their personal interest in the spiritual.

Generally speaking, there are no distinguishing characteristics that would clearly determine them, as they are incarnated in the Earth plane. There are those who will know within their hearts as they awaken.

Let us back up a tad here.

It is important to point out to your readers that there are many starseeds and lightworkers on your planet now ***who are not yet awake****, who are not yet performing their chosen work. For the veils* (of consciousness) *dropped so heavily and they became so enmeshed* (in outer world activities) *that they have not indeed awakened as quickly as was anticipated.*

It is important to understand that the gathering of emissaries from other planets and stars is for the purpose of stabilizing and increasing the strength and energy of the vibratory rate and the light about the planet. And this is in part why, since your year of 1986, there has been a steady increase in the inflow of higher vibratory rates and greater light for the planet itself and for the inhabitants thereon. As the numbers increase, of those emissaries who are about, there is of course the greater availability of the higher vibrations being directed, focused particularly on your planet or the planet which you inhabit. Do you understand?

✦ Yes.

There are too many groups to name, but what is occurring on your planet now is that there are so many of the higher vibrations, that those who have had the opportunity in the past to be in your planet space if you will, who were of a lower vibratory rate and nature, ***are no longer able to come into that space for they cannot sustain themselves in that environment.*** *It would be something like a human being attempting to sustain itself in an environment where temperatures were hundreds of degrees higher or where oxygen was either not available or greatly diminished.*

✦ I understand.

And so it is a natural occurrence. It is not that there has been a decision made to block them. It is simply a natural occurrence.

✦ Well, I think that will be sufficient and I thank you for it.

Allow us to give one more bit of information to you.

✦ Oh, indeed.

*And that information is that **there are indeed too many groups to list**. If you were to attempt to name them all you would lose your reader and you would still not succeed, for there are those of course from Sirius and those from the Pleiades. And many other groups from smaller and larger and more distant stars and planets as well.*

✦ The Pole Star and the Great Bear, the Big Dipper?

Indeed. These though have been here in the Earth planet almost forever.

✦ All my life!

Even longer! But some that are here now are quite new.

✦ I would welcome any other bits of information.

No indeed, that was sufficient. It was merely to give you the understanding that it is not possible to quantify, define, and list them all. And they have no desire to be recognized. They are here for higher, greater purposes and while they may at some time, work with one particular incarnated individual, or one group of individuals, none of those who are here now are seeking recognition in any way.

✦ I thank you for that information.

And we thank you as well. You may trust your intuition, and we speak to both of you. You may trust your intuition implicitly. And we are delighted to have had this opportunity to share with you this morning. You are the focus and recipients of great positive energy at this time for all who are here are offering that.

✦ I am very grateful.

As are we all. It is well to remember to thank yourselves. And if there is nothing more we offer our appreciation, our applause, our love, our light, and our blessings. And we are through for now.

✦ Thank you one and all.

This book contains enough information to bring any reader to an awakening of the existence of the Universal Spiritual Picture, even though it only touches upon the entirety of spiritual truth

In this excerpt Melchizedek makes it clear to *me* that I should make it clear to *you* that I am only *touching upon the whole of the truth* in my description of the picture of those in the higher realms who watch over the Earth

School. It is truth, but it is only part of the entire detailed truth, which is too large and complex to be contained in a library of books.

I thought I had made this clear in the preface, but it must have been apparent to Melchizedek that it would be of benefit to many to clarify it again here, for if it were not important to restate that information here, he would not have made an issue of it.

The point that Melchizedek makes is of course true of every chapter in this book. There is no end to information related to the higher eternal spiritual life. What is included in this book is truth, but it only touches upon the entirety of the truth. So please do not believe that this is all there is.

My original intention was and still is to offer that which will best enable readers to awaken to a rather complete understanding of the true meaning and purpose of our physical life on Earth (in relation to the Cosmic life of God and all the many minions of God in the Hierarchy of Godness) as it has been given to me through Cathy's verbal readings and my journalings. My further intention is to provide this understanding in a single volume rather than in a five-foot shelf of books. My wish is to bring sufficient information together into a single volume to create a tapestry (not a photograph) of the Universal Spiritual Picture. I know through my intuitive path that there is great value in creating a larger spiritual understanding in a single book, for a large percentage of the world's population is now caught up worse than ever in the overly busy outer world rat race.

I also know that bringing such information to the public in piecemeal volumes leaves an understanding of the larger spiritual picture only to those who already have an existing deep inner motivation and dedication to find the time to read hundreds of volumes of highly esoteric, arcane information, and then to put it together into an understandable whole.

My purpose is to relay enough of the message given to us by the Beings of Light to allow all readers to catch a glimpse of the larger spiritual picture of who we humans are, why things in the Earth world are the way they are, what we are truly doing down here, and how we can find our way back to conscious Oneness with God.

> *This chapter is intended to provide a generic picture of the assistance that is available from the higher realms of God that exist above our third-dimensional, physical level of consciousness*

To receive divine assistance on our individual paths back to conscious Oneness with God, we must first awaken to the existence of the larger spiritual picture. It is then required that we make a long term commitment to God, of our own free will, to make our spiritual path the highest priority in our lives. Having made a sincere commitment, all that is then required to receive the greatest degree of assistance possible is to request it. Some may ask how to actually request information or other types of assistance from divine Beings of Light who live in the heavenly realms of God.

As already given, there is no specific verbiage to be used. I will offer here what I have used only for the benefit of those who have never before communicated directly with those in the higher realms and who therefore may be a little unsure of how to go about it. This is only one way, but it will serve as a generic example.

Considering that my higher self, my soul, and my divine Spark of God Within are all higher realm aspects of my own Beingness, I always felt it would be wise to first ask for their help. So I would start my day with something along the lines of, "I call upon my higher self, my soul, and to the greatest degree possible at this moment, my Divinity Within, to assist me in my daily activities and in my progress along my spiritual path."

I felt that it then would be wise to call upon my Guardian Angels and Higher Guides and ask for their assistance in a similar manner. These are the Angels and Higher Guides who have been assigned to assist me personally to find and harmonize with the Spark of God within my soul. We can communicate with all higher beings using only our feelings and thoughts if we wish, as we may do in silent prayer. They know, moment to moment, all of our feelings, thoughts, attitudes, beliefs, and actions like the Santa Clause mythology, if you have ever wondered where that came from.

After receiving the three readings used in Chapter 2, I now (in addition to the above), "invite the Angelic Realm to participate fully in my daily activities," as Sananda, St. Germain, and Archangel Michael have suggested. Archangel Michael has assured us that the Angelic Realm has a corner on the market of inner joy and lightheartedness that they are only too happy to share with us if we wish. Sananda has also offered that such a request made to the Angelic Realm opens the door to greater angelic synchronicity in the events of our daily lives.

Then finally, whenever I am about to use one of the spiritual tools created by the Archangels or Ascended Masters, I usually call in the one I knew who had created it. Lately though when I prepare to write, I make an additional request such as, "I invite or call in all appropriate Ascended Masters and other Beings of Light who are interested in the co-creation of this book, to assist me in my efforts."

The point is simply to ask for help from above without being overly concerned with the verbiage. The request itself opens the door of free will and allows the Beings of Light to assist us. It costs nothing, and its value is priceless. As long as our commitment to the path remains in place and our intentions remain in harmony with our soul's higher good and the higher good of the Universe, our requests will bring us the most powerful assistance possible within the constraints of the Universal Laws that are part of the Earth School.

Our ways of communicating with these divine Beings of Light are strictly up to us as individuals. Right and wrong are concepts created by humans on Earth in an attempt to control the behavior of other humans in a most non-divine way. Right and wrong have no meaning in the higher realms. We are each on our own in the manner in which we personally choose to invite, request, or call upon our higher friends for help.

By continuously asking for assistance from the higher aspects of our own beingness, our Guardian Angels, our Higher Guides, the Angelic Realms, the Ascended Masters, and appropriate Beings of Light in other heavenly groups, we are expanding and increasing our conscious awareness of these divine invisible aspects of the spiritual life while we are still carrying out our third-dimensional practical activities. This increasing conscious awareness of the assistance available from the various divine minions of God in the heavens above, while active in our daily lives, is already a sign of progress along our path.

These Beings of Light cannot change us. They are not permitted to carry us along our spiritual path. They cannot grow up for us. If we desire greater harmony, peace, joy, unconditional love, and meaning and purpose in our lives, we are responsible for changing ourselves so that the Universe, through these Beings of Light, brings us those things naturally (in accordance with the Universal Laws of the Earth School).

If we wish to move back to heavenly and blissful conscious Oneness with our God Within and therefore with God, the All That Is, we are each responsible for changing our personality's habit patterns to be in harmony with our soul and with our God Within.

Due to the Universal Laws originally set up in the design of the Earth School, these Beings of Light cannot change us, but they can surely assist us, in many seemingly magical ways, to change ourselves, and they will do so if we open the door of free will and permit them.

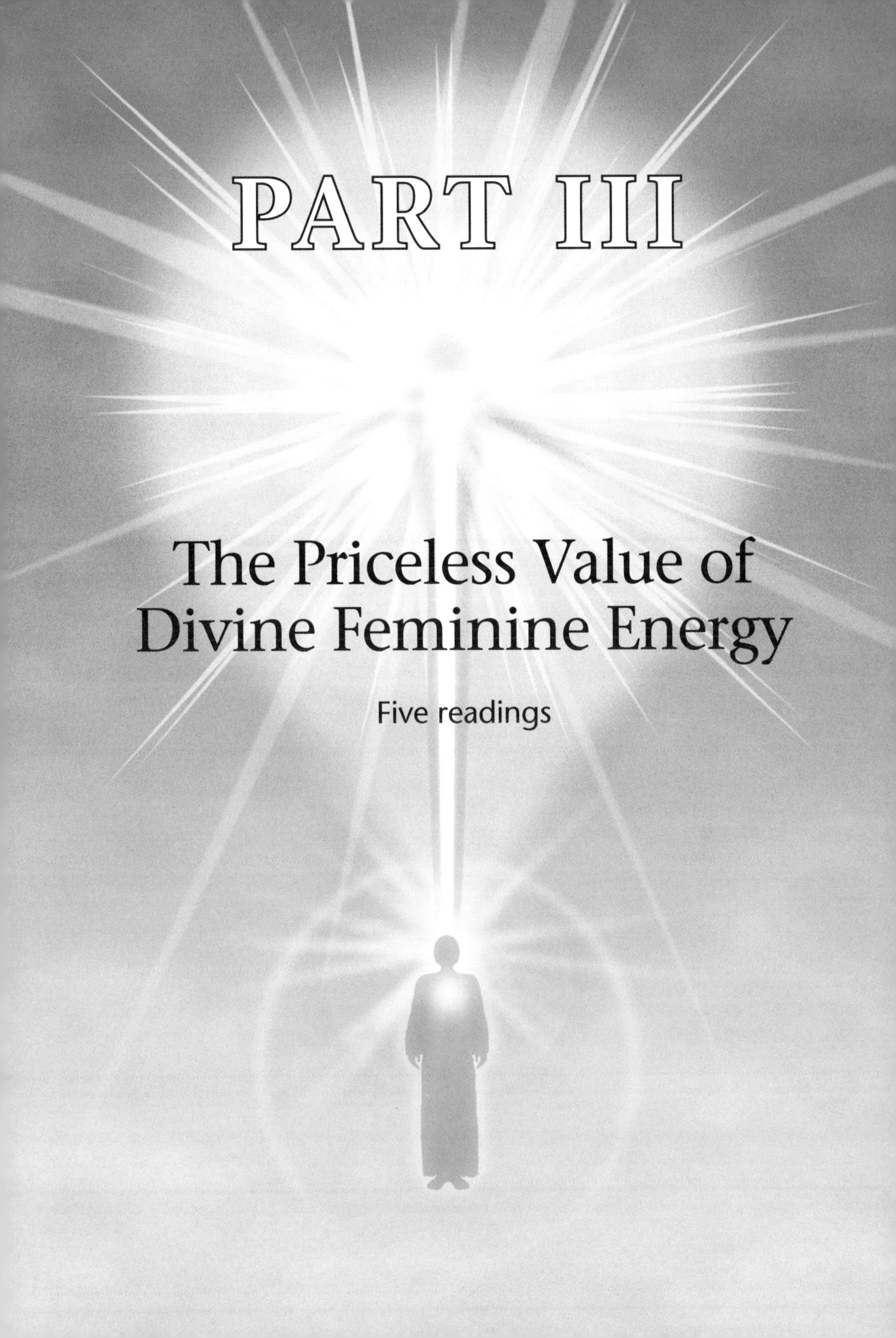

PART III

The Priceless Value of Divine Feminine Energy

Five readings

CHAPTER 14

My Personal Background

Prior to Receiving This Feminine Energy Information[1]

Much of the information presented thus far has been old (i.e., the fact that we are not really merely our body and its personality, but indeed have three distinct aspects to our beingness). Some of it is ancient (such as that pertaining to the Universal Laws). However, this information on the importance of and the extremely high spiritual value placed upon divine feminine energy by the Beings of Light in the heavenly realms above us is relatively new. It is still not widely known to many who may have been on the spiritual path for some time. While it is common knowledge to those Beings of Light in the Angelic Realms and in the Great White Brotherhood above, who would assist us in our evolution, at present it is known by relatively few humans currently incarnated in our third-dimensional Earth School.

What is it that is known by so few humans? That there is a Universal requirement for those who wish to make substantial progress on the spiritual path back to Oneness with God to integrate divine feminine energy into their daily lives sufficient to form a relative balance between their feminine and masculine energies. This requirement exists not only for those who have intentions for Ascension in this lifetime, but also for any who intend to live far into the new millennium and any who would like to be able to reincarnate during the next thousand years of the Golden Age.

---

1 Why am I providing information about myself here? Because I have been asked to do so! More precisely, in response to my questions about the content of the book, it was strongly suggested that I do so. I was told that my own experiences with this information would be of benefit to the reader. In offering some of my experiences, it is also necessary to provide some information on my personal background so readers can know from whence I was coming, my starting point.

My original introduction to the value of feminine energy through my dreams

My earliest introduction to the personal value of integrating feminine energy into my daily life occurred in the early seventies. I had become very interested in the spiritual path as a result of having been introduced to a book about Edgar Cayce and in learning of the nature and accuracy of the information that came through him in his trance-state readings. A part of that information was that dreams were one of the soul's most natural ways of communicating with the personality to which it was attached.

In my resulting study of dreams and their interpretation, I was drawn to the works of Carl Jung.[2] As a result of my strong interest, I quickly learned to interpret and understand most of my dreams to the point where I could connect their content with the actions, thoughts, feelings, attitudes, and beliefs that I had manifested in my daily activities just prior to receiving the dream. I also became aware that Jung had identified within the psyche of human males a *feminine* inner aspect that he named the anima and within the psyche of human females a *masculine* inner aspect he called the animus.

I had two things in my favor in learning about dreams. Part of my strong interest in dreams came from my personal viewpoint that since I had no obvious "psychic" abilities, I might just as well study something that didn't require any and that would help me grow spiritually, regardless. The other thing was that I was not afraid of learning more about myself. I believed that there was a very real advantage in knowing everything I could possibly discover about myself so that I might change whatever I found that no longer served me well. I believed we all could change any part of ourselves if only we were able to see the things that needed to be changed for our own higher good, and if we also understood the benefits in making a change.

My Shadow Dream

After gaining an understanding of my soul's dream designs and gaining faith in my personality's ability to interpret them, I began having a repetitive nightmare.[3] Jung called this particular type of nightmare a shadow dream because the traumatic factor in the dream, the focal point of the

---

[2] Carl Jung had already discovered many higher spiritual truths for himself (as had others with similar interests and benevolent spirits who constantly focused their attention on understanding the higher reaches of the mind of humankind).

[3] Nightmares are very important dreams. If we don't understand the meaning of an important message given to us in an ordinary dream, our soul will give it to us repeatedly, indicating that the message is very important to our long-range happiness and

dreamer's fears, often appears as a dark shadow, unidentifiable. The shadow represents or symbolizes an aspect of ourselves of which we (as our personality selves) are quite unconscious, thus we see a shadow symbol instead of something we could more readily identify within ourselves. The shadow symbol often represents an aspect of ourselves about which we are afraid of learning—fearful that we might not be able to do anything about it (even though we obviously can).[4]

I tried interpreting my shadow dreams using the same standard methods that worked so well with my everyday dreams, but I knew I wasn't catching on to the real problem behind them because they kept returning. I never did find a direct way to interpret them. They just kept coming back until I *really* wanted to know what the shadow was in my life. Then one morning, while the fear was still fresh in my mind (and the perspiration fresh on my brow), *I suddenly knew, intuitively and unmistakably, that the shadow represented my emotions! I was traumatized with fear at opening to my emotions! I was deathly afraid of having, feeling, or showing gentle, kind, or loving emotions. I was terrified of the vulnerability that opening myself to gentle emotions might create!*

Oh well, so much for my personality's macho facade!

The immediate effects of bringing gentler emotions into my life

As I began to make a conscious attempt to allow myself to feel my gentle emotions again (in public), I found Jung's anima/animus symbolism very helpful. My dreams began to show an increasingly closer relationship between me and an unknown beautiful dream woman to whom I immediately felt powerfully attracted. The "me" in my dreams truly represented my soul as usual, and the woman in turn represented Jung's anima, the feminine energy found within every man. It seemed to my personality that there was nothing wrong with my promoting a closer relationship with this beautiful woman of my dreams by bringing my gentle emotional side into my daily life once more (especially since my wife understood dream dynamics as well as I did and knew it was not a third-dimensional woman).

Within weeks I discovered that I could carve and sculpt quite well in various types of wood and large pieces of gemstones with no previous outer

---

growth. If we still don't make the effort to discover the true message, our soul may present it in a nightmare that makes it much more difficult to forget or ignore. When we finally catch on to the real meaning or message, the nightmare will not be repeated.

4 Our soul would not waste its effort providing us with information about ourselves if we, as our personalities, truly were unable to do anything about it. Souls are not dumb! They live at levels of consciousness and awareness that are quantum leaps higher than those of our human personalities.

world experience or background whatsoever. The interest and ability just suddenly seemed to be there! The results were quite amazing to my friends and me.

I also began remembering songs provided to me in my dreams by my soul (from its previous repertoire of experiences), complete with words and music. These were no little junk tunes. They were beautiful, catchy, lyrical melodies complete in every way. My personality did not have the ability to read or write music so nothing ever came of them, but the ability to recall them from my dreams is still present.

As soon as I began making a conscious effort to allow gentle positive emotions, feminine energy, back into my life, innate artistic abilities were manifesting that I previously had no idea existed within me. It was obvious at that time that the uncovering of these artistic abilities was directly related to my attempt to integrate more of my anima, or feminine self, into my daily life.

My Regression to the Masculine Extreme

However, some years later in 1984, due to another traumatically painful episode in my rat-race outer world career,[5] I went back to the old way again. Once more I gave up on the outer world and built the shells or walls around my heart that I thought were necessary to shut off the potential for any more externally-caused emotional pain. My regression lasted about five years (still working at a survival job designing and implementing computer systems, of course). My inner interest in the spiritual and metaphysical side of life continued, but I kept it to myself. I still read all the new books that attracted my spiritual interest, but my outer world environment rarely saw anything but my tough guy persona as I carried out my daily rat-race activities.

Cathy's and my married life continued status quo until 1989 when Cathy, in an attempt to seek higher information helpful to pulling us out of the doldrums, read a new book and immediately began receiving information from her Guardian Angels and Higher Guides and transmitting it verbally. I followed her success with my own as I began journaling information from my higher self, my soul, my Divinity Within (and my Higher Guides).

Well, talk about a boost in motivation to really get back on the spiritual path! There is nothing like being able to receive information directly from

---

[5] Since 1964 my survival jobs have all been related to computers. I have been a mainframe programmer, an application system designer, a database designer, and a manager of those who carried out similar functions. In the 1980s I moved with the rest of the world into the design of application systems that would function on mini and personal-sized computers.

the higher realms above about oneself and the nature of the spiritual path to rejuvenate one's interest in the spiritual life!

My re-introduction to the value of feminine energy through information received from the higher realms above

My re-introduction to the value of feminine energy was provided in response to personal questions about my own spiritual growth in a reading by Cathy in the early nineties. I was asking about the meaning of a particular dream I had with a horrible content that I couldn't quite grasp or relate to through normal interpretive techniques. The answer I received was that indeed all the characters in my dream, whose actions I couldn't identify relative to my everyday life, were parts of me. They were subpersonalities that had very dominating, overly masculine attitudes that denigrated almost all forms of femininity they encountered. In response to my continued questioning, I was told that I was far overbalanced toward the masculine energy extreme. I was also told that in order to make any further significant progress toward my spiritual goals and ideals, I must integrate more of my gentler feminine energy into all aspects of my life until I had achieved a more even inner balance.

It was after receiving this information that I realized that other than including gentler emotions I didn't really know what feminine energy was, much less why it was so valuable and necessary for continued progress along the spiritual path. Over the next several years I learned that this masculine imbalance was not just my individual isolated personal bent, but rather a generalized symptom spread across the entire planet in women as well as men.

All of this personal information is presented for the purpose of letting you know where I was coming from when I was first given this information from Beings of Light in the heavens above describing the critical importance for all of humankind to integrate more feminine energy in the new millennium. I want to be certain that you understand that I was definitely not born and raised as an expert on the subject of the value of feminine energy in our inner lives.

Personally, I wish that I had been so lucky as to have that as an aspect of my early conditioning (now that I understand more about it). But nnnnnoooooooooo! My cultural conditioning and outer world education had provided my personality (from third grade on) with a set of thoughts, feelings, attitudes, and beliefs that were something like these:

- Masculine was always better than feminine.
- Logical thinking was the optimum decision-making tool. Emotions only clouded my "perfect and logical" solutions to problems.

- Activity was better than passivity, because it got more done in the physical world.
- Appearing strong and tough was better than being some kind of a girl-kissing sissy and getting beat up all the time.
- Being unemotional was better than showing love and opening self to the possibility of suffering the emotional pain of being rejected.
- Anger was a great way to handle fear. It created an adrenaline rush sufficient to handle most potentially violent situations.
- If someone confronts you, allow yourself to become angry and let him know that you are ready and willing to fight. Mostly, they won't.
- Pay special attention to the details in the external world around you in order to be ready to react to trouble. It might lie just around the corner.
- Be alert and apprehensive always. Expect trouble, and you will always be ready when it comes.

This is not a complete list, but enough to provide the gist of my internalized conditioning and the habit patterns of feelings, thoughts, attitudes, beliefs, and actions that I adopted from my outer world experiences.

Surprise, Surprise

At the same time that I held these inner habit patterns, I was still very interested and sincere about making progress on my spiritual path. I could understand in my higher mind much of what Christ was trying to explain to his disciples and quite a bit of the arcane Ancient Wisdom that was not included in the Bible. I understood at a very deep level that unconditional love, divine love, was the most potent healing power on Earth and the ultimate solution to all of humankind's problems. I just did not see the effect, the impact that my personality's unconscious feelings, thoughts, attitudes, beliefs, and actions were having on my spiritual progress!

There is one other major point I want to make before I bring in the information on the benefits and value of integrating feminine energy into our lives.

When I first received the feminine energy information through Cathy's readings, I could not bring myself even *to desire* to integrate into my life what I defined, felt, and thought of as feminine energy. My own painful, hurtful, and negative experiences with girls, young women, and mature women, in all sorts of situations throughout my life, had given me my own personal opinions and feelings about things feminine. I certainly did not desire to integrate what I felt and thought were the negatives I perceived.

So, as I focused inwardly on this personal dilemma, I received from my higher self[6] a rather complete experiential understanding that allowed me to move ahead and has served me well ever since. I include it here because I believe it may be of use to anyone who has even the mildest of negative attitudes about the opposite sex, whichever gender that may be.

Distinguishing between our culturally defined ideas of feminine energy and those defined by the divine Beings of Light

The understanding I was given in my journaling session was that the feminine energy being spoken of by the Ascended Masters was *divine feminine energy,* not that defined as feminine by either the culture or me personally. In meditation, when I considered the difference between divine feminine energy and my hypersensitive personality's negatively-biased version of third-dimensional, outer worldly feminine energy, it made all the difference in the world. When I was able to view it from above, from the higher perspective of my higher self or soul level, I could easily discriminate, objectively and clearly, between divine feminine energy and that which I had personally experienced from and through the human personalities of members of the feminine gender. From the higher perspective I could see, feel, and understand the difference, like day from night. Then and only then could I grasp the true positive value of, and the spiritual need for, the integration of divine feminine energy into my life. Only then could I even *desire* to move toward the integration of feminine energy back into my life.

The same understanding helped me discriminate between *divine masculine energy* and the third-dimensional kind, which I had acquired and manifested personally throughout my life as a form of self-protection. It didn't take a lot of meditation to experience, see, and feel the difference internally. In this way my desire increased tremendously and I began to move toward the release of the negative masculine ways that had become so natural (so unconscious) to my personality and to replace them with more divine, more positive masculine energy and ways.

For me this ability to discriminate between divine feminine/divine masculine energy and that which I had personally defined from my own experience was absolutely critical to my spiritual progress. I feel that this same discrimination may be of help to others.

---

[6] In this case, the higher self refers to an aspect of the soul that is easier to reach and to experience than the full soul. In other situations, or in someone who had already moved into their soul level of consciousness, the higher self might be an aspect of the Spark of God Within or any other synonymous term you prefer. In all cases the higher self is an easier-to-reach step up from where one is in the present moment than the next full step up to a higher level of consciousness and vibration.

The Ascended Masters have made it clear that none of us will make it back to conscious Oneness with God without the divine feminine/masculine balance in our lives. It is a Universal requirement. The gentleness and unconditional love that Christ was able to manifest when he was still in body was part of the effect of the divine feminine and masculine balance within him.

About the Feminine Energy Readings

Understanding the feminine energy information received from above will make clearer:

- Why the world is the way it is today
- How we each may make our own personal lives more joyful, peaceful, and fulfilled
- How we may move more quickly and efficiently along the spiritual path back to conscious Oneness with God

Looking Ahead

In the next few chapters I will include excerpts from five readings provided by two Beings of Light, Athenarious and Thenous, whose specific heavenly area of expertise is that of divine feminine energy. In these excerpts I will include most of the ordinary dialog that transpires in our readings to show some of the flavor of the questions and responses, and the conversation that goes on in between, even though these readings were far from typical. Because the very purpose of these five readings was to receive information for inclusion in a book, as opposed to receiving answers to various personal questions posed within different subject areas, there is much less interplay than usual. Nevertheless, you can see there is often a refining or redefining of questions and answers until each party has an adequate understanding of what the other is requesting or offering.

If the Ascended Masters simply answered a question as I first posed it, the response often would not cover what I had really wanted to know. Why? Because my questions, posed in context of a human vocabulary and syntax, are often not precise enough. Because our third-dimensional language is based largely on physical life, not spiritual life. It is therefore too primitive. The current level of human understanding of the Universal Spiritual world behind the physical world is too meager to address properly many of the higher spiritual issues and their nuances.

It is similar to a child asking the parent, "Where did I come from?" and receiving a lecture on sexual union and procreation. When asked if she understands, the child replies, "Well, Jimmy says he came from Pittsburgh and he wants to know where I came from."

Or it may be like the situation of someone born and raised in the climate of Savanna, Georgia, talking about snow with an Eskimo from the Arctic who has seventeen different words for the many various types of "snow" in her world. There are two completely different levels of understanding to be surmounted.

CHAPTER 15

The First Feminine Energy Reading

An Overview of the Current World Status Relative to Humankind's Inner Masculine/Feminine Energy Balance

This is an excerpt from a reading by Cathy received from Athenarious on 8/17/96.

Welcome to our world. You may call me Athenarious.

✦ Thank you for coming.

Indeed, you came to us.

✦ Okay.

And you are most welcome. Ours is a world you might compare to or consider a school of higher learning, of higher education. We here have tremendous harmony and tremendous peace. There is little structure, but great availability of information and experience. This is new to you and initially there will be perhaps an acclimating experience for the semantics of your world are neither rich enough, encompassing enough, or broad enough, and so there may be some initial difficulty in bringing that which we would offer into your language. Nevertheless, we will do our utmost to assist. If you have questions, you may proceed now.

✦ I desire now to begin my lifework in world service in a more active way, having been prompted by Arthruss a week or so ago, who said it was time to begin to focus on what suits me best just as I am, in doing that. The analogy was that—I don't seem to remember just now—(my personality mind had suddenly drawn a blank).

Physicians and rotation.

✦ Yes, thank you.

(This was a reminder of an analogy that Arthruss[1] used in a reading prior to this one. Arthruss had described the situation in which hospital interns are given rotational experience in their early service to allow them to discover what it is that they truly desire, truly will enjoy, in their practice of medicine.)

✦ I determined that I would like to begin my life service in the activity of writing a book. Perhaps two, perhaps more. I have had that idea for some time but never felt adequately prepared, and I guess because of that belief, I wasn't. It took me a while to realize that Cathy and I, from our positions of her verbal readings and my journaling, may have access to information from the higher realms that is not yet understood by many and may be of use to others. And I'm not sure I felt that way before, completely. I knew that we had bits of interesting information—

You really had some growing and evolving to do.

✦ Yes. When I first thought of writing a book, it was more or less from the personality level or maybe my higher self level; and that would have been about it, using the information received but writing a book from that level. Now I believe I can write from my higher self or soul level with guidance from and through my Spark of God Within, at times.

✦ Now I want to know what you, from your perspective, I'll just say the Universe, would like to have written in a book or two or more. And any other information that would be helpful along those lines.

In actuality there are several issues or topics that would be readily forthcoming, but while there is much information to be given and some of it is segregated into rather specific areas, the openness which you offer has brought something of a consensus **that initially there is a great need that can be filled here**. *There is a great void in bringing in the greater feminine influence, a feminine awakening, if you will. For we find, as we observe humanity incarnated in the third dimension, that there is little of the richer, higher*

[1] Arthruss is a member of the Intergalactic Council who has helped me personally in many of my dream state experiences. I consider him a soul friend, a friend of the spirit.

qualities, the useful and practical and applicable feminine qualities, being brought in or being manifested.

The world is currently in a state of extreme masculine imbalance

For particularly in your country and in a number of the other more "advanced" cultures and societies on your planet, we find that the **feminine** *has fallen away, and that even those who are of the* **feminine gender** *are encouraged, coerced, pushed into developing the more* **masculine attributes** *of their personalities in order to live the "good life," if you will, in order to fit what is currently seen as the appropriate mold for success, for evolution even. You are at the zenith of a patriarchal era and this soon will pass, but for now it is at its apex in terms of acceptability, even to the extreme of admiration and adoration.*

And of course this means, for one thing, imbalance, and imbalance is always the antithesis of harmony. It is the antithesis of true health. It is the antithesis of inner awareness. For attunement and awareness, opening to the higher realms, the higher planes, and working toward lifting the veils of consciousness truly requires balance, truly requires harmony; and by and large we do not find this to be the overall ambiance of your planet at this time.

And so we would offer a work that would assist and entice those who are incarnated in the third dimension to seek the balance, to reawaken the feminine within them, to find the treasure there, to find the richness there, to not only bring into the light and into the conscious awareness but to lift up in an equally exalted state those qualities which are of the feminine. In truth, you would find that if you had the more feminine characteristics imbued within the political leaders of your time, you would make tremendous gains with dizzying speed in bringing your planet to a place of peace and harmony, to a place of cooperation, to a place of Oneness *of humanity, a joining together of goals, a seeking out that which is like, that which is similar, and focusing upon that as opposed to the incredible focus that appears in the aura of humanity today.*

The focus of humanity today is heavily slanted toward the negative, all that is "wrong," and we put that in quotes, all that needs fixing. If mankind, incarnated in the third dimension, were permitted to move along its current path and were not nudged, encouraged, pulled, pushed, whatever the Universe is able to do to seek this greater balance and to use these remarkable feminine assets, ***you humans would actually think yourselves to death, and you would think your planet to annihilation****.*

Not a pretty sight, not a pretty thought. And there is a very small, minute even, percentage of those who are currently incarnated, who have conscious awareness, who would ever believe that this scenario (nuclear holocaust) very recently loomed on your horizon. And you were speeding toward it with all the energy and effort that you could put into it. Fortunately there are those, however minuscule the number, who have the awareness; and there are those on this side who have, if you would accept a colloquialism, who have been busting their backsides (etheric, spiritual backsides to be sure) *to turn the tide, to turn the influence, to turn the stampeding horde. Of course, we must do this without ever negating the free will of each entity, and so you see the enormity of the task.*

✦ Yes. But I find it kind of strange that I myself would be or could be a channel for bringing this, or attempting to bring in this awareness of the benefits—

Indeed, you are all too perfect for you have your own personal need of this. You are all too perfect a channel for this information. Can you not see that? You will have the interest, you will have the desire for you have awakened to the need.

✦ Okay.

And you have begun in fact, and you know this, to make these corrections within your own consciousness, within your own being.

✦ I would feel better if I had already achieved the balance.

Then you would not be the perfect channel. For you see, if you had already achieved the balance, you would more likely be the perfect personality to write the book, but in this way you are the perfect channel to receive the book.

✦ Okay.

And we come to you with this topic because you are so open to it, because indeed you are the perfect choice. For you will test the information given, in much the same way that others will test it when they read it, and that will assist us in presenting it more perfectly.

✦ Okay.

This excerpt may seem quite short, but actually there were several personal questions preceding this extract that were not directly relevant to this subject area.

Summary

In this first presentation, Athenarious made the decision to include the topic of feminine energy in order to fill a great need that exists in the world today. It focuses on the need for an awakening of the masses to the value and benefit of increasing the feminine influence in our personal lives and in our third-dimensional world.

This information declares clearly that the majority of the population in the United States and other "advanced" countries is far overbalanced toward the masculine extreme, in women as well as men. It points to this masculine energy imbalance as being responsible for much of the negativeness present across the world today. Included in the definition of masculine activity is that of *thinking*, and Athenarious offers the observation from the heavenly perspective above that left to our own design we humans would literally think ourselves to death.

The generic picture presented is that domination by the masculine, the worship of the masculine, has reached its apex. Athenarious indicates that we have gone about as far as we can go toward the masculine extreme, and now there is a great need for an increase of the feminine to create the balance needed for inner joy and fulfillment, meaning, and purpose in our lives. In general this reading creates a context into which the information in subsequent readings can be placed.

Thinking: My Personal Experience

It was in a reading by Cathy four or five years prior to this that I had first heard that thinking was not perceived from the heavens above as something of the highest value for making decisions. At that time I was stunned! I was amazed and appalled! I couldn't believe it! My personality wanted to know what else is there? What are we supposed to do, act without thinking? I just could not grasp what kind of activity could be more beneficial.

I was good at thinking. I had learned from experience that I could hold my own with others in almost any kind of intellectual pursuit. I was happy with my ability to use logical reasoning processes in my outer world activities. I thought that logic and reasoning were the *ultimate* decision-making tools. At first I simply could not understand what could possibly cause thinking to be perceived as an inferior decision-making tool. It took me a while to adjust to the mere idea that something could be better.

What was recommended as being better than human thinking was intuition, the ability to receive divine intuitional guidance. My personal reaction was, "Wait a minute. Intuition is something only women have and it's really only good for things like finding the car keys when they happen to be where they do not belong."

Well, to that when asked in my next journaling session, my higher self gave me this message.

Not so fast, Boy Wonder!

What we are talking about is not just for members of the feminine gender. It is called feminine intuition, but only because it requires qualities and abilities that are of a divine feminine nature, such as passivity. Divine guidance cannot be received by masculine, left-brained thinking or reasoning. *Thinking* is the antithesis of receiving divine intuitional guidance.

Intuition requires that personality mind thinking be *stilled.* Intuition requires that the personality mind be quiet and passive, awaiting the still small voice of divine guidance that comes from and through the Spark of God that lies within the soul, above the personality. Intuition requires that the single line of communication between the personality and soul be still and thus open for input, not busy with inner static, small talk, or thinking. Other than that requirement, everyone has the innate ability to do it.

Well, to me, receiving divine guidance through intuition sounded good! Something worth trying! I was somewhat surprised to hear that feminine intuition is not just a feminine gender capability. I had previously accepted information from the Edgar Cayce readings saying that anyone could do what Cayce did, but that was speaking of unconscious readings. The idea of anyone placing great importance on intuition truly was new to me. I had never linked the concept of receiving divine guidance with intuition. Just as I had never connected "enlightenment" with intuition. It all sounded good, but I still felt a bit of a letdown to learn that human thinking was seen from above as an inferior tool for making decisions or knowing truth.

However, let down or not, it didn't take a lot of meditation to understand and realize that intuition would allow each human on Earth to be guided by his or her Divinity Within, rather than by the uncleared personality filled with its egocentric, biased, outer world, man-made information that was adopted from its outer world conditioning and education.

Intuition is for receiving *divine guidance* and information that is best for one's higher good—in the moment. I was told, "Try it, you'll like it." So I did, and I do. To the extent that I am successful, I like it very much. When I am not successful, I know what it takes to get it back again (stilling the personality mind) and then it's back to the fundamentals.

CHAPTER 16

The Second Feminine Energy Reading

Laying the Groundwork for an Expanded Understanding of the Value of Integrating Divine Feminine Energy

This is an excerpt from a reading by Cathy received from Thenous on 10/6/96 with Athenarious nearby and Creighton as guide.

Welcome, it is most pleasant and delightful to see you again. I am Thenous and Athenarious is here also.

✦ Well, good afternoon to you both.

Indeed!

✦ As I told Creighton (pronounced Kryton), we wish for this book to have the material that you most wish it to have, to contain what it is that you see as most important, most helpful to us humans now in lesson. We have no particular format in mind and we don't know exactly what would be best. So we're looking for material, but we're also looking for a format, a design that you wish us to follow. So please let us know anything along these lines that you wish to convey to humankind.

Indeed we embark upon covering a rather large subject, one that is for all intents and purposes foreign to the concept of those who are currently incarnated in the third-dimensional plane. In addition we receive a message from Creighton that you will find yourself working on two volumes, two books, rather simultaneously, rather concurrently, for it has come to our attention that you have made significant progress in work on what you would call your Book One and that part of the information that we would cover here will also be included in that volume.

✦ That's interesting!

Why do you say that?

✦ The two books at the same time! Because I wanted first to furnish the public with Book One that would, without going into great detail, bring anyone who suddenly became interested in the spiritual path in the future a rather complete synopsis, the Universal Spiritual Picture in a nutshell, so to speak. And of course in that volume this enhanced value, or valuation, of the feminine energy will be included, which I believe, is that you allude to when you say it is rather foreign to our third-dimensional world here.

Indeed, that is the case. What we wish to do at this time is to take an overview of the subject itself. Hitting perhaps highlights of that which would be included in both volumes. If that is—

✦ Oh, indeed!

The masculine way

Very well. Let us begin with that which you actually know, that which you have actually experienced and are aware of and that is; that currently in today's world, there is the predominance of mental control, mental activity. The mind's logical processes are held in quite high esteem, virtually worshipped by some and used as a measurement of the value of an individual, a measurement of "intelligence," a yardstick for rating, for ranking entities, and not only ranking their capabilities, but their very worth.

Particularly within the corporate structure, but also within the worldview itself we find that the mind (the personality mind) *reigns in the area of politics, in the area of government where craftiness is considered of value, is applauded, is indeed considered a necessity. Manipulation is a way of life, a way of expression, and those who are refined in these "skills," in these "arts," are venerated and held in esteem and find themselves to be quite successful.*

All of this is quite a natural occurrence. It has come about in a most natural way and is at its zenith at this time, as a result of this epoch or this time being the epitome, the apex, of the masculine, patriarchal age in the experience of your planet and of those beings who are incarnated upon it. The shift (to a higher dimension) *is at hand and it may seem rather abrupt to some. It is important therefore to offer tools which will permit entities that are currently involved in third dimension incarnation, currently immersed in the glory of mental activity, to begin to see, to glimpse at least, another aspect, another perspective.*

It is important to know and to state that within each being there is the potential for balance, for harmony, for bringing the feminine aspect into the fore, for integrating and smoothing out the clashes, the seeming dichotomy between the two (our inner masculine energy and feminine energy). *For success in the spiritual world, in spiritual development, in the spiritual aspect of the third-dimensional plane, and success in the physical material aspect are truly enriched, truly expanded, truly reached, not by an overwhelming propensity toward the mental and the masculine, but by a smooth and harmonious blending of that which is masculine and feminine.*

We have promoted negative, aggressive emotions without a true understanding of their effects upon us

For eons the emotions have been viewed in rather a strange manner in our perspective. Those which are more destructive in nature, those which are more divided from or removed from harmony, are those which have been accepted and those which have been encouraged. We speak of the emotional component of competitiveness, the emotion of anger, the emotion of that which leads to a sense of superiority and of winning.

Indeed these require reaching into the depth of emotions, of the emotional body, which is available to the human spirit, available to those who are currently incarnated in the third dimension. But this is just a small part of the emotional picture. And it is a twisting of reality, for even ***fear*** *has been considered a positive in the sense that it brings about such a strong adrenaline response that it often triggers heightened mental activity and leads to the protection and the preservation of the "human race."*

Each of these emotions which we have named, carries with them power, strength, and a rush of energy, and they are accepted by the masculine culture as being necessary, as being required for survival, for preservation of the individual races, for preservation of lifestyles. And we find that it is this division, this selecting of these particular emotions that most encourages, and most influences mankind to separateness, to bigotry, and most clearly to bringing about wars, fighting, division, and destruction.

Greed is another. Certainly greed is based in emotion though it very much takes over the mental body, as do all of these that we have named. They consume an entity and they consume the mental body, feeding it with power, with drive, with ambition, with strength, with tenacity. Is this clear?

✦ Absolutely crystal clear!

And so it cannot be said that there is **an absence of emotion**. *It cannot be said that the emotional body has been exiled; though many who are proud of their mental capabilities will indicate just this. There is the feeling, the belief, the concept that there has been the purification of the emotional body,* *there has been the taming of the emotional body, and there has been the emotional control.*[1] *But in fact, if the observer is clear in his eye, he will see that in many of those masculine traits, much of that which is worshipped is fueled by the* ***emotional body****, and often by an emotional body that is very close to being out of control, hovering dangerously on the edge between control and chaos.*

And so truly it is ***not*** *that there is a lack of emotional activity. It is* ***not*** *that there is a lack of inclusion or use of the emotional body. It is more that there has been the division in the emotional body, and those aspects of it that are considered to be "feminine" in nature have been suppressed, have been isolated, or exiled, however you wish to portray it.*[2]

But know this, all of these emotions, all of these feminine emotions are active in every human being, and if they are not allowed to manifest in the consciousness, they do in fact manifest in the unconscious. They manifest in the dream state and their manifestation, their activity, is not unknown to those who attempt to cultivate and to be masculine. And very often, however strong the attempt to ignore it or to bury it, the awareness of this feminine activity generates a fear state within the entity and this fear state causes a strengthening of the dichotomy within the emotional body.

The effects of this situation are to cause the greater defending of an entity against the feminine and the greater strengthening of the masculine activities, the masculine persona. And for the majority of those beings who are incarnated in the third dimension, particularly those who are in positions of power, those who are in positions of strength, those who are in the political arena, those who are in the military arena, those who are corporate giants if you will, the leaders of corporate giants, there is the shutting down of the intuitive process. There is the blocking of centering with the divine within.

Again we find all of this building and sustaining divisiveness, the belief in scarcity, the requirement to fight, to compete, and to sustain self and self's position at the expense of others. The perspective of the entities who find themselves in this situation is that there is only so much success, only so much glory, only so much material wealth available.

This dichotomy in the emotional body is highly destructive to emotional relationships. It is highly destructive to harmony among nations, to harmony among individuals, to harmony among those who outwardly, seemingly work on the same team, if you will. And the overall aura that is visible to us from our perspective, is fear, not strength, not courage, not mental acuity. **Fear** *is the dominant and the primary driver of humanity at the ultimate state of involution.*

---

[1] This is precisely what I felt and thought about myself!

[2] We haven't excluded all our emotions from our daily activities; we have excluded only our feminine gentle, kind, and loving emotions while adopting and promoting the masculine emotions of competition, violence, and aggression.

It is not our wish, nor is it our assignment, to paint a dismal dreary picture. Our wish, our desire for participating in this activity is to offer a path, to bring light to a situation that is generally gray, if you would perceive its aura, but which at worst is filled with spikes and thunderbolts of red and black and yellow when the anger is most active, when the fear is most prominent, and when one is scrambling, struggling, and scraping to achieve, and to maintain once achievement has been reached.

And still the entities who are in this state, who compose a large segment of the world's population, who appear to be in such a dire situation, are only one step away from salvation, one step away from enlightenment. They need make only one shift. They need only ***desire*** *to shift for there are hundreds of thousands of those in the Angelic Realm who stand ready to assist each and every entity who is interested in even the smallest way to opening to expanded consciousness.*

As our personality selves, we live in a world of total illusion, and we promote illusions about ourselves

For you see, there is an illusion. There is an illusion of happiness. There is an illusion of success, but deep within each of these entities (at his or her soul level) *one by one, never as a group, but within each individual entity, there comes the eternal question, why does all this not bring me the fulfillment that I expected?*

Great care is taken to hide this inner unhappiness from all others, all of those external to self. Great care is taken to hide this inner questioning. Great energy is put into the front, the facade of achievement, of success, of happiness, of completion, of fulfillment.

And yet you may rest assured that not one of these entities truly experiences happiness, completion, and fulfillment in his or her life experience.[3] *For as we have stated previously, quite a vast number of those who are in*

---

[3] This is a main part of one of the greatest lessons that the Earth School has to offer all humans. Entities who live or exist at the *personality level of consciousness* cannot experience these divine emotions in physical Earth life. The idea that we can is an illusion. The experience of true happiness, completion, and fulfillment is illusory and temporary at best, for these emotions all require unconditional love and unconditional love does not exist at the *personality level* of consciousness in the third dimension. However, it does exist at the *soul level of consciousness* when an entity re-establishes harmony with its Divinity Within. Unconditional love can be transmitted from Angels, Archangels, Ascended Masters, and other Beings of Light in the higher realms because they live at a higher level of consciousness than that of the largely egocentric human personality. On Earth, only those entities who have evolved to the point where they have brought their personality consciousness into harmony with their soul, and their soul into harmony with their Spark of God Within, can become sources and/or channels of divine love once more. This is the way out of the illusion and back to the reality of Oneness with God.

feminine form have adopted this precise (masculine) *pathway in order to succeed, in order to be competitive, in order to be accepted and to achieve worldly, third-dimensional gains.*

And what is the answer? It is not as one might suppose a torturous struggle to rid self of negativity and to shift consciousness dramatically with thought, analysis, and effort. For at this time, in this age upon your planet, there is such a tremendous influx of light, such a tremendous influx of higher vibration, of energy, that there need only be the desire, the reaching out and the awakening to the awareness, to the understanding that true happiness, true fulfillment, and true success are found on a different path, on a different ladder, on a different course of action, being, and living.

The spiritual path back to the ability to receive divine guidance through our soul's innate feminine intuitional pathway is the answer to all outer world illusions

The world, the population thereof, must come to recognize that there is available to it a tool that is so enormous, so profound in its capability, in its facility for creating harmony and success for each entity that it has no equal. But that tool is not through the mind. That tool is not available to, nor can it be accessed through the mental body. It is the antithesis of the logical process, of cunning, of craftiness, and of manipulation. The opening to, and the welcoming of this tool into the consciousness of each and every entity will create an expansion which is beyond comprehension for those who are currently immersed in the belief, in the worship, of that which is masculine and that which is mental.

The tool is intuition.

The fact of the increased light, of the increased energy, the increased vibratory rate, and the increased attention of all of the Angelic Realm means that there need only be the slightest shift in consciousness to create the opening to intuitional input from these entities. And remember please that each of these entities has with him or her at least one Guardian Angel and one Higher Guide who have never lost their attunement, never lost their awareness, their perspective.

Help is available, and the channel, the avenue for receiving that help, is through **the heart**. *There need only be the desire for, and the true and willing surrender to, guidance from within* (at the heart's level of feeling). *Power, personal power, of a nature unimagined is available to each and every one who makes this shift, who chooses this shift. Intuitional guidance will bring with it the magic of the greatest magicians, the energy, the light of a whole host of the Angelic Realm and more than this, peace, peace within, which ultimately will lead to peace without. This shift will bring about a balancing of the emotional body. It will allow that which is not atrophied, that which is still vibrant, still available, still filled with divine energy in each* *and every entity incarnated on your planet to be resurrected, rejuvenated, and evolved into a divine balance.*

This shift is the shift to the spiritual path, to the return to conscious Oneness with God.

It is the shift to the path of **spiritual evolution**. *It is the promise of quantum leaps along the path of evolution. It is the promise demonstrated and offered through the life of the Christ some 2000 years ago or so. And it is the shift back to divine love.*

It is important to note here that this shift in consciousness, this movement toward balancing the emotional body so that the masculine and the feminine are in harmony, will be the greatest breakthrough in medical healing that has ever been known in the third-dimensional plane.

If you look with clear seeing, with clairvoyant understanding and awareness, at the entities that we have described (those who are overly balanced toward the masculine extreme) you will find that the chakra system is very much out of balance. The third solar plexus chakra is greatly enlarged and violently active in many of these. The base chakra in many is also enlarged. In some the second chakra is very nearly, appears to be very nearly, in a state of atrophy. And the heart chakra is abnormally small. The throat chakra may or may not be enlarged depending on the activity of the lower will. The third eye and the crown chakra are quite small.

Negative emotions and inner emotional disharmony are THE cause of all disease

For all that we have described, the imbalance that we have described in the chakra system, in the emotional body, in the activities in the mental body, all of these lead to **disease, dis-ease, within the body**. *But particularly the imbalance in the emotional body where you have anger, and you have aggression, and you have greed, and you have fear dominating, you also have disease. And this imbalance will show itself eventually in a third-dimensional way in the physical body of each of these entities.*

There is the wearing out, the wearing down, and the over activity of the adrenal glands that is destructive to the physical. The liver and the kidneys are required to work tremendous overtime in cleansing toxicity from the system, for these emotions which we have described create great toxicity within the physical body. The building up of plaque, of cholesterol within the arteries is also a function of being closed down to the life force energy that comes through the crown chakra. Indeed many of these entities receive their life force energy only through the solar plexus. And frequently they receive it by drawing it from others, not from the natural attunement to the Universe.

Positive emotions and a loving spirit bring good health

Your most prevalent killers (diseases) *in the medical arena will not even exist in the new millennium. In fact those entities, who for whatever reason do not recognize the value of making this shift in consciousness, of making this surrender, this inner attunement, will not exist in the third millennium either, at least not in the third-dimensional plane.*

The vibratory rate, the energy fields will be too high and too refined, and these entities will not be able to sustain physical bodies, nor will they be able to incarnate during the time of the millennium. We do not define the millennium as beginning in the year 2000. The millennium is at hand and there is already the shifting to the higher vibratory rate, to the higher levels of energy of the third millennium, and it has been dramatically evident since your time of 1986, and it will continue to increase year by year.

As you move toward this, you will find a tremendous increase, the medical profession will find a tremendous increase, in those diseases that are of the nervous system, for it is the nervous system that is the true conduit of the electrical activity, of the vibratory rate of the planet. And the nervous system of those who do not choose to make this shift will be unable to sustain the electrical activity inherent in life in the third dimension on the Earth plane.

All can choose to make the shift to the spiritual path and the inner harmony it brings us

Much that is unseen and that the majority of those in human form are quite unaware of is going on at this time, in the higher dimensions and on the inner planes, if you will. And there will be the opportunity for each entity, through his or her own Guardian Angel and Higher Guide, to make the choice, to choose to make this shift, for the impulses (the inner nudges) *will be stronger. The external happenings, those* (seemingly coincidental) *accidents, if you will, will be more frequent in order to jolt or jar the entity into an awareness, into an awakening.*

Many have already chosen to not take this path, and you will see a resulting increase in mass exodus (of students) *from your planet in the form of major catastrophes, plane crashes, deaths in earthquakes, floods, and other natural disasters, and by those who succumb to plagues of whatever nature.*

A warning here! It is not appropriate to portray that all who leave in these scenarios are those who have chosen not to make this shift for there are still those who leave naturally when their mission here is complete and they are ready to move on to a mission in the higher planes, in the higher dimensions. And it is important to make this clear when you write about such things.

Even young children who leave this plane often do so because their mission is complete. Or because their scenario has changed to the point that they know that they cannot complete their mission in this life experience and they do not wish to waste a lifetime, if you will. And so it is important to offer these various reasons for a soul leaving an incarnated form.

Those who do leave because they choose not to participate in the higher vibratory rate are not lost. They will be given opportunities to continue their work on other planes on other planets, in other Universes where the vibratory rate is more compatible with that which they are able or willing to accept at their current state of spiritual development. Do you have questions?

✦ What about after the millennium? Will some of the entities that have not been allowed to come in during this millennium be permitted to try again?

Yes. There will be a time for that.

Summary

In this reading, when I heard that I would be working on two books at the same time I felt kind of overwhelmed. I am not a published writer. I can't even type except for the hunt and peck method. Once I spot the key I want I'm on it like a cat, but then I have to find the next one, and the next, and so on. I am now learning to touch type and have built my speed up to nearly twenty words a minute, but of course I cannot sustain that kind of pace for long periods of time. So the news about working on two books at the same time was quite a shock. Luckily for me, it was just a misunderstanding on my part. What was truly meant was that the information being given would be useful for both of the first two books.

Thenous' perception from above, of humankind being at the apex of masculine imbalance, led me to a further bit of enlightenment. For several years I had noticed signs of a planetary movement of consciousness toward the feminine, toward that which I was learning was feminine. A greater sensitivity toward the natural environment, an increased number of sightings or appearances of Mother Mary, a broadening acceptance of healing touch and therapeutic touch in hospital settings, all were telling me that a global change was taking place. This caused me to ask of my higher self or soul, in one of my journaling sessions, if the New Age shouldn't more properly be called the Feminine Age.

In essence the answer was a rather definite NO!

The new age might accurately be called the Age of Balance, but not the Feminine Age. Because we are currently at the extreme of masculine imbalance, movement toward a true balance will require an increase in feminine energy. To many, the increase in feminine energy, as it becomes noticeable in our culture, may make it appear that we are moving toward a feminine age, but that will not be the case!

An extreme imbalance of feminine energy is no more beneficial, for the higher good of All Life, than what we now experience as a result of the extreme imbalance of masculine energy. The ideal is the balance of these two energies within each individual and across the cultures of our planet. The current movement will be toward the balance so that in the near future and throughout the next one thousand years, each of those on Earth will be able to receive divine guidance through the passive feminine intuitional ability and will be able to carry out that divine guidance using the active masculine energies. All humans will be in harmony with the divine will of their Divinity Within.

Balance is perfection! Balance is the Ideal! *Neither extreme is the Ideal!*

In the next decade or so there will come a dramatic change in humankind's attitude toward good health

Thenous makes clear that the population of the Earth today is suffering from an extreme imbalance toward third-dimensional masculine energy, in both genders. She also makes clear that this masculine imbalance is the cause of the obvious global tendencies toward violent, aggressive behavior of human against human.

She offers that the remedy for these violent global symptoms lies in the integration of divine feminine energy sufficient to form a balance within each human. Such a balance opens the door to the reawakening of our soul's innate ability to receive divine intuitive guidance and information from our Divinity Within. It is easy for all to see or to imagine the tremendous difference there would be in a world of humans guided intuitively by their Divinity Within as opposed to a world of humans guided solely by their personality minds, conditioned by and filled with outer world habit patterns, as we have today. This is the great shift in consciousness that is taking place now, which will change our Earth School life in the near future in this, the Golden Age.

Perhaps not quite as easy to see or imagine is the difference in our own *personal health issues* that an inner balancing and harmonizing of divine masculine and feminine energy will bring us. Thenous states that creating such a harmony within will bring us the greatest breakthrough in medical healing that has ever been known in our third-dimensional physical world.

Knowledge of the positive correlation, the direct connection, *between emotional imbalance and disease* will bring a dramatic change in attitudes toward illness. Those who have a disease will come to know that the cure lies within them in the mastery of their emotions.

The concept of healing will expand far beyond today's orthodox medical focus on the treatment of the physical symptoms of disease. The new focus will be primarily on the maintenance of good health. The maintenance of good health will shift our focus of attention toward the *emotional and spiritual causes and effects of disease* in all aspects of our beingness—physical, emotional, mental, and spiritual. True health will include inner joy, inner harmony, and the inner love of God, love of ourselves, and the love of others. True health will be a result of an evolved inner balance of divine masculine and divine feminine energy. It will not include the maintenance of a facade of happiness at the personality level of consciousness.

True knowledge and understanding of healing and the maintenance of good health will come from divine guidance received from the heavenly dimensions of God above, not from the personality level of human consciousness as it is today. Receiving such divine guidance intuitively will be commonplace.

Healing in the future will become partly educational and partly therapeutic. In all cases though, the individual will be helped to understand that the root cause of his or her illness is the problem of holding certain negative habit patterns within. It will be understood by the masses that (in accordance with the Universal Laws of Cause and Effect, Like Attracts Like, and Manifestation) the personality's negative thoughts, feelings, attitudes, and beliefs all cause *disease* to manifest in the physical body if held consistently for too long a period of time. The precise cause of any illness will be readily available through divine intuitional information, as will the prescribed path back to inner harmony and good health.

Healing centers will be available to provide the spiritual education, treatment, and spiritual tools that help people to understand and release the specific negative thoughts and feelings that caused their particular disease and to replace them with those which will cause inner spiritual harmony and good physical health. Individuals will be helped to help themselves back to balance and good health within and without and to maintain it afterwards.

From the higher perspective of the soul it is easy to see many of the changes to come in the near future, when the understanding of Universal Laws and the divine truth about the Univeral Spiritual Picture encompassing all our third-dimensional life become commonplace. Illness will be short-lived when we all can ask for and receive divine guidance from our Divinity Within.

CHAPTER 17

The Third Feminine Energy Reading

The Benefits of Integrating Divine Feminine Energy into Our Daily Lives

This is an excerpt from a reading by Cathy received from Athenarious on 10/12/96.

Welcome and love to you all. This is Athenarious.

✦ Thank you for coming.

Indeed, we thank you for coming.[1] *I understand that you have questions.*

✦ I have a question about the content of something in the previous reading, "Many have chosen to not take this path." My question is why have they chosen not to take this path? Because they perceive it as too difficult?

Because they do not perceive it at all, perhaps?

Perhaps it is better to state that they have not chosen to take this path. It is not inaccurate to say that they have chosen not to take the path, but what that includes is that the choice has been made at a level of consciousness which is such that there is the understanding that there is no potential, there is no likelihood that the entity in question will open sufficiently to

[1] It took me a long while to learn what was meant by this comment. It meant that Athenarious, in this case, was thanking us for moving our focus of attention, our level of consciousness up to their (plural) level for communication purposes.

that which needs to be received and perceived in order to move ahead along this path.

The choice has been to remain too much in the mental, to remain too externally oriented, and the belief system of such an entity is too firmly rooted in personal, personality, lower will, control of his or her life experience. And there is the recognition or the understanding at the soul level from the Higher Guides and from the Guardian Angels that there ***is virtually no potential*** *for this to change in this life experience.*

✦ I see.

Some will leave because they have completed that which they came to do in this life experience.

✦ And you stated that in the next paragraph.

Indeed. It is important to offer that information.

✦ Okay, that answers my question. Please offer whatever you have in mind for today's session.

We have discussed sufficiently, for now at least, the current state of consciousness in your culture, the imbalance toward the masculine, the fear of opening to the feminine, the misunderstanding of the talents and skills of the feminine. For indeed if there was the understanding, if there was the ability to perceive that which the opening to the feminine and the integrating of those skills into the life experience would so greatly facilitate (such as the goals of harmony and peace, peace within your planet, peace for those who inhabit your planet), and if the dominant masculine consciousness could be aware of the magic available through integrating the feminine, there would be a stampede to learn to use these talents and skills.

At the same time there would be ***great difficulty*** *in learning to do so for, with that as the goal, most entities approaching from that aspect would find it virtually impossible to release their personal requirement for mental control. They would want to access and use the skills and talents of the feminine, under masculine, mental, lower will control. And this would not work in any case. It would not accomplish balance and harmony. And the potential magical approach, the potential ease and indeed instantaneous creation of that they desire, would elude them.*

The positive effects of integrating divine feminine energy sufficient to achieve a good masculine/feminine balance

Let us speak now of the positive aspects of integrating the feminine and achieving balance and harmony within each individual entity. We will state that which perhaps may be obvious to some but will not be obvious to all. The integration of the feminine and masculine, the harmony, the blending in a harmonious fashion which will be the result of such activity, will endow those in third-dimensional form with outstanding health, with strong immune systems, with vitality and long-term lingering youthfulness, for the degeneration of the cells of the human body is directly related, can be directly related, to the imbalance, to the disharmony, between the masculine and feminine aspects. For indeed it has been scientifically proven that the cells in your body today are not the same cells that were in your body several years ago. Indeed some areas of cells replace themselves in a period of months. Nevertheless, you perceive what is known in the third-dimensional world as the aging process. Think about this. If you have, in effect, a whole new body, then why does an entity continue to age?

✦ I have no idea.

It is because ***the disharmony and the imbalance within the entire system*** *are imprinted into each cell through its rather short lifetime, and the new cell is a replica of the cell that is dying or has died. And so the cells, after they are created, learn if you will, of the imbalance in their environment. And the imbalance in their environment affects them in such a way that the next cell that is generated comes into being with a greater awareness of the imbalance within the environment. And so there is the perpetuation of the aging process in the new cells as they are created, for they are created with this greater awareness of this imbalance. Is that clear?*

✦ Yes.

The imbalance also makes the physiological aspect of an entity incarnated in human form more susceptible to disease because there is already disharmony within the system. Do not misunderstand, for disease and illness serve their purpose in the third dimension as great teachers, as great influences upon the entity to learn those lessons which it came to learn and which it must succeed in learning and in overcoming if its mission is to be completed. Important to note here is that it is not necessary to go to the extremes of becoming ill in order to learn a lesson, but many who incarnate into the third dimension unknowingly choose this path by resisting learning the lessons in an easier fashion.

And here we could begin to write yet another book and we will not do that. For we feel it is important to maintain the subject at hand. But is that clear?

✦ Yes.

Perhaps the greatest tool of the feminine aspect is that of ***intuition****, that of inner knowing, that of being aware of a higher truth, a higher knowing from a perspective that is much broader, much clearer, and much more attuned to truth, if you will. Intuition is certainly an aspect of the feminine and it is an aspect that must be developed by those entities who will move into the* *next millennium. Intuition is a tool that will serve humanity beyond all description.*

There is never a time, there is never an activity in the third dimension where intuition would not be an incredibly valuable tool, an incredibly valuable activity in daily living. In survival, but more importantly in spiritual development in the evolution aspect of this designed Earth experience.

The involution process is ending and aggressive souls will no longer be able to maintain physical bodies on planet Earth

For the involution process will soon be completely eliminated from the experience of the planet itself. Currently there are still those entities that incarnate into the Earth plane who are in the involution cycle [this was in 1996]. With the coming of the new millennium this will cease entirely. Only those who are in the evolution cycle and only those who have made good progress, who are in the upper portions of the evolution cycle, will find themselves able to manifest bodies, to create bodies which are compatible with the higher vibratory rate, the ambiance, the environment of the new millennium. And so you see that it is ***absolutely required*** *that the feminine be integrated and balanced with the masculine.*

Another point. Intuition works very well when you are living in the moment. Intuition is not a tool that is useful in living in the past or living in the future. For intuition is that information which you need ***right now****, in the present moment. This is the information that flows freely through the intuitive channel. And so it is important to practice being in the moment. It is important to practice maintaining your consciousness in the moment. Is that clear?*

✦ Yes.

And do you find that helpful?

✦ Yes.

Very well. It is important to us that this information be given in such a way that it will be of assistance to those who are ready to awaken and move toward integrating the feminine into their consciousness. And perhaps to those who might be caught before they are so indoctrinated into the culture that the feminine is dominated almost to exclusion by the masculine.

✦ Okay, then before we go on there is something I used personally from our last session with Thenous. There was some information I found very interesting, but I cannot say I am absolutely clear on it because of my own personal experience, my perspective, where I am now. I'm not sure that I completely understand. And it was the paragraph that said this.

This is an excerpt from a reading by Cathy from Thenous on 10/06/96 (the week before).

It is not as one might suppose, **a torturous struggle** *to rid self of negativity and to shift consciousness dramatically with thought and analysis and effort. There only need be the desire, the reaching out and the awakening to the awareness, to the understanding that true happiness is found on a different path, on a different ladder, on a different course of action and being and living. The tool is intuition.*

End of Thenous' 10/06/96 reading. Continuing with Athenarious' reading.

✦ I am certain I do not understand this clearly because for me the torturous way *is* the way. That's the way I have chosen, or that I seem to have chosen.

Indeed, it is the masculine approach. The mental approach.

✦ I have worked with this since I started transcribing the feminine energy tapes, for I have understood it in the following way. We have adopted these negative habit patterns during our involution phase. To resolve their current negative effects has meant to me to observe them, to identify them, to know them, to understand their etiology, to determine that which would be more harmonious, and then to release the old negatives and replace them with that which is more positive, which creates greater inner harmony between my personality and my soul.

✦ I could see no other way, so I asked the question internally of my higher self or soul and received this understanding in a journaling session.

If one attunes to one's higher self or soul, and through intuition constantly receives guidance from one's own internal connection to God, the All That Is, then what comes in as guidance will be that which is true and pure and good. If one follows that guidance for a period of at least 21 days, there will be the overlaying of whatever has been there with the new habit patterns. And all this will have happened without the detailed analysis, the trying to understand the subpersonality's old mission and new mission and all of those things that it takes to do it the hard way.

End of the journaled material. Continuing with Athenarious' reading.

✦ Is this something of which you will speak later? Is this glimpse of mine what you meant when you said it is *not* as one might suppose *a torturous struggle*?

Indeed, it is very close to that which we meant and we suggest that these are the kinds of things you will wish to include in your book as your own experiences based on this material. It is going to be important that your book include these kinds of things if those who are growing and experiencing third-dimensional life forms are going to be able to relate in a way that will allow them to perceive this information as being ***something that they can incorporate into their life experience****, rather than just a philosophy which they can espouse and believe in* ***but not practice****.*

✦ Yes, okay. When I asked about a format before, I probably didn't make myself clear, but that is exactly what I was asking about.

Ahh!

✦ My question should have been, should I include these kinds of connections with my own torturous struggle? And so now you have answered that.

Indeed, we apologize. We thought we had made that clear in describing that the reason that you are the perfect channel for this information, and that you are the perfect author for this book, is because you will use that which is given, because you have chosen to seek to integrate the feminine into your experience, and in using that information you will be able to relate your experiences and your movement, your growth, your understanding of the information that is given, in such a way that others will be able to relate also.

✦ Okay.

It is imperative that this be a large part of that which is offered and expressed through this book.

✦ Okay, good.

Otherwise we could have chosen any channel that would willingly write down the information that we give. But you are in the perfect stage of your own growth, the perfect place to be able to relate to and present this material to those in third-dimensional form in such a way that they will say, "Well, he was able to do this and this is how. And so I too may be able to do it in similar fashion if not in exactly the same fashion." Is that clear?

✦ Yes.

Good. With regard to that which you received we would make two minor adjustments. One is that rather than to say, "in at least 21 days," we would recommend that you use 30 days.

It is not that it is impossible to do that in 21 days. It is that it is more likely for it to occur in a broader range, in a greater number of incarnated entities, in a period of 30 days.

And the other addition we would make is that yes indeed that which you learn can "overlay" that which you have done, but we would prefer that it ***replace*** *it, and it cannot replace it unless that which you already have is* ***released****. And you do not need to know the details of what you are releasing.*

✦ Okay.

You need only know that it is a hindrance to you, it is a block to your growth, or it is something that impairs this blending, this integrating, and this wholeness. And that in overlaying, the new habit patterns really ***are filling a void****.*

✦ Yes, okay.

For it is the releasing that creates the void that must be filled.[2] *Attachment is a very important aspect and one that we will deal with in greater force, if you will, at a later time.*

And so again we will state that intuition is a very important tool. And it is a tool that is only available through the feminine aspect of self. Intuition works through the ***heart****. The information is received through the heart. And yes, of course, the information is acted upon by the mind,* ***but it must be received through the heart, for that is the connection****. The soul to the heart, the higher dimensions to the heart. Through the crown chakra, through the third eye, into the heart. Very important that this is understood. Because initially it will not be something that human entities are familiar with experiencing. Though in all probability each and every one would be able to remember a time in their current life experience when they did have this experience, though they may not have taken appropriate notice of it. Is that clear?*

✦ Yes, and I've had intuitive— —thoughts I wanted to say, —

Understandings is a good word.

✦ Okay.

Or knowings is another good word to use.

---

2 The possible existence of residual negative energy from our personality's old negative habit patterns is the reason that Athenarious needed to make the point she did regarding the difference between "overlaying" old habits with new, as opposed to "releasing" and "replacing" old habits with new. The new spiritual tools (chapter 21 and appendix A) will remove any negative energy left over from the old ways, if we first release the old creating the void, and then replace them with the new, as she said. However, if we mentally just overlay the old with the new, the negative will still remain within us and will simply be covered over with the new. This would not create as stable a situation for our new habit. Merely overlaying the old would leave it within us and make regression more likely. This is an important point.

✦ Relating to people's childhood experiences, before we humans get so bent out of shape down here. That some of those can bring back the memory of what the intuitive experience is like, especially in the playing mode. A three- or four- or five-year old in the playing mode seems to be a good example. Or maybe I should ask you if that is the case.

Indeed it is. And we recommend that you include this information in your book as you discuss intuition, as you use that material which we are offering. This is a partnership. This book is co-creation. We will help you to make certain that you do not go astray.

✦ I appreciate that, thank you.

But in fact you will find that you can trust yourself much more than you believe that you can. To a far greater degree.

Passivity is feminine

Very well. Now one aspect of the feminine nature is that of ***passivity****, and probably it is the aspect that has caused the feminine to receive the greatest rap, if you will, the greatest black mark within your culture. For your culture, in its masculine and mental dominance state, is very much attuned to action, to activity. Do things, fix things, correct things, create things. But please understand that creation does* ***not*** *begin with activity.*

Creation begins with inspiration. Creation begins with inner knowing. It begins with a deep inner understanding and you can only get this through the feminine aspect. You can only get this through intuition, and intuition works in a passive mental state.

Now there will be those who say no, that isn't true. There are many instances where intuition has come to those in crisis, who are very much in action, but I tell you this. When that inspiration came, the moment that inspiration came through, ***the higher mind was quiet*** *and the lower mind was preoccupied to the point of not being truly in control of the consciousness. Is that a clear concept?*

✦ Yes. And in my experience it has been mostly when there has been the giving up by the personality, by the personality's recognition that this is something beyond the ability of the personality to handle, to accomplish, without the help of a higher power.

Correct!

✦ The surrender to the fact that whatever the emergency situation, it was seemingly beyond the control of the personality of the individual, who then, in surrender, had the new insight or understanding.

Or it is when an entity enters into a crisis situation, coming to the rescue perhaps, having had the inspiration (in a passive state) ***before*** *his activity. So there are both. But surrender is incredibly important and that entity who comes, if you will, to the rescue and has had the inspiration first has already surrendered, has already opened to a higher power. He is not in his ego mind at the moment that that knowing comes to him.*

Can we prove this? Not in a third-dimensional way. No we cannot. And we have no desire to, for those who are interested will be able to have the experience. They will be able to have the knowing, and be able to experience the subtlety of that shift in consciousness.

Passivity equates to attunement and also equates to surrender (of the personality to divine guidance). *Physical activity can occur simultaneously with a passive mental state. And here is your optimum blending, to be able to be* ***physically active and mentally passive****, simultaneously.*

How passivity works in the reception of divine guidance

Now in these cases of physical activity and continuing intuition, you will find that there is quite a correlation in the mental state between activity and passivity. There will be activity and there will be just this little break of passivity. And then there will be activity. Thoughts will be flowing, then a little break. Thoughts will be flowing, and again a little break. ***And it is in each one of those breaks, those gaps, if you will, that inspiration and intuition come through.*** *Anyone can train himself through practice, through exercising awareness to note that this in fact does occur and happen for him or her. Anyone can learn to focus in on those gaps.*

Now in a state of meditation or in a state of quiet contemplation, there is not that thought, gap, thought, gap. There is gap and the intuition comes through then. But generally speaking in meditation and contemplation there is very little physical activity occurring at the time that these two are occurring.

Not that they cannot occur simultaneously, but when they do it is, generally speaking, in an entity who has achieved a fairly high level of spiritual growth and attunement. Is that clear?

✦ Yes. As you were speaking of the ability to have activity and passivity at the same time, I was reminded of a book on inner tennis that Cathy and I came across some twenty-five years or so ago. The gist of the book seemed to be an excellent example of that premise. It indicated that the activity that takes place while the higher mind is passive and open to receive, is probably an activity that is superior to that when the personality mind is active. Where we might use the phrase to the effect that "unconsciously" one is doing the right thing without even *thinking* about it. Where the mind is so far above the activity that the best strategy to use, how to play your very best, is intuitive. In this situation it's not even as though you have a human opponent, you are simply keeping your eye on the ball and responding to inner guidance, like a child perhaps playing in the sand.

Indeed, that is correct. And "unconscious" is probably good terminology for those in the third dimension, but really he is in a state of ***higher consciousness****. The mind is not unconscious; it is of a higher consciousness. He is not unconscious of what he is doing; he is at a higher consciousness in what he is doing.*

✦ Yes, I see.

An example of extreme[3] feminine energy imbalance

A person who is unbalanced toward the feminine will receive great intuitive insight and great intuitive information ***and do virtually nothing with it****. And so the masculine is certainly important in the third dimension and we do not wish those reading this book to believe that we are rating the feminine as a higher aspect. They are equal. The balance needs to have both integrated in an equal way, and we stress the feminine only because it is so lacking in your culture today.*

✦ There was an element here with which, in my own experience, I had a lot of difficulty, and the only way I was able to get around it was for me to be able to distinguish between let's say "third-dimensional" feminine and "divine" feminine, "third-dimensional" masculine and "divine" masculine energy. In other words, our cultural idea of feminine would differ from the view of feminine energy from where you stand now. Down here the culture takes something like an average of the attitudes, feelings, thoughts, and actions of a group of individuals, whose gender is female in this case, and then forms an attitude about that generic group. And the same with the masculine.

Indeed.

✦ And the result of that is far different from what one perceives as masculine or feminine at the Angelic State or the Ascended Master State. I truly could not even *desire* to be feminine or to integrate feminine energy until I made this distinction.

---

[3] This shows the effects of an imbalance toward the extreme feminine side. It emphasizes that the true need of humanity is for a balance between the two, so that we can use our divine feminine (passive) talents to receive divine intuitional guidance and our divine masculine (active) talents to put that guidance into practice in our third dimensional world. Man or woman, we need a blending of divine feminine and divine masculine energy within our Beingness if we are to reflect Divinity in our lives.

And it is an important distinction for indeed we are discussing here the ***divine feminine and the divine masculine****, and it is important to state that early on in your book. We are looking for a balanced entity who can achieve spiritual development, full-expanded consciousness, awareness of the higher dimensions, and awareness of the greater concept of who he or she really is.*

It is important to note that that which is measured by your culture as feminine activity really includes a great deal of ***masculine overtone****. It is a poor mix. Perhaps you could say that it is a product that includes artificial coloring and artificial flavoring.*

And perhaps we will stop for now.

✦ I thank you very, very much.

As we thank you. And we offer our love and our blessings and we wish you the greatest harmony in your lives and your daily experience and we are through for now.

Summary

There are many benefits to be accrued by attaining a balance of divine feminine and divine masculine energy, especially for those who choose or have chosen the spiritual path.

Athenarious mentions continued youthfulness and freedom from disease. I already understood that all disease is caused by combinations of negative emotions held for long periods of time, but I really had no idea that signs of aging were part of the picture. I had never thought of aging as a disease, but of course it *does* bring us a fair amount of noticeable dis-ease or lack of ease. Personally, I never jump the fence anymore. I always go round by the gate. Perhaps if I had created a more even energy balance in my life at an earlier age I would still be playing tennis and looking good while doing it. (Well, perhaps I've gone too far.)

The greatest tool of our feminine aspect is that of intuition. This includes inner knowing and the awareness of divine guidance and higher truth from a perspective far above that available to the personality level of humankind at its current stage of evolution. It includes what might be called enlightenment wherein each of us can simply recognize our need to know or understand something, anything, still our personality mind, and suddenly *know and understand* that which we are seeking.

Athenarious tells us that intuition works especially well when we are neither dwelling in the past nor worrying about the future, but living right now in the eternal, continuous moment. This is what all those who raise their vibrational rate to be compatible with the increasing rate of the planet will be doing in the near future of this new millennium. To live fully in the moment requires a certain degree of spiritual growth to the point where one has such a trust in God (and all God's minions) to provide inner guidance and information, and a faith in self to be able to open and receive it, that she or he need not worry or be concerned with either the past or the future. Intuitional higher guidance will be available to all who have brought their personality, their soul, and their Spark of God Within into harmony and are therefore attuned always to God.

Athenarious also provides a clear picture of precisely how the aspect of passivity works in attaining higher guidance through intuition. Our personality minds are almost always busy, unless we have already taught them to be still at will. In the moments when our personality mind is busy thinking its own thoughts, there is no possible intuitive input. However, when our personality mind is still even for a moment, inspiration and intuition can come through.

This stillness may be the result of our learning to still our personality mind, or it may come in emergency situations as a result of our personality's mind becoming overwhelmed by the size or seriousness of the emergency at hand, to the point where it does not know what to think and shuts down. When the personality mind surrenders to the enormity of the situation before it, its giving up or perhaps shutting down automatically creates the stillness that opens the door to divine guidance. You can see by this that our friends in high places are always available to help us, if we only learn to still our personality mind. When we learn this, we need not wait until we are confronted with a life and death emergency to receive higher guidance.

Athenarious points out clearly that it is a balance between divine feminine and masculine energy that is needed. Too much feminine passivity will bring the intuitive insight and information to an individual who may in turn do nothing with it. Knowledge not used is, of course, worthless. A balance of the two, where our feminine energy passively brings in the information and our masculine energy actively uses it in the outer world, is the optimum we humans can reach.

Intuition is a tool that is available only through the feminine aspect of ourselves, and then it is delivered through the heart. Much of humankind has developed such constant habit patterns of *thinking* (at all times, in all places) that they have become largely unfamiliar with the experience of holding divine gentle feelings in their hearts. Any who have created protective, defensive shells around their hearts may need some help from above (always available for the asking) to remove the shells, as well as a little practice to bring their hearts back to the point of feeling, experiencing divine positive, gentle, and loving emotions again.

In reading of these requirements (i.e., a balance of divine feminine and masculine energy, an ability to still the ever busy personality mind, and an open, feeling heart) remember, there is always help available from those in the higher dimensions of God above. Each and every condition, which we may find within ourselves, can be released and replaced by using the spiritual tools created just for this New Age.

For now, just remember you are a student in the Earth School learning how to return to conscious Oneness with God (if and when you choose to do so). Rest assured that God has provided a way back that includes assistance for every possible condition that any mortal man or woman has ever created for him- or herself. Returning now is easier than it has *ever* been since the creation of the Earth School.

CHAPTER 18

The Fourth Feminine Energy Reading

Some Exercises for Integrating Divine Feminine Energy

This is an excerpt from a reading by Cathy received from Thenous on 10/13/96.

We welcome you again to the peace and warmth of our lovely area. I am Thenous.

✦ There are no special questions we wish to ask at this time. Our visit today is just to continue what has already been offered for the book.

Very well, if you will give us just a moment.

Defining and identifying that energy which is feminine as opposed to that which is masculine

The feminine and the masculine energies manifest themselves in the third-dimensional plane as that which is called the yin *and the* yang, *as a differentiation between right brain and left brain activity, and as a polarity, yin being feminine and yang being masculine.*

Right brain activity is more the feminine, the creative, the passive, the receptive, for it is through the right brain that information such as we are transmitting today is received. And it is here that creativity in the form of paintings and poetry, most writing, and other inventive and creative activities including composing and the playing of music is dominant.

*In the left brain you have **logical thinking** and you have third-dimensional **activity**.*

*In our session today the information that is being received is being received in the **right brain** and the speaking of that information is of necessity controlled by the **left brain**. And so there is the constant shifting between the right and left.*

*One of the rewards, one of the outcomes in becoming balanced in the feminine and the masculine energies is not only a tremendous increase in harmony and a tremendous increase in the ability to experience peace, but also that there becomes that which is called **whole brain awareness**. This is what must be accomplished in order for there to be the third-dimensional living, the third-dimensional activity occurring simultaneously to the attunement, to the receipt of intuition, to the listening within, to the harmony, and the expansion of consciousness. For the expansion of consciousness requires and/or facilitates access to the higher realms, to the higher dimensions. And these realms are accessed primarily through the intuition, through the passive activities of meditation and in the Dream State and in the Trance State.*

An equal balance of divine feminine and divine masculine energy is the ideal

However, there are those entities who are too heavily invested with the feminine, and this does occur with those who begin working along the path and choose to move into a channeling type of activity or even the psychic reading activity. For in psychic readings the information is also received through the right brain and reported through the left brain.

It does occur that there are those who become so dominant in the right brain, who become so heavily imbued with the feminine, that while there is tremendous attunement to the higher levels, and there are wonderful experiences of the higher planes and higher dimensions, there is an inability to bring this back into third-dimensional living and third-dimensional activity (into the personality).

And so there is the dichotomy in the life of such an entity. And the two lives indeed are quite separate. The life that is lived in the third dimension in the waking state and the life that is lived in meditation, in the dream state and in the trance state, are quite separate and there is very little blending.

*This is **not** conducive to spiritual development though many believe that it is. And the reason that we say this is that the purpose of incarnating in the Earth plane, in the third dimension, is to become so balanced, so harmonious within self and so attuned that there is a return to the original state* (of being a soul attuned or in harmony with the divine Spark of God within it).

The original state was not dominated by either the feminine or the masculine, but really exhibited a total blending, almost a neutral portrayal of these two aspects for there is no polarity within the ascended beings. There is no polarity in the higher dimensions and in the higher planes. Is this clear?

✦ It is to a certain extent. I mean it's crystal clear up to the point where you are now, but when you say *no polarity* I have a hard time understanding that and feeling it.

Indeed, as you have a difficult time understanding that there is no time in the higher dimensions.

✦ Yes.

This is very much because you are ***in*** *the third dimension, because you are* ***incarnated*** *there and to whatever degree the veils are still dropped for you, it is not possible for you to have the experience of timelessness or the experience of no polarity. However, many of you do have the experience and you do find that in the meditative state that you have no concept of time. That when you finish meditating, when you come back into your daily conscious awareness, you have no sense, until you look at a clock or other timepiece, as to how long you have spent in the higher dimensions.*

✦ Yes.

This is an experience of timelessness. Also one of the great lessons, once achieved, is the concept, most difficult to grasp in the third dimension, that because there is no time, there is no past, and there is no future. Everything is occurring at the same moment, everything is simultaneous, and so in fact the "past" can be changed as well as the "future" being changed.[1] *But this is an area that is not germane to that which we are currently discussing. It is merely something that adds to the understanding of how difficult it is for those in the third dimension to comprehend the higher dimensions,*

---

[1] If I choose to address this issue further, I will include it in part V, Our Changing Persectives, Seeing From Above. For now I will only add that the appearance, the illusion of time and space, was included as part of the original design of the third-dimensional Earth School in order to provide, to create, a world, an environment, in which the lower conscious personalities of our lost or entrapped souls could experience life as we now know it and gradually increase their desire to evolve back to the original state of conscious Oneness with God. Without the illusion of time and space our personalities could not experience reincarnation with its sequence of lives all eventually affecting the soul with those experiences. Now you will also understand (as in the case of Saul of Tarsus) the reason that once the awakening and commitment to the path have taken place *the past doesn't matter.* When the Earth School experience has had its effect on any student to the point where the human has awakened and committed to the return path to conscious Oneness with God, the past is no longer important. At that point the school has done its job, and only the student's return to God is important. Neat!

the wholeness, the Oneness of entities who are not incarnated in the third-dimensional plane.

For those of you who are mediators, who have experienced and/or practiced meditating regularly, we offer this experiment.

A light body meditation exercise, part 1

If you will sit quietly and relax your body in whatever way you are accustomed to doing; we could here go through numerous relaxation techniques, but we will not at this point. It is however, important to relax your body and bring yourself to a state of peace and near tranquility, so that there is quiet within the consciousness and within the cells of the physical being. If you will do this and focus upon the solar light. Just perceive this, imagine this, if it is more efficient for you to do it this way. Imagine that the solar light is above you and is streaming down to you and around you in something of a channel or a vertical tunnel.

Allow this light to flow into your being, allow it to flow in through your crown chakra, and to proceed or travel through each chakra in turn. The third eye, the throat, the heart, the solar plexus, the second chakra, and the base chakra. (See the cover illustration.)

This visualization should bring to you an experience of greater, deeper relaxation, and a sense of warmth. The solar light is indeed a living being. And you can perceive it in a similar way to your actual physical sun.

Now once you have brought this light in through each one of your chakras, then feel or visualize the light disseminating throughout your entire being so that every cell of your physical body is filled with this light. Then experience the light moving from your base chakra upward, in front of your being, in front of your body, and entering back into the heart chakra and flowing up through the throat, through the third eye, and through the crown so that it is coming back up through and above the top of your head and falling down about you as a waterfall.

Now this light, this solar light is very warm. It is very comforting, very soothing and it brings with it a sense of security, of protection. Allow this light to fall down about you so your entire being is in the center of this waterfall of light. Now breathe in, taking deep breaths all the way into the area of the solar plexus, filling your thoracic cage, breathing deeply, and slowly.

As you breathe in the light and it fills your being, imagine or visualize the light expanding beyond your being in every direction, expanding into your light body, filling your light body at least three feet away from your physical body, as an extension of your physical body, and you may do this up to thirty feet if that is comfortable for you. Having done this, be very quiet and very aware of the qualities of this light and of your expanded state.

Now in the expansion of this light nothing interferes. It can quite easily expand through furniture and walls, floors and ceilings, trees if you are outside, any object. Nothing impedes the expansion of your light body as you visualize or imagine it occurring. Please remember to practice this and all exercises in an area where you feel comfortable, where you feel protected and safe. And where you will not likely be disturbed.

Now when your light body is expanded to its fullest extent, continue to breathe deeply, slowly and rhythmically, allowing yourself to absorb this experience, to absorb the richness, the warmth, and the love, the divine love, which is inherent in this solar light. Enjoy this experience until you feel completely comfortable, completely filled and surrounded, until the cells of your being feel flooded, filled with this light. You may remain in this state for as long as you like.

The purpose for this part of this experiment is to give you **the experience**, *to give you the firsthand knowing and awareness of what it feels like to be a part of the solar light, to be attuned with the solar light. And this beginning can be the jumping-off point if you will, for other experiments and other experiences. Or it can be used alone for as long as you desire to stay in this space, just being aware of the love and the comfort, the warmth and the peaceful vibratory rate of this light and this experience.*

As with all other meditations, if stray thoughts occur or interfere, merely allow them to float away. Release them from your consciousness and focus again on the flow of the solar light into your being, through your being, and expanded out beyond your being.

A light body meditation exercise, part 2

Once you are comfortable with this experience, once you are comfortable with this experiment, then you may move on; and when you are in this state, when you are in your expanded light body and in the consciousness of this attunement, then allow yourself to float upward, to move through the tube of light, through the channel of light, through the conduit, whatever you desire to call it and move up to the solar planes (soul planes).

At this level on the solar plane there is wholeness, there is whole brained awareness. There is the experience of openness in the consciousness, of attunement to the divine and what you are really doing here is meeting your own soul. Meeting that level of your own being, which can be attuned to throughout your Earth experience, throughout your third-dimensional experience.

Be aware that you are welcomed by your soul, that you are loved by your soul. Experience being wrapped in the warmth and protection, the love and the acceptance, of your own soul. And now begin to look through the eyes of your soul. Look at yourself. Look at your life experience as it is now. As it is in the current moment. If you have issues, if you have questions, if you have challenges within your life experience, bring them now and lay them out so that through your soul's eyes you may perceive them with greater clarity, with greater understanding, and with an awareness of truth. As you look upon these issues, as you look upon these challenges, you may be aware of a new perspective. You may be aware of insights that you have not previously had or experienced. And you may be aware of actual answers to questions, to challenges, to issues in your life.

However, it is not necessary that these answers, this broader perspective, come to you while you are in this meditation. Just absorb the warmth and the love and the comfort that is found on this plane. And the acceptance of you (your higher self's or soul's acceptance of you). *You will find that the acceptance is true, wholehearted, clear, and without reservation. The answers, the clarity, the new perspective on your life's issues and challenges may come to you over the next several days. And they will come to you as intuitive insights.*

Stay in this situation; stay in this place, this space, for as long as you desire. And when you are ready, thank your soul for its love, for its comfort, for its presence in your consciousness. And if you are prepared, if you are ready to offer a commitment to grow, a commitment to move forward, a commitment to release some of your issues and some of your challenges, make this commitment now. And if you are not yet prepared to do this, then merely thank your soul and express your appreciation for that which has been offered to you, and your promise that you will consider all the information that comes to you as a result of this experience. And then move back into your third-dimensional consciousness; move slowly through the tube of light or the channel of light and allow your consciousness to return to your physical being.

As you experience this happening, begin to breathe deeply and be aware of your light body returning to a more normal state and size, until you are comfortable with where it is as an extension of your own being. Breathe in three times and as you exhale each time breathe out any energy that you do not want, anything that is not compatible with the state that you have experienced. On the third inhalation, as you exhale, breathe out through your feet and visualize, or know, or feel, or experience the light flowing down into the Earth. This is for grounding. This is to assist you in bringing into your waking conscious state, into your everyday activities, that light, that warmth, that love which you have experienced in this experiment.

Then open your eyes and stand up and stretch until you feel comfortable and centered once more within your third-dimensional being.

You may do this exercise as often as you desire, but we recommend that you do it at least once a day for at least seven days. You can become, through experience, so comfortable with moving into this state of consciousness that you need not follow each and every step, so comfortable that you need not even be in a state of meditation. You may be able to bring this consciousness to you, or move into this state of consciousness, in your daily activities.

A self love exercise

For those of you, and there are very many of you in the third-dimensional plane who find a sense of unworthiness, who find a sense of being unloved by self, we recommend that you stand before your mirror (and you can do this when you are brushing your teeth or preparing for the day), look into your eyes, and repeat to yourself, I love you. I love you unconditionally. I love you without reservation. I love you with complete, wholehearted, divine acceptance. This is an exercise that you will wish to repeat for at least 30 days. And you will be quite amazed at the results of this activity.[2]

Do you have comments or questions regarding this?

✦ Not regarding what you have given.

Very well. You may find that when you have questions, when you have comments, that they come at times that would be most appropriate, for your readership is likely to have similar questions and a similar need for answers.

(Hinting to me that it is my intuition that pops them into my mind and that I should look now to see what is there for me.)

✦ Okay. Then I will ask this. Is our first mission down here to become our soul, to begin to identify with our soul self, so that we simultaneously experience being our soul at the same time as we understand that we have this body and manage to handle it in accordance with the harmony that we experience in the soul state? Is that our first mission? Or something like that?

The first requirement on the way back to conscious Oneness with God is waking up to the Univeral Spiritual Picture

Well, we find it rather difficult to number the missions, if you will, because in fact the first requirement is to ***wake up*** *to the fact that there is something more than your physical environment, something more than the third dimension, and something more than your mind, your emotions, and your physical body!*

Back to your question. There is often given the intermediate step of becoming one with the higher self prior to becoming one with the soul. And this is quite effective, for the higher self is very much representative of the

---

[2] You will find it much more effective if you do this exercise with *feeling, with feelings.* Use your imagination, and use the memory of your light body experience to see yourself as your higher self or soul, speaking and feeling these words aimed at your personality. Experience them coming from your higher aspects down to your personality. The effects are those of creating a greater inner harmony and a greater sense of well-being among your personality self and all the higher aspects of your beingness.

soul. It is very much an emissary, if you will, a liaison between the third dimension and the solar plane, the soul level. And the higher self is a handy and more acceptable way (more acceptable to our personality's level of consciousness) *for entities to move into expanded consciousness.*

But once there is the slightest awakening, once there is the slightest desire to move beyond the third dimension, help is instantaneously available, and each entity will find himself or herself drawn along the appropriate path. For there are differences and there are those approaches which appeal more to one entity than to another. Is that clear?

✦ Yes, yes it is.

And primarily this is because of the experiences that have accrued during the involution process and the beginnings of the evolutionary process. It very much depends on where the entity is when he wakes up. Waking up is not a level of consciousness. Waking up occurs at various states of consciousness. Is that clear?

✦ Yes.

And so as soon as the entity wakes up it is necessary for him or her to move forward from where he or she is. And the old adage in your third dimension, when the student is ready the teacher will appear, is quite accurate.[3] *It is based on fact for indeed that is the way that it occurs. Now the teacher may be a Higher Guide or a Guardian Angel and they may begin their work through a book, a movie, a video, a poem, a flower, a sunset. This is why there is assigned to every incarnated being at least one Higher Guide and one Guardian Angel. And generally speaking the guide for an entity is a guide who has been with that soul over numerous incarnations, eons of time if you will. And so there is a very great connection, a very great awareness, of what it will take and when precisely the soul, the entity, is ready and open to receive that information.*

False starts? Indeed. For the Higher Guides and the Angels attempt to make progress through any opening, however small, and the information, the guidance, the inspiration is not always received.

Back that up! The information is always received but it is not always known (to our personality).[4] *The entity is not always aware of receiving*

---

[3] Every feeling, every thought, every word or action or desire that we have ever had as our human personality is known *immediately* by our higher self, our soul, our Divinity Within, our Higher Guide(s), and our Guardian Angel(s). This is why help becomes available as if by magic at the moment "the student awakens and is ready."

[4] As our personality we are not always aware of our soul's having received information. We must create a certain degree of harmony between our personality and soul to be certain that when the soul is given information from above, the personality will know it too.

the inspiration, the guidance, or the information. But the Higher Guides and the Guardian Angels have as their entire mission bringing that one entity to the point of awakening and then assisting them onward on their path. And so they are ever vigilant, and ever active, and ever aware and present.

✦ Can you give us some examples of how they might help? How one who is yet unawakened might experience the receipt of that information or inspiration?

Almost one hundred percent of the time it is through the emotions. Almost one hundred percent of the time it is a sense of joy, a sense of elation, a sense of oneness with something that occurs in the external. A sunset, a mountain, a poem, a passage from a book or an entire book. But it is a response through the heart chakra, one hundred percent of the time.

It is not through the mind. The emotion may trigger thought, and the emotion may trigger mental activity, which is reflective, which is focused on the inner as opposed to the external, and so of course the mind plays a part. But the key, the beginning point, is always through the emotional body and always through the ***heart chakra****.*

✦ Thank you.

Indeed. Many of you have probably heard the phrase or seen the expression, "stop and smell the roses." And this is an outstanding exercise for attuning the heart chakra, for what we are really focusing on here is bringing in the feminine and reawakening that which in many cases has been cast aside, held away, stifled. What we are really doing here is opening the heart chakra, stimulating the heart chakra, getting entities and individuals to be aware that inspiration comes through the ***heart*** *and to experience that inspiration as something they are more and more aware of. So that it does not pass unnoticed.*

We are using whatever an entity finds to be particularly beautiful, particularly harmonious, and often we find that this is some part of nature. Individuals in the third dimension tend to experience a very heightened state of joy, and elation, awareness and peace by natural scenes. Waterfalls, rock formations, sunsets, mountains, your Grand Canyon, a fledgling bird, the young of any animal. Sometimes an insect, a grasshopper, a dragonfly, but very, very often it is nature. A manifestation of or through nature that touches the heart in such a way that it may open it. For many it is music, or a beautiful painting, or dance, the experience of dancing oneself or watching others dance, ballet, or any other form of dancing.

Now all these are right-brained activities and so you might truly say that stimulating the heart is also a matter of stimulating the right brain into activity, or at least into awareness and receptivity. Is that clear?

✦ I've never made that connection, but as you speak it, without the receptivity it hardly seems likely that one would experience the feeling in the heart.

Indeed, and that is the point that we wish to make here. Because left-brained awareness, left-brained seeing, left-brained experiencing cannot be substituted. There must be an integration of the feelings, of the emotional body. It cannot merely be a logical thought, or a thought process. This is the difference between knowledge and knowing.[5]

✦ Without the feeling, without the right-brained receptivity, from my own experience in the past, it would probably have resulted in a judgment, a scoring of the dancing perhaps. Such as "They were excellent" or "I would give them a 9.3," but that would not result in the feeling of inspiration through the heart.

Correct! Quite correct. And that is why merely observing something is not adequate. Because it is possible to observe with the mind, it is possible to observe with a cold eye if you will, with a calculating eye, with a discriminating eye. And these are well thought of in your culture today, but they will not bring the feminine into your experience. And if the feminine is not brought into the experience then there can be no blending, and there can be no harmony. The peace that passes understanding is very much received through the feminine aspect of the being. It will flood over into the mental and it will encompass the entire being, but it is received through the feminine aspect of the being, through the right brain and through the heart.

An exercise to bring the feminine into the consciousness

And so to where we were originally heading with this.

Another exercise that is excellent for those who desire to bring the feminine, the experience of the feminine, into their consciousness is to spend time doing that which you love, that which you find beautiful, and that which you find touches your heart. Walk in nature. View art in a museum. Listen to music. Attend a play, a movie, the ballet, whatever brings beauty into your

---

[5] *Knowledge,* especially man-made knowledge, is largely left-brained memorization of the hypotheses, concepts, and current beliefs (created by other human personalities) that we are taught or conditioned toward, and which may have *no* relationship to *Truth as received from above. Knowing* includes a personal feeling experience. Example: Take the left-brained, intellectual, verbal or written description of the difference in taste between an apple and a pomegranate as opposed to the actual *feeling experience* of tasting both. Once you taste them you *know* the difference. But reading and memorizing the written description without the personal experience leaves you only with man-made intellectual *knowledge* that you have accepted as an accurate description from other human personalities. Accepted or not, you know *nothing* until you experience it for yourself.

experience, and while you are involved in that activity, pay attention to your heart. Be aware of how your heart responds. Be aware of activity within the heart. And also be aware of how that experience and how your response to that experience affects the rest of your physical being and your mind. In other words open yourself to a fuller awareness of the experience that you are having.

Be more consciously aware of that which is occurring within, in addition to just experiencing the joy. Be aware of experiencing the joy, and how the joy comes into your being. And be aware of how it affects your portrayal of yourself. When you are in that state, when you have had that experience or are having that experience, how do you manifest yourself? Who is the you that is touched by this beauty? Come to know that part of yourself, and to understand and appreciate that part of yourself, and to accept that part of yourself as valuable and essential to having harmony in your entire being.

A pragmatic Christ Light exercise

And now let us offer a practical exercise for those of you who are involved in business affairs or any kind of activity that is normally dominated by mental activity, by measuring and planning, and preparing, and thinking, and scheming, and laying out. This is a method, a way of softening, of bringing the feminine into these kinds of activities without becoming the third-dimensional equal of effeminate, or soft, or without being considered wimpy, if you will.

When you know that you are going into a situation where you expect that there may be conflict or you expect that there may be tension, or adversity of any kind, or even just a situation where there is the potential for the mind to be dominant in each entity who is present, then the morning before (or if you do not have that much advance notice, as well as you can prior to entering into the situation) see in your mind's eye, visualize the situation occurring, visualize the players who will be involved, and (using the power of your imagination) fill the room or the area with light. Visualize the light of the Christ, the Solar Light, filling the room or the area. Send a rose-colored light from your heart to the heart of each entity who is in the room or who will be in the room, and visualize the light or the Being of the Christ standing behind each entity. And then when you go into that situation, that meeting, or that experience, take notice and be aware of how this affects the atmosphere, the environment of the meeting itself.

And in using this exercise, one very certain fact that you can know is that whatever activity occurs and whatever the outcome of this meeting or this exchange, it is for the highest good of each of the entities involved. You can know this with certainty. And if you find yourself involved in an unexpected situation, particularly one where you may be experiencing tension or hostility, adversity or anger, you may very quickly do the same thing.

Surround those involved with the light, send the rose-colored light to each heart, and bring the Christ Love and Light to stand behind each of the entities. Practice this and see if you do not begin to recognize the pattern at work. See if you do not begin to recognize a softening. Quite often there will be a very surprising difference in the activities of those involved in these situations. Do you have questions regarding this?

✦ No, I do not. (long pause) Does this activity in our conscious state, bring in the activity of our Angels and our Higher Guides? And perhaps the Angels and Higher Guides of those involved on the receiving end of our visualization?

Yes, indeed it does, and in fact it invites the activity, the presence of the higher selves and the souls of each of these entities. The environment will be such that there will be the greater openness and the greater opening of all entities involved to input from their higher consciousness. Though they may indeed not be aware of it at all.

✦ And the environment will be set for the optimum higher good for each individual?

Quite correct. And recognize that if the immediate outcome is not that which you individually judge to be correct, or judge to be for the best, you should keep track (of it over time). *You should watch and see if it does not happen later that indeed it is the best outcome for the highest good for each one. For this is not always obvious at the moment that the meeting or the activity occurs, or is even concluded. Is that clear?*

✦ Yes.

And, if the outcome is not in accord with that which you believe within yourself to be the truest and the highest, it would be well to follow this so that you can learn the validity and the value of bringing in the light and the Christ Consciousness.[6]

An exercise of sending higher love light to others

Another very helpful exercise is one that you may find is not something you can adequately achieve on the first or second or thirteenth try. Still, choose a day, and during that day each person that you greet, that you meet, or that you interact with, send the rose-colored light to that person's heart and offer a (silent) *blessing to them at the beginning of your interaction. And see if*

---

[6] I also had had some prior experience with this Christ Light exercise in a couple of potentially vicious business situations. What occurred immediately was not what my personality had hoped for, but the long-range results turned out to be two of the most totally surprising, beneficial, long-lasting, and soul-fulfilling situations I have ever enjoyed.

you do not have an awareness through this, overall, of a difference in your day, a difference in the outcome of your day, and frequently a difference in the interactions themselves.

Summary

In general, after age seven, we humans have already quite completely identified with our physical body and its growing personality. We have already begun to think and feel ourselves to be only the physical body, its emotions, and its personality mind.

On the spiritual path one's ego or personality gradually becomes cleared of its disharmonious and aggressive tendencies until it harmonizes with the soul to such a degree that in essence it becomes relatively transparent to the soul. This harmonious transparency of the personality allows the natural divinity within the soul to shine through our personality without being discolored (by uncleared outer world adopted attitudes, thoughts, feelings, and beliefs). The soul is able to bring the Divinity of its God Within into itself and then to manifest it into the outer world through the now harmonious personality.

I am overjoyed that Thenous included this light body exercise in this reading, for it can bring you the actual feeling experience of being your soul, and of experiencing being in the light body of your soul. It can show you how it feels to be your soul, what is meant when you read of being your soul, including the feelings and the insights and understandings that come from your soul's higher perspective in life. It may require a little practice, but it will be worth the effort.

The goal of the spiritual path is to help all who are interested to grow in awareness and in the ability to *Be* in this higher vibrational soul state always. This state of consciousness offers a higher perspective, a higher viewpoint. It is like observing your body and your personality from above while feeling the experience of being in your light body. It can be described in many different ways, but that is how it seems to me at this moment.

It is blissful. It is a feeling state, a floating or flying state. It is a state of higher consciousness. It can grow to be a state of higher knowing. In this state you can know your higher will, your higher mind, and the unconditional love of your higher heart.

The light body experience is a glimpse of our natural soul state, the state in which we were originally created by God. When we experience the feelings associated with this light body state sufficiently, through practice, we can return to it directly, by simply remembering the feelings and going to them just as we can do with any fond memory of the past, as in reminiscing.

Our Earthly dilemma is largely a matter first of identity, and then of knowing which of the three aspects of our beingness we truly *prefer* to identify with, to become again, and to be.

At any moment in our life we can choose to identify with either our personality or our soul. As our soul, we can know directly the nature of the Spark of God, the Divinity, that lies within us. As our soul, attuned to the Divinity Within, we can open our intuitional path to receive divine guidance and/or divine love. We can learn to resonate internally with the divine love of God and to transmit that unconditional love and light into the third-dimensional world wherever we may be.

But how do we regain the experience of knowing how it feels to be one's soul? Through exercises like this! For only with the experience of how it *feels* to be our soul self will we have access to the *inner knowing* that is needed to make enlightened decisions for ourselves.

Especially for those readers who, like me, may not previously have been well versed in the arts and skills of the divine feminine energy's feeling realms, practicing exercises like this can be of immeasurable help in regaining the experiences which provide the motivation that makes it easier to move along the path. Intellectual knowledge alone does not and will not move us along our path of spiritual evolution.

The spiritual path is not intellectual, and intellectual progress (memorization of man-made facts) by the personality mind is barely relevant to soul growth. All spiritual progress requires practice and the practice must include and involve the feeling experience of that which is being practiced (i.e., the feelings invoked by carrying out the new habit patterns which are more in harmony with our Divinity Within).

For this reason, experiencing the feelings of being one's soul again is totally relevant to progress along the path. Experiencing the unconditional divine love of God at our soul level brings joy to our soul, and sharing that joy and love with those we meet in our third-dimensional world creates an even greater joy as we begin to regain the feelings and the knowings of who we really are and what we really are doing down here.

Why is this experience so helpful? Because it helps us to *remember* our original experiences as the souls we once were and can be again. We are remembering our soul's higher consciousness experiences of inner harmony and the peace which passes all understanding. We are regaining experience with a fearlessly loving state of higher consciousness that may become our new ideal, a new preferred way of Being. The feelings of these higher states of consciousness alone can motivate us to seek to become our souls once more, so that we can bring that experience permanently into our life in the third-dimensional world.

All this is ours, if we choose it.

CHAPTER 19

The Fifth Feminine Energy Reading

The Power to Create Heaven on Earth Requires the Feminine Intuitional Ability for All of Humankind

This is an excerpt of a reading by Cathy received from Thenous on 10/25/96.

I am Thenous, and we shall move forward with the information for your book.

As within, so without. A statement, a concept offered in many spiritual writings. Perhaps more clearly stated, "As a man thinketh in his heart, so is he." But to date the explanations given have fallen short of bringing the clarity of this message home to those entities who are currently incarnated in the third dimension. For indeed the concept of "As a man thinketh, so is he" brings forth the understanding and the ideas that what is present within the heart of an individual entity is that which he manifests within his personality or through his personality. And this indeed is true.

However, we wish to expand here for we wish to bring to the awareness of those who would read this book the understanding of the power, the personal power, involved in this concept. It is important that we in this dimension, in every way we are able, help bring a clarity of understanding to those incarnated in the third dimension so that they are empowered and that they create their own experiences, their own lives.

We each have the individualized power to manifest, to create, or to recreate our own lives

Of those who are in the third dimension and share with each other in the process of their spiritual development, who share their experiences, their understandings, and their ideas, it is often said that the focus upon the external is too great and should be turned, so that the primary focus is within. And this is a concept that we certainly endorse.

However, we believe that it is important for there to be the understanding that what is external to an individual entity can also be very useful. An awareness of what is external to an individual entity is of great value and has great use in terms of that entity's spiritual development. For if you look through your physical eyes and you look at that which is external to you, you can be certain that you are looking at a perfect reflection of that which is within you. Is that clear?

✦ Yes.

We each have created our own little worlds through the Universal Law of Manifestation

This is really a very important concept because it opens the way. An understanding of this concept opens the way to personal empowerment and tremendous individual growth. Each entity incarnated in the third dimension has not only the opportunity but also the responsibility to create his or her life in the highest order precisely as he or she desires. Because whether there is a conscious awareness of this law, whether there is a focus and an understanding of this Universal Law of Manifestation or not, ***it is working****.*

Each individual entity is creating his own life experience every moment that he lives*. Now consider the implications of this and consider the value of being aware that this is occurring. For many, for the vast majority of those incarnated in the third dimension, there is not the awareness that they are expending energy and attention and effort each moment, creating the world around them.*

We have already addressed the concept that many incarnated entities see themselves as victims. But what or who is the victimizer?

✦ We humans see it as "outside" forces. We blame "others." Plenty of blame to go around. That's when one learns the extent of a human personality's truly creative nature (finding others to blame).

Indeed, and we very much wish for there to be a clear understanding and an internalizing within self for each entity who comes in contact with this information, the knowledge, the understanding, that they, each and every one of them, ***are in control of their lives****. And this is how the magic works! This is how miracles occur!*

For in truth there are no miracles![1] *In truth everything that occurs in the third dimension follows Universal Laws. Nothing is outside of the Laws of the Universe. True, your scientists do not yet comprehend and have not yet documented the Universal Laws. They have found many of the seeming orders within your Universe and they have come to a much greater awareness and understanding of how the Universe works in the third dimension. And there are many who are now further expanding their consciousness and becoming quite aware in the area of quantum physics that the third-dimensional laws are a very limited and very small part of that which actually enfolds and guides your world, your third-dimensional world.*

Thoughts are things. Thoughts are very, very powerful things. Thoughts coupled with emotions create that which you experience. They do. It is not possible to have a thought, particularly one which is coupled with a strong emotion, that does not create within your third dimension a change in vibrational rate, a change in energy, and in fact a change in the objects and entities toward whom or what those thoughts are directed.

And the spoken word is even more powerful. It is really not possible to convey the tremendous impact that the spoken word has in your third-dimensional world. And one of the reasons that this is true is that the subconscious mind of every entity believes every word that it says.[2] *If you were to say you are getting a cold, your subconscious mind will believe that and it will go immediately to work to make sure that all the physiology in your physical body understands and receives that message. Much of this has been proved through the use of hypnotism. A third-dimensional subject can be hypnotized and told that he is being given an apple to eat. And you can give him an onion and he will eat it and he will believe, he will experience through his physical senses of smell and taste that what he is eating is an apple.*

✦ On this matter I requested and journaled an understanding of this, how the thoughts and feelings combine to manifest that which we think and feel. The analogy my higher self gave me related to a

---

1 From the perspective of the Beings of Light in the higher dimensions, those things which appear as miracles (to those of us down here) are *not* miracles. They see them as simply the natural result of a soul's living in attunement with the Divinity Within and reaping the automatic rewards of God's Universal Laws. Our problem lies in the fact that humankind, living largely in the personality state of consciousness, has little or no awareness of the Univeral Spiritual Picture or of the Universal Spiritual Laws that comprise it. In this ignorance, by harboring negative feelings and thoughts, we create our own hell on Earth when we could be creating our own heaven.

2 This is why affirmations are so often recommended to those on the spiritual path. However, affirmations will prove to be much more effective if and when we allow ourselves to *feel* the message behind the words. Merely repeating the words in an unfeeling, rote manner has much less effect in the manifestation of miracles in our lives. The feelings behind the words are the real power.

photograph that was made into a slide to be shown on a screen. *Thoughts* actually were like the negative or the slide, and the *feelings* were like the powerful light that would shine through the slide and make, or manifest, or create the image or picture upon the screen. I don't know how accurate this is or if there is a better analogy, but in that one it seemed as though the thoughts were not as powerful as the feelings. This is a subjective thing with me but can you clarify that for me?

First, let us state that any entity who has a thought has ***feelings*** *that go with that thought. What you are saying is quite accurate. A thought that had no feeling attached to it would have no power. It is the combination of the two that optimally causes manifestation.* ***The emotion, the feeling, is the power.*** *It is the impetus, and the thought is the vehicle. And the spoken word is merely an extension of that. The spoken word includes both thought and emotion.*

What you have with a thought is an etheric form. Those who are clairvoyant are quite capable, many of them, of seeing thoughts and how they project themselves into the environment, into the atmosphere. Words are more the third-dimensional manifestation of thought and feeling. Is that clear? Is that helpful?

✦ Yes. Thank you.

The information given to this point, from our perspective, clearly encourages attunement.[3] *For if one is constantly creating his or her own world, then it seems that the desire would be to create the greatest happiness, the greatest peace, the greatest harmony, and the greatest joy. When one is attuned, when one is centered, then indeed these are the desires. For these are soul desires, harmony, balance, joy, peace. These are desires of the soul.*

And the expression of the soul comes through intuition, comes through the feminine, through the heart chakra. Now there are many who will say it comes as thoughts, and we will say to them that by the time they perceive it, it may be a thought, but its original entry into the human form, into the third-dimensional entity is through the heart chakra. Physically it may be experienced in the right side of the brain, but its first impetus, its first receipt is in the heart chakra, and it is a feminine tool.

Intuition is a feminine tool. It is one that needs quiet and passivity, attunement and clarity of purpose. Your intuition will guide you in that which is for your highest good, that which your soul desires to have manifest in the

---

[3] Attunement with God assures positive and loving feelings, thoughts, and actions at all times, in all places and under all circumstances. Such attunement is possible with clear guidance from the Divinity Within through our natural feminine energy's intuitional path.

third dimension, and that which will benefit your growth and your spiritual development as well as your physical third-dimensional well being. Often it is intuition that prompts the action that appears as the miracle.

Is it not wonderful to recognize such empowerment? Is it not wonderful to know that as an incarnated third-dimensional human being you have the avenue, the channel, and the power to create your own world? And the answer to that question is yes; it is both wonderful and frightening.

For many, this concept comes with an abundance of fear, and it comes with an abundance of guilt. For the individual who is first becoming aware of this Universal Law of Manifestation, this truth, is very likely to look around himself or herself at the world they have created and experience a sense of despair, a sense of anger, and possibly guilt. And then later, once these have settled in and passed, there may be the fear. Because while there is the understanding or the awareness now that there is this empowerment, there is not necessarily the confidence that there is the knowledge or experience in how to use it. Is that clear?

Disbelief as a convenient defense mechanism of the personality, a way to avoid accepting the responsibility for creation of all that we may find in our own personal worlds

✦ Yes, it is, but you haven't addressed the matter of disbelief. When one would hear this in our culture, as I understand it, a very large percentage of the population would simply disbelieve it because they already believe that they are the victims and that outside forces are creating their victimhood.

Indeed, that is correct. And the disbelief is rather an attractive choice.

✦ Yes.

For if they were to believe that this is true, then all that we have just stated quickly falls into place. Disbelief is a protection—

✦ A defense mechanism?

Correct. And it works actively and powerfully to separate entities from their own souls, from their own empowerment. But for the true seeker, disbelief cannot be maintained. Because once this concept comes into the conscious awareness, it is a sign that the entity is ready, that the soul is making inroads, that the light and the love of the higher self and the soul will quickly fill and follow any path created and opened to them by an entity's conscious receipt of this concept.

Whatever experiences you have had, in this lifetime or another, that bring a sense of anguish or guilt or despair or self directed anger, the answer from the higher dimensions, the answer from the Universe is, "Just let it be okay." There are no accidents. Everything that occurs, everything that an entity does, moves him or her in the right direction for learning the appropriate lessons and for moving onto the spiritual path and coming back to Oneness.

It doesn't matter if the choice may not have been of the highest order. What matters is that the lessons are learned, that there is the peaceful and calm acceptance that any and all activities ever experienced have gradually moved him or her toward the higher good, and that now anything that is in the consciousness can be released. It can be blessed for the opportunity given and released back to the Universe to be returned to its etheric parts as molecules and atoms, protons, and neutrons, and re-used.

Everything is energy, and energy is recycled by the Universe. The energy that was in the cells of an entity who dabbled in darkness may now be the energy that expresses itself in the saint, or the teacher, or the healer. Every cell within the body of a third-dimensional incarnated being is replaced, some in seven years, some in less that a year. And it is all just pure energy. It's all just God Force if you will, and you can choose to mold it and form it in any way that you desire.

But the transformation is always through the heart. The real transformation is always in the emotional body first, thus the importance of being attuned to the feminine and the importance of bringing the feminine power into your conscious awareness and your conscious experience.

Divine love casts out all fear, and divine love resides and flourishes in the heart and manifests itself through the ***emotions****, and* ***then*** *the thoughts, and* ***then*** *the words.*

The personality's conscious brain mind alone does not have the tools to deal with this information

If the (personality) *mind is in control when an entity comes to look at that which is external to himself as that* (little world) *which he has created, the personality mind does not have the tools, does not have the wherewithal, to deal with this situation in a healing manner. The personality mind will judge that which has occurred, and that which is before it, and will elicit the emotions of guilt, the emotions of fear, the emotions of anger as it logically perceives that the actions of the entity have created something other than that which the entity desires, something other than harmony, something other than peace and joy.*

And the personality's mind will reinforce ***disbelief*** *because it cannot grapple with that which sets before it as truth. And this, in and of itself, may create the crisis situation which allows the soul of the entity to lead, to encourage, to move the entity into the direction of desiring and seeking inclusion of the feminine balance, the use of the intuition, and the opening of the intuitive channel through attunement to the higher realms.*

There is no mental path from the third dimension to the fifth dimension. There is no mental way, no mental path of attunement to the Universe, to the God Within. It simply cannot happen.

You've heard the concept that those who would come up must first hit the bottom.

✦ Yes.

And it appears to be very true. Particularly in the involution cycle of your planet. Now however, there is a better way. There is a greater opportunity because the planet itself has transitioned to a point where the light waves and the higher vibrations have been flowing in for ten years now. And the environment in which the soul is incarnated is no longer an environment of involution. It is now an environment of evolution. It is an environment of evolution at a greater speed, at a greater rate, so that soul activity and the activity of the Angelic Realm and of the Higher Guides and the Ascended Masters can reach more easily and more deeply into the third dimension. Is that clear?

✦ Yes.

And so now there is not the need for the entity to hit bottom; there is not the need for intense pain either physical or emotional in order for the shift to occur within a soul. And the shift itself can happen quite instantaneously. It can happen viewing a sunset. It can happen planting a garden, harvesting the fruit. It can happen reading a poem, reading a book, or watching a movie. And the Universal forces are quite active in producing, influencing the production of products in every media to meet the needs of those whose consciousness are responding unconsciously to the increased vibratory rate and the increased light that has become the aura, if you will, of your planet.

The timing of the new millennium, present today, makes it especially important to understand the value of integrating divine feminine energy into our lives now

And so today, in this time frame, it is even more important for there to be available an understanding of the tools of the feminine, an understanding of the need for balance, an understanding of the requirement to embrace that feminine part of self which has been shunned and shut away and cut off to whatever extent. And we find that many who are currently incarnating in the third dimension will not suffer this problem. They will not go through the masculine dominance that those of you who are currently in adulthood have experienced. Because the ambiance of the entire planet is shifting toward the feminine in such a way that it is creating the greater harmony and the greater balance for the planet itself.

Part of the important message here is that entities who choose consciously to continue to ignore the feminine, to continue to adore the masculine, are going to find themselves incapable of residing in the Earth plane in the third dimension without experiencing greater and greater degrees of disharmony, more and more medical issues, particularly those of the nervous system.

The attuned, the benign, the balanced, the meek shall inherit the Earth due to their ability to receive divine guidance which allows all to know how to remain in harmony with our God/Goddess Within, and God, the All That Is

And the message that we wish to offer is that the divine feminine is beautiful. The feminine is wholesome. The feminine has attributes which, embraced and integrated into your consciousness, can allow you to move quickly, peacefully, and harmoniously through your current third-dimensional experience. Indeed, seeking and achieving a balance between the masculine and the feminine, learning to appreciate and applaud passivity and inner attunement, a demonstration of divine love, is the only way to shift into the next millennium with any sense of peace and harmony.

For indeed a large part of the reason for offering this information at this time is that the millennium is basically at hand. The time frame for the shift of the planet itself and the time frame for the quite remarkable changes that will occur in the environment is now short by your standards. And it is our desire to see all succeed, to make the shift and to experience the blessings that are available in wholeness.

If it were possible to make every living entity clairvoyant for three minutes so that they could see what is available (how their lives could change and how they could be lived with a sense of attunement and harmony and wholeness), there would be a tremendous influx of those who are eagerly and rapidly seeking to move toward the light. Because the view from our perspective is so awesome, it is like the shift in fairy tales from scullery maid to princess.

The difference in the life that is lived in a predominantly masculine consciousness and that which is lived in a balanced harmonious consciousness is indescribably dramatic. We are speaking here of the actual third-dimensional manifestations in the life experience, not just the shift in the consciousness, not just the ability to experience the higher dimensions through meditation, but the ability to experience the higher dimensions ***in waking conscious states.***

It is the experience of having love and peace be the primary everyday experience of every entity incarnated in the Earth plane. Harmony, cooperation, joy, all of these are an integral part of the life experience of the balanced whole entity. Clear and conscious reception of information from the higher realms, from the Guardian Angels, from the Higher Guides. A true consistent knowing of what to do, what to choose, and how to go about it.

It is our hope and it is our desire that the state of third-dimensional experience, of living, is one that would be very attractive particularly to those who are seekers on the path, for it is a vision that the souls of all offer up as truth and potential reality.

And it is a fact that those who do not choose this state of being as a goal will very soon, within the next decade, surely within the next two decades, ***find it impossible to remain in the third dimension****. And please understand that that is an acceptable choice. That is okay. It is just that those entities will have to continue their experience elsewhere. Have we made a coherent and reasonable message today?*

✦ Yes, thank you.

Thenous' summary

Allow us to summarize here. When the thinking moves from the personality's lower mind to the soul's higher mind and heart, then will the tool of intuition be fully functional. And then will that which many have chosen to label magic have full play, full activity within the external experience of the entity. If there is harmony within, then that which is drawn to the entity will be harmonious.

Does it mean that there will be no disharmony in the third-dimensional world? No, because there will still be those entities who think disharmony in their hearts. But whatever disharmony there is will not affect and cannot penetrate, the aura of the entity that has harmony as his or her basic sense or state of being.

If one uses the perception of that which is external to assist in gauging where he or she is internally, this can be a tremendously useful tool. Particularly for those who are moving along the spiritual path, who have made the conscious decision and commitment to do that. For as soon as disharmony is experienced externally, that seeker will look within to find what is amiss, where the attunement has varied, where it has shifted? And conversely, those who understand this concept can use it quite vitally and vibrantly to create that which they choose to have within their external experience.

If you would have love, if you would have harmony, if you would have joy, if you would have peace in your external world, then first choose it in your heart, first find it within. When these become the large part, the most consistent part of your state of inner being, then they will become the most consistent part of your external environment. And those who find the balance, those who choose wholeness, can be involved in any situation, can be physically, geographically located in any place, and that which occurs for them will be harmonious. And the harmony will be clearly perceived by them as coming from the highest level. And you yourselves as channels here have had this experience of perceiving the same situation from various levels of consciousness and recognizing the difference. Is that not so?

✦ Yes, it is.

And so we encourage you, the readers of this book, of this material, to experiment with this shift, to make the choice to incorporate the feminine, to bring it into your consciousness, and to make it a part of your focus in your daily activities. Try it, you'll like it.

And with that, unless you have other questions, we are through for now.

✦ There are no other questions, and I thank you very much.

Indeed, you are most welcome and we appreciate your time and attention. We offer our deepest love and light and blessings from our hearts. And we bid you good day.

Summary

This last session on the value of feminine energy, by Thenous, reviews several higher realm spiritual issues and summarizes them into a brief description of some of the potential benefits of an increased integration of the feminine attributes, abilities, and skills sufficient to establish a balance of feminine and masculine energies within the individual.

As I came to my desk this morning to finish this section of part III, I meditated as usual to set myself up to receive higher guidance through my intuitional connection to my higher self, my soul, and my Divinity Within. I invited in my Guardian Angels, my Higher Guides, and any Archangels, Ascended Masters, or other Beings of Light who desired to co-create this book. This is what came through my Divinity Within and my soul. It is quite different from what I had already planned. It is addressed to all readers including me.

My Journaled Summary from My Divinity Within

Feelings.

It is all about feelings, feelings, feelings.[4]

[4] Repeating anything three times is a sure sign from the Beings of Light providing the information that that which is repeated is very, very, very important. It is kind of a

The light body experience is all about feelings. Living as your soul, living in harmony with your God or Goddess Within is all about feelings. You cannot transmit, give out, or express that which you do not first *feel,* so it's all about feelings.

To control thoughts, first control feelings

It is not about thoughts, for they come second. Whatever thoughts you may have at any time, you have already had that same type of feeling first. This is why it seems so difficult *to learn how to control your thoughts.* You are not looking correctly at that which creates the thought, the *feelings* that you hold which create the thought. You are not aware of the appropriate cause-and-effect dynamics.

If you desire and choose to have positive loving thoughts, *first create or find within your heart, positive loving feelings* and then the thoughts will come too. If you lose those positive feelings, you will lose the positive thoughts.

It is all about feelings!

Manifestation

Relative to the manifestation of that which you desire in your life, if you have negative thoughts of limitation or poverty, it is because you have those negative *feelings* first. Knowing, in accordance with the Universal Laws of Manifestation, that what you *feel and think* is created in your world around you, you try to use that information to create positive thoughts. But you often put the cart before the horse, the thoughts before the feelings, and are therefore unsuccessful in holding positive thoughts for any length of time. However, by first creating or finding the positive feelings within your heart, you can *sustain the positive thoughts forever,* or as long as you choose to sustain the *feelings* that create the thoughts.

The difficulty arises when you do not understand the dynamics of the feeling and thinking processes. The difficulty arises when you denigrate or negate the value of the creative power of the feminine trait of feeling in your culture.

When you denigrate the feminine, you show that you have no idea of the immeasurable value of feminine energy in your individual lives across the world, in our Universe, and in the Cosmos. In your ignorance, you create your hell. With your newfound knowledge, you can create your heaven. When you know the *cause,* you can control the *effects.*

---

standard way of indicating this. It is like a college professor stamping his foot resoundingly to indicate to his students that it is time to take notes.

It is all about feelings, feelings, feelings.

The world needs to know which comes first. It needs to understand, to know and to *feel that feelings* are the more valuable to humankind because they are the creators and maintainers of the thoughts.

And the divine feelings are a feminine quality.

This is the value of one of the feminine aspects.

Passivity

You now understand that passivity, which is also a feminine quality, is necessary and required for intuition to be effected. You *cannot* open the path of intuition with thoughts, with thinking, or with any activity of the personality mind. It won't work. It cannot work!

To open the doors to your ability to receive divine guidance, divine truth, divine understanding, and divine knowing (of how things work, what will be best for your higher good, for the higher good of others, and for the higher good of all life) *feminine passivity is required.*

Passivity holds the line open. Passivity makes intuition possible. An active personality mind that is constantly busy thinking, plotting, planning for the future, or equally busy remembering the past, *precludes and prevents intuitional input.* All you can receive with a busy personality mind is additional personality mind guidance, the same as you have had all your life.

To receive divine guidance and information requires passivity, and therefore passivity is another type of feminine energy to be valued.

Feminine intuition is for the inner reception of divine guidance *and* divine love

If you desire the ability to receive divine guidance, you must integrate sufficient feminine energy into your life to form a relative balance with the masculine. You must first realize the value of the benefits that divine guidance will have in your life. Then you must practice passivity sufficiently to make it such a strong habit pattern within your life that you may call upon it whenever you wish.

Intuition is of priceless value to your individual life just for the purpose of receiving divine guidance, and intuition is a feminine trait. But the intuitional path is *not* just for the purpose of bringing you divine guidance. It is also the path for receiving the feelings of unconditional love from your God/Goddess Within and all other minions of God, the All That Is.

Intuition is the path for bringing you all messages. This includes messages such as that you are understood intimately and loved unconditionally.

Intuition provides the path for you to commune and communicate with your Divinity Within. That communication may include guidance, if that is what you seek, but it may also include the resonance, the feeling expression, of your love for your Divinity Within and the instantaneous feeling response of the requited unconditional love (for you) returned from your Divinity Within.

Whenever you invoke your feelings of love for those divine qualities that you have always known were the qualities of Godness, Goddessness, or Absolute Goodness for the higher good of all life, you will feel an immediate response of unconditional love back to you through your open intuitional path, your heart.

This is the way you receive God's love. You extend your love for God to God. God immediately responds and sends divine love back to you. You can set up a constant rapport this way. You can receive God's love for you anytime you choose to feel love for God.

You can set up a consistent resonance of divine love by consciously being aware of your love for God, for Godness, for Goddessness, and for Absolute Goodness for all life everywhere. It is unfailing. And as you resonate with this mutual love you are filled with it. Your cup will run over, and you can transmit the excess into your environment wherever you are. You can send it at a distance or nearby. You can simply shine it into the atmosphere or direct it to someone or something specific.

In this way you discover what is meant by the expression that it is better to give than to receive, for the transmission of unconditional, divine love to others causes a glorious feeling inside, in and of itself. Sending it causes an inner experience of unconditional love the same as receiving it.

The ability to receive the divine love of God through the feminine intuitional path can make you into a kind of perpetual motion device, for intuition connects or attunes you to God, the infinite source of all love in the Universe. With infinite divine unconditional love coming into you and through you at your beck and call, you can become a channel (seeming to the outer world like a source, but truly being a channel) of divine love and light into your world.

This is possible only through intuition, a feminine ability.

And it is possible only through passivity, a feminine trait.

Is this sufficient?

I will answer here and say, yes, this is certainly sufficient to show the value and importance that divine feminine energy can have in the lives of each of us as individuals, as students here on Earth.

As I send my consciousness upward into the higher perspective of my soul and my Divinity Within, I can see and feel and know that all this is true. I have experienced it myself to a certain degree and yet it still seems incredible to my personality. It still seems inconceivable that such a small change in the focus of our attention toward the integration of divine feminine energy can have the potential to bring about such a complete, joyful, and fulfilling change in our individual human lives, and therefore to the lives of all of humankind on Earth.

I know from my own experience that even a small increase in feminine energy can act as a catalyst to bring inner joy and meaning to the life of one who at one time could not even understand what there was in life to possibly be joyful about. For without positive feelings and without intuitive guidance, there can be only limited progress along the spiritual path. Without the progress along the path, toward becoming and being one's soul, there cannot be the direct, immediate communion and communication with the God or Goddess Within. And without that I would be lost (again).

It has truly transformed my inner life already and I can tell you that I am a long way from achieving a true balance. And that is important to know. We are not required to be perfect or to achieve a perfect balance in order for intuition to come into and to benefit our lives, but we are required to achieve a modicum of feminine/masculine balance.

A glimpse of the future effects of a good balance of divine masculine/feminine energy on our planet Earth

So I know personally of the benefits that feminine energy can bring to the life of an ordinary individual such as myself. And by sending my consciousness to the higher perspective of my soul and my Divinity Within, I can also see the changes it can bring to our entire planet, our entire Earth School. The integration of feminine energy to the point of enabling divine intuitional guidance to come into the lives of all Earth's inhabitants will bring a shift in the level of the world's consciousness of colossal, quantum leap proportions.

It will be a shift away from a world controlled by human personalities who do not yet know that they are parts of God and who are still guided primarily by their personality minds filled with naturally learned but disharmonious habit patterns. It will be a shift toward a world inhabited by souls (still having human bodies) who understand the larger spiritual picture, the Universal spiritual nature of life, who have largely cleared their personalities of negatives, who know they are each parts of God, who are in communion with and are guided by their Divinity Within, who live their lives at very high, joyful, loving rates of vibration, who are in harmony with their divine guidance, and who are aware of and are fulfilling their souls' purposes in this life.

With a balance of divine masculine/feminine energy, we can all become sentient, sensitive beings who live our lives attuned to and guided by our Spark of God Within, knowing and joyfully fulfilling our soul's purpose, for the higher good of ourselves and the Universe, of our own free will.

This will be the new paradigm for life on Earth in the Golden Age. It will come into effect because of the increasingly higher frequency of light and vibration that is a part of the Earth planet's (the Planetary Logos') shift to *its* higher consciousness and because of the increasing balance of divine feminine/masculine energy, which brings divine guidance to the souls of the remaining inhabitants.

This millennium marks the time in the evolution of humankind when the personalities of many are consciously ready to call their souls to them and begin to create harmony among their personality, their soul, and the Spark of God within their soul. The ability to receive divine guidance will facilitate this spiritual growth and the creation of this inner harmony beyond words.

Understanding the value of the effects of these feminine energy changes makes it easier to see how it will finally be possible for divine love, divine understanding, compassion, kindness, benignancy, helpfulness, benevolence, inner peace, and inner harmony to come into the lives of all the inhabitants of the Earth School in the near future.

It will be the Golden Age, the Age of Balance, and it will be wonderful to experience.

PART IV

The Spiritual Path Itself

Creating Harmony Among the Personality, the Soul, and the Spark of God Within the Soul

CHAPTER 20

Attachments

The Habit Patterns that Cause Our Inner Disharmony

All mortal animal habit patterns that our human personalities have learned or adopted from their outer world environment, which cause ***disharmony*** with their respective soul and Divinity Within, are as attachments that hold us like a magnet to the limited, physical, third-dimensional, human life on Earth.

Chapter 9, Evolution, describes spiritual evolution as including, primarily, the release and replacement of any such disharmonious habit patterns. Our souls were pure and perfect before we became entrapped in physical life and before our resultant personalities learned habit patterns that were not in harmony with the higher aspects of our Beingness. Therefore, conceptually, it should be easy to see that by clearing our personalities of that which causes and maintains disharmony with our souls, we automatically move our personalities into ever increasing harmony with our souls and the Spark of God, which lies within our souls.

To increase your own inner harmony, bring harm to no one

Attachments may include overt habitual addictions (or aversions) to physical, outer world things that we have used and adopted in the past as substitutes for what we felt was missing from our inner lives. Forms of attachments to physical things may include our habitual use of tobacco, alcohol, drugs, or even an addiction to sex (rather than a simple mastery of it for use when the occasion is right and with harm to no one). Basically, it is the issue of "harm to no one" that is most important to understand here. Bringing harm to anyone on Earth, especially to self, is that which is always in discord with our soul and therefore always creates inner disharmony.

Our souls are Beings, with bodies of light, which live at a much higher level of conscious awareness than we, as just our personalities, can experience in this physical world. Considering the Universal Picture of the meaning and purpose of life on Earth as a school experience which leads us eventually to awaken and return to being our souls again in conscious Oneness with God, anything that hinders the progress of one's self or of others causes harm. And anything that causes harm to anyone, including self, immediately causes disharmony between the personality and the soul, which of course knows everything we feel, think, believe, or do.

Does everything in our personalities cause inner disharmony? Nope. Whenever we feel impersonal love for ourselves we are helping our own personality to move into greater harmony with our soul. Whenever we feel impersonal love for others we are helping the personalities of those others to move into greater harmony with their respective souls and, we are creating increased inner harmony with our own soul.

Whenever we think kind thoughts of ourselves or of others, we are creating greater harmony with our soul. Whenever we feel and manifest divine attitudes or beliefs into the world around us, we are helping anyone in our little world, and thus we are increasing our harmony with our soul. Anything that we are manifesting in our daily lives that enhances others' perceptions of themselves or that helps others to move toward knowing themselves as parts of God brings them increased inner harmony, brings us increased inner harmony, and leads us along the path toward our higher conscious Oneness with God.

By the same token, anything we do to denigrate or diminish another's perception of him or herself brings us instantly into a state of inner disharmony with our soul. Whether such entities allow our personality's negative attacks to influence their own self-perceptions depends upon their state of spiritual evolution. If they are living in a relatively high and secure state of soul consciousness, they will be above any such external personality opinions. However, regardless of the effect on the other person, our personality's act of unkindness will instantly create disharmony with our soul.

We may hide our intentions from others but never from our soul. This is how we humans create and maintain our own inner discord, emptiness, and depression. Because our soul knows our every feeling, thought, and intention, there is only one good way to avoid this.

The solution is to release the personality's attachments to habit patterns that cause us to react in negative ways to outer world circumstances and to replace them with habits that are in concert with our soul and Divinity Within. When we have refined or spiritualized our own personality to a great enough degree, we can live our lives here on Earth in joy and fulfillment, as our soul selves, attuned to and in conscious Oneness with God.

Personality clearing or refinement is our path both to our joy in the fulfillment of our soul's purpose while on Earth and also to our Ascension.

One piece of good news is that we need not be absolutely perfect to Ascend. However, we are required to demonstrate, while here in the Earth School, that we, as our soul selves, are in control of our personalities to a far greater degree than the personality is in control of the soul.

Less overt types of attachment to habit patterns that cause inner disharmony

Therefore, with all that said, attachments to disharmonious habit patterns may include any of the personality's habitual ways of feeling, thinking, and acting plus all our habitual beliefs and attitudes toward everything in our outer world which when manifested bring harm to self or others. For examples, see Table 20-1.

TABLE 20-1 Less Overt Forms of Attachments to Disharmonious Habit Patterns

Types of Habits	*Examples*
Emotional habits: habitual ways of feeling	Feelings of fears of any kind, feelings of anger which stem from fears, feeling the need to judge either self or others, feeling the need to dominate or attack others, feeling the need for aggression, retribution, or revenge, feeling the need to suppress or repress feelings that the outer world has made taboo, or feeling the need for competition to prove worthiness, etc.
Mental habits: habitual ways of thinking	Thinking that *thinking* is the highest and best method of making decisions (intuitive Divine Guidance is better!), thinking that masculine aggressive behavior is the best for one's own higher good, thinking that receiving information and guidance from our Divinity Within is only possible for a few "special" humans, thinking that man-made information is better than divine information received from above
Habits of belief: habitual ways of believing	Believing that all the things we were taught from our outer world education are *true,* believing that Democrats are best, believing that Republicans are best, believing that the Chicago Cubs never could win a World Series (miracles happen). These are man-made illusions, not truths!
Attitudinal habits: feelings and thoughts combined	Thinking and feeling that competition and winning are beneficial or of any true value and importance; thinking and feeling that gentle, nurturing, feminine emotions are worthless

Attachments to physical world life can include anything we have learned or adopted from our outer world that causes our personality to be in conflict with our soul, thus hindering our growing, and knowing, and understanding the immense Universal Spiritual Picture of life in the higher dimensions of conscious Oneness with God.

Attachments can include habit patterns either of addiction or aversion

Another important point is that attachments are attachments whether they are addictions or aversions to earthly things or ways. You may "love" a kind of thing or way of behaving and I may "hate" that same thing, but we both remain personally attached to it until we release it and replace it with a new way of feeling, thinking, or acting that creates harmony among our personality, soul, and Divinity Within. That attachment may be replaced with an impersonal, nonattached feeling derived from the higher perspective of our soul (far above that of our personality). From the higher consciousness and perspective of our soul, we may see, feel, and know that any habit to which we are attached is simply a part of our Earth School environment and in reality, in and of itself, is neither negative nor positive.

The only true negative involved in any of our earthly situations is whether or not we adopt and form a habit pattern that causes continual inner disharmony with our soul. The only negative is whether we attach ourselves to a habit that hinders or prevents our personality from growing—in consciousness—back to the level of our soul in conscious Oneness with God.

In viewing attachments from above, you will find that your higher self or soul is much more impersonal and divinely detached than your personality, especially at the beginning of the evolutionary phase. You will also find that the love experienced at the level of your soul and the Divinity Within your soul is far more divine, impersonal, unconditional, and inclusive than the conditional so-called love of the personality. Soul love is the higher and deeper love for all of humankind that you may have experienced at special times in your life.

My Personal Experience

When I first became aware of the concept of attachments being like magnets, which hold us to our earthbound condition, I could not understand why I was not already floating and flying above my body and its personality. In my mind I was not "attached" to anything on Earth! I was pretty much disgusted with everything, and frankly, except for Nature, I disliked or hated most of it. I saw it all as quite painful and meaningless. Therefore, I was certain that I had no attachments to hinder my progress along the path. Then in a reading by Cathy I was given the message from above that hatred of something can be as strong an attachment as an addiction to it! My reaction was something like, "Well, well, well!" (Euphemizing of course!)

My personal realization at that time was that I now had a lot of cleaning up to do, a lot of releasing and replacing. And it was true. What made it ten times more difficult for me was that at that point on my evolutionary path I did not know of the new spiritual tools that were available to me.

Why did I not know of them? Because I already knew of one way and it never occurred to me to ask about a better way. That's the way consciousness expands. You have to grow enough to know enough to ask the higher questions. Oh well! Pain is the great educator!

The spiritual path definitely does not mean recognizing attachments to things and attempting to resolve the situation by fostering a dislike or hatred of them. To do so would only keep us firmly attached to them.

In my personality's own experience I had to learn the hard way that the appropriate way to handle even such a mundane (but stressful) situation as leaving a survival job that I hated was first to learn to love it and everyone in it, impersonally, just for what they are, nothing more and nothing less.

From our soul's perspective we humans are all parts of God who have lost awareness of our soul selves and our Sparks of God Within. Unaware of our souls, our personalities are acting out habits, which they have learned from the outer world and believe are best for them. They are simply not yet fully awakened to the Universal Spiritual Picture and the higher reality that indeed they are all souls, parts of God, on their way back to conscious Oneness with God.

After learning from a reading of the requirement related to leaving a job situation, it took me a little over a year to achieve this impersonal feeling toward my coworkers. When I did, it was only about six weeks before a series of synchronistic events allowed me to leave my survival job with divine blessings and assistance from above in anything I chose to do in fulfilling my soul's purpose. In general, when we leave a situation in this manner, we will receive the highest degree of serendipitous, synchronistic help from the Angelic Realm in finding what we have wished for in our next job situation (if we open the door of free will by asking for their assistance).

Attachments to discordant habit patterns are like magnets

Attachments can be seen as magnets that hold our personality's consciousness, attention, and focus on those aspects of the outer world to which we have the attachments, as opposed to our being able to focus (with a single eye) on the inner world where our soul and Divinity Within live. These magnets are what hold our personality's attention on the outer world of the Earth School. These are the things that come between our personalities and our God Within. Attachments are those things that prevent or hinder our personality's consistent focus on our true identity as souls, attuned to and in harmony with our Goddess/God Within.

It is in the releasing and replacing process that we remove the magnetism that holds us firmly entrapped and focused primarily on our personality's outer world, third-dimensional, Earth life existence. Releasing attachments and replacing them with higher, more impersonal, more divine feelings, thoughts, attitudes, beliefs, and actions toward all of life allows us to move upward to the higher, more expanded consciousness, awareness, and more divine feelings of our soul *all while still having a physical body.* In this evolutionary process we are moving our personality's consciousness up to the higher level of our soul where we can once more have a close conscious connection to the Spark of God within our soul, and thus to God, the All That Is.

An excerpt from a reading by Cathy, on attachments,
from Archangel Michael on 8/27/00.

It is appropriate and good that I, Archangel Michael, be the one to speak on a chapter such as attachments, for often am I called upon and, when I am not, often ***should*** *I be called upon to work with an entity to sever attachments. I am quite efficient at this and depending on the nature of the attachment and depending on the true willingness of the entity to release attachments, then it may take only a period of thirty days of Earth time, and perhaps less. It is not harmful to call upon me to sever attachments more often than is necessary. For I can clearly see what is needed and when it is needed, but* ***I must be called upon****, (keep in mind the free will aspect). I must be called upon to sever these attachments.*

If one was able to view attachments from a psychic, shall we say, or an etheric perspective using the third eye, one would see that these are cords, sometimes like threads, sometimes like heavy cable, coming out from various areas of the physical body of the entity who would be free. I am merely describing this so that you can know that there can be an entity who has cords coming from many, many different areas.

It matters not to me whether the attachments are threads or cables. My sword is sharp and it will sever them all. It is important here for you to mention to your readers that severing attachments does not mean ending relationships. Attachments, as are being discussed in your book and in this reading, are those which are negative in nature in that they tend to draw energy from the being to whom they are attached. They diffuse focused attention, they interfere with concentration, and certainly with single-mindedness or single sight. Do you understand?

✦ Yes.

Relationships are improved when attachments are released. Now, that improvement may mean that the entity to whom one is attached may move farther away in the physical or it may mean that the entity may move closer in the physical. You may use examples of this if you wish. Examples where there's such an attachment to an entity that the ***attachment itself*** *drives that entity away (release of this attachment may bring the entity back, closer again). Or perhaps where there is such an obsession with being in that entity's presence, or being involved in the decision making of that entity, overshadowing* (controlling) *that entity's life, that it drives the entity away. These relationships will decidedly improve when such attachments are removed.*

Attachments have a tendency to grow back, which is why it is important to ask that I sever them more than once. It takes an extremely strong individual, strong in focus, strong in mind, strong in will, strong in connection with divine will to be able to sever an attachment once and have it remain gone. But it does happen.

Grievances

One of the quickest ways to form an attachment and one of the greatest ways to feed an attachment is to hold a grievance. It is imperative that there be no grievances held within the consciousness of the entity seeking spiritual growth, spiritual development, movement to higher levels of consciousness. Do you understand?

✦ Yes, and this is where forgiveness plays such an important part?

Forgiveness exercise

Correct. It is really important that forgiveness exercises be performed. And one very simple one is to make a list of all those against whom you have a grievance. Do not stop until your list is complete. You will be quite surprised, and this is good for your book. An entity may be quite surprised at grievances held from experiences long in the past and grievances held toward those long since passed over and no longer in the physical plane. An entity does not have to be incarnated in order for a grievance to be released and forgiveness to be applied. And many will find, in fact most will find (if they are true to their exercise, to their desire to forgive) that as they go through the list, they must include themselves. (We must forgive ourselves.)

When the list is completed, it is important to go through each and every individual in a meditative state or at least a state of very quïet mind. A state in which the Christ Light has been brought in through the crown chakra, and the heart chakra has been activated and the love can be felt to flow through. And then, when the entity truly feels love and forgiveness for the other person, or for the object, or for the circumstance to which the attachment is secured, it is important that the entity speak the words, "I forgive you, I forgive myself, I forgive the circumstance, the action, the feeling, whatever the grievance is based upon, and I release it."

The releasing can be done in any way that the entity finds comfortable.

- *The grievance may be placed in the violet flame and burned.*
- *It may be allowed to float up and be carried away by the angels.*
- *It may be encased in a balloon and allowed to float away.*
- *We find that the use of angels to remove what may often appear to those who have inner vision to be soot or ash or darkness of some kind, perhaps even in the form of smoke or a cloud to be carried away by the angels, is a very good way.*

Whatever is good here. There is a tape that has been made called, Healing With the Angels, *which is very effective for releasing grievances. And this tape is by Doreen Virtue.*

Also when an entity is going through severing attachments and forgiving grievances, it might be well to work morning and evening with the tape, Clearing the Chakras, *also by Doreen Virtue. This tape is made to be quite effective if used over a period of fourteen days with regularity.*

There are no attachments, which are good. *The very definition of attachment makes it something that is not desirable to the seeker on the path, to one who would be healed. For severing attachments is a very healing experience and often brings healing to the physical, emotional, and mental bodies of the entity who enters into this exercise.*

✦ I once thought I had no attachments because I disliked so much about the physical world experience except Nature. I therefore thought I was free and clear of all attachments. When I learned from a reading that aversions were very powerful attachments, I immediately understood that I had a great deal of work to do.

And that is well to use in your chapter as your own experience. But some of the strongest attachments are those that ***appear to be love****.*

✦ "Personal" love. (Conditional love).

Correct. Often between a parent and a child. Sometimes between two adults. Very often we find that these love attachments are of the nature of living one's life, at least a part of one's life and often a significant part, through another. And these are the attachments that entities most often do not wish to sever. They will argue with you that these are ***positive****. They will* *argue with you that they are* ***love*** *and all of their arguments harbor the fear that if the attachment is cut, they will have no life of their own.*

But it is not always a spouse, it is often a child, and occasionally a sibling. Very often it is a child. Sometimes it is a parent. Sometimes it is the child who has the strong attachment. Usually you will find that those attachments run both ways. It is important to have your reader understand that severing the attachment from self is sufficient. It is not necessary to concern self with whether or not the attachment is severed from the other entity. That is the other entity's issue and within his or her free will to deal with.

✦ I understand.

It is true that the entity who is being psychically severed, shall we say, will have an awareness of that, will have an experience of that. Very often one will find when one is severing attachments that one or more of the entities whose attachment is being severed will call or write indicating that they were thinking of the entity and missing them, feeling lonely, needing them. For they will be aware that the attachment has been severed at its source.

✦ Okay. Anything else you would offer on attachments?

Do make a very important point of grievances and how they form ***instantaneous attachments****. And how continued grievances strengthen and thicken the cords of attachments.*

✦ Hold no grievances.

Forgiving grievances! *Be clear that it is human, shall we say, for grievances to come to mind, for grievances to occur. The important thing is to release them immediately and to send love where the grievance has gone. It is important to do that.*

✦ Okay. I'm now looking at the questions that I had written beforehand. In the book I mentioned using the Golden Rule to help us determine a new habit pattern with which to replace the old. We've spoken of releasing the old, but they also need to be replaced. The releasing creates a void and we need to fill the void with a replacement habit. I mentioned using the Golden Rule to help us determine a new habit but now in this session I'm asking if there is a better way.

State your Golden Rule.

✦ As you would have others do unto you, do unto them.

This is good but ***it is not sufficient in and of itself****. And here is the pitfall. And it is often a pitfall. Suppose one does not love oneself. Suppose one believes that he or she deserves to be punished. Suppose an entity has low self-esteem and then treats others as he or she believes he or she should be treated.*

✦ I see.

What we are saying here is to use the Golden Rule, it is an excellent tool, but include this information with it. ***Love self.*** *Often the greatest lesson to be learned in the entire path of an entity's seeking and growing is* ***to love self****, to have an appreciation for self, to be kind and gentle to self. Do you understand?*

✦ Oh, yes. Yes, personally it's been the greatest millstone around my neck.

And you might be quite surprised to find that it is the greatest millstone for the greatest number of seekers. In fact, there are very few who have a sufficient appreciation and love of self, ***because they do not know who they are.*** *Low self-esteem is prevalent in the third-dimensional world. It is everywhere in action.*

So here I learned that the Golden Rule is useful in determining good replacement habits, but only after we have released attachments to any emotional habits of feeling extremely low self-esteem (learned from our outer world, not from God) and replaced them with feelings that are more in harmony with the unconditional love that our soul and Divinity Within feel toward us (as partners with them along the path back). Then, for those who have a modicum of self-esteem or self-love, the Golden Rule will serve as a guide for replacement habits, as will your intuitive flashes and your nightly dreams.

In short, the Golden Rule states that if we dislike certain types of behaviors being done to us, doing them to others will automatically cause disharmony between our personality and our soul, disharmony within (whether anyone else ever learns of it or not). We may choose ***not*** to show our inner disharmony to others in our own little worlds but we will experience it nonetheless in our inner world. We can never hide anything from our soul and our God/Goddess Within, and it is harmony with them that will bring joy to all three aspects of our Beingness.

Using the spiritual tools described in the next chapter will obviate the need for a detailed analysis of how and where we acquired our disharmonious habit patterns in this life experience or in previous lifetimes. That is one of the most wonderful features of these tools. We need only to know for ourselves that we have a habit pattern we no longer desire to manifest in reaction to certain outer world events. The description of the spiritual tools in the following chapter will make clear how we can release and replace habits easily and effectively, if we are sincere.

Self Validation

After we have made a release and replacement of a disharmonious habit, we can look in our own heart for personal validation of its effects. The heart is the body's intuitive connection to the soul. The soul lets us know immediately how it feels about our personality's intentions and actions through our *heart*. Using our imagination we can relax, focus on the new ideal habit we have chosen, and passively open ourselves to receive and experience the resultant feelings our soul brings to us. If focusing our attention on the new habit pattern brings us a warm, positive, inner feeling in the region around our heart, we have increased our inner harmony!

In my own experience, I had difficulty at first in noticing such feelings because in my youth I had built so many defensive, protective shells around my heart. However, those shells were created from habit patterns too. Because they were habits, I was able to release and replace them with new habits of faith and trust in the higher (and more effective) spiritual protection of the white light of the Christ Spirit of God above (rather than my personality's third-dimensional, offensive/defensive ways). The spiritual protective ways not only have done a better job of protecting, but also have simultaneously allowed me to experience the gentler emotions that my personality's third-dimensional defensive ways did not. In a relatively short time my feelings returned.

Is this releasing and replacing process worth the effort? For those who have made the choice the answer is quite clear, and it becomes even clearer as the process of spiritual evolution continues.

Even in the illusory physical world it is known that there is no sacrifice in giving up a penny to gain a fortune. In the real world of the soul in the higher dimensions above, the perception is that there is no sacrifice in giving up the pain and unhappiness found in all the disillusionments of the temporal physical world in order to regain all we originally had as free will souls in the eternal joy, harmony, and bliss of unconditional love in conscious Oneness with God.

CHAPTER 21

How to Release and Replace Attachments to Disharmonious Habit Patterns

Using New Spiritual Tools

This millennium is to become the Golden Age in which the world will see the evolution of a new kind of sentient human being—a being who is in this world, who has a physical body, but who is simultaneously living in a higher consciousness, at a higher dimension as a soul, and is able at any and all times to receive divine guidance from its Spark of God Within. The personality of this new type of evolved human will be cleared of that which is not in harmony with the soul and Divinity Within. Above all earthly circumstances, these souls will so love the divine feelings of inner bliss and harmony (a part of their higher conscious Oneness with God) that they will do nothing, they will carry out no outer world activities that they know would diminish or destroy their divine inner harmony in the slightest way.

Because of the nearness of this great event, spiritual tools have been created by some of the Archangels and Ascended Masters who watch over the Earth School. These tools were designed to speed up the evolution process by making the releasing and replacing of disharmonious habit patterns much quicker and easier than it has ever been.

> *A description of the new way of releasing and replacing negative habit patterns en masse (using spiritual tools created by Archangel Michael, Saint Germain, Augmenton, and other Beings of Light for the New Age)*

A spiritual tool is a method or process created by Ascended Masters, Archangels, or other Beings of Light that makes it easier for us humans to free ourselves of our negative or disharmonious habit patterns and to replace them with those that bring harmony between our personality and our soul. The Beings of Light who create these tools always stand behind them and see that the necessary etheric and spiritual dynamics are taken care of whenever any human uses them.

I will include here the three tools that I have used most frequently since they were given to us several years ago. The remainder of the tools that have been described to us will be included in appendix A (to avoid giving the reader, as offered from above, the feeling that she or he is drinking from a fire hose; too much at once). In this way the list will be available as a reference if and when anyone is interested.

These three basic spiritual tools, when used together, accomplish all that is necessary for the releasing and replacing of habit patterns that create disharmony within. (So does the vacuum tool of Archangel Michael described in appendix A.) They render my old detailed, analytical, and time-consuming way entirely obsolete. Once we commit to the spiritual path and begin to seek the greater harmony with our soul and the God/Goddess Within, our intuition and our dreams will bring us the feeling awareness of personality habits that are not in harmony with the higher aspects of our beingness. When we know, even generically, which negative habit patterns we wish to transform into positives, these three tools used together will release them (providing us with a clean sheet so to speak) and allow us to replace them through our practice of our newly chosen positive habits that will move us more quickly, more smoothly along our path and bring greater inner harmony and divine love into our lives.

Tool 1: Created by Archangel Michael who uses his etheric violet sword for the cutting of our psychic cords of attachment to old negative habits

In a state of meditation, rise up as high in spirit as you are able in the moment and silently call in Archangel Michael.[1] Give him five or ten seconds to make his connection. State your intention in plain words (this can be done silently of course). Then simply ask him to use his violet sword to sever all cords of attachment to whatever habit pattern(s) you wish to

---

[1] It is recommended by all Beings of Light that in all such exercises and in all meditations we use our very highest imaginative powers. Some readers may have to go back in time to recall the strength of the imagination that was perfected before seven years of age, when we were still living as our souls and before we became "educated" by our outer world environment to believe that we are only our body and its personality. If use of the imagination seems strange to you, please remember Christ's saying that unless we become as little children again we shall not enter into the Kingdom of Heaven. It is not well known to the masses of humankind, but the *imagination* is one of the *most powerful tools* that we can use for creation through the Universal Laws of Manifestation. If you look at your own little world from the level of your soul, you

release, whatever it is that you have discovered that hinders progress along your spiritual path, whatever no longer fits who you are now or who you are becoming. Below I offer an example, using one of my first major negative outer world habits.

> I call upon Archangel Michael. (Short pause.) I desire to release some of my old negative habit patterns. I ask Archangel Michael to use his violet sword to cut all cords of attachment to all my past fears relating to opening my heart to others or in the presence of others, all my fears of making myself vulnerable to emotional pain, and all anger and judgment that stem from these fears.

That's it! That's all it takes! Any psychic cords of attachment to all related habit patterns that you may have had for years will immediately be severed. You can be as generic as you wish. The more general your request, the broader will be the span of effect of Archangel Michael's attachment severing activities. However, if your intuition has given you information about a certain problem area, it would be wise to address that problem specifically. This tool allows for the release of any habit patterns that you no longer desire to have by cutting the etheric cords of attachment to them. Any habitual ways of negative feeling and thinking, or any negative attitudes and beliefs stored in our personalities or in our souls, can be released simply by our conscious desire and intention to let them go and by our request for Archangel Michael's assistance in cutting the psychic cords of attachment to them.

And he makes house calls! No matter who or where you are in outer world terms, if your sincere intentions are to release these negative habits and to cut the cords of attachment which tie them to you, it will be done. And if you allow them to grow back again (by not diligently focusing upon their positive replacement feelings and thoughts) and later desire once more to sever your attachment to them, Archangel Michael will joyfully do it again, and again. For his mission is to help all humans back to conscious Oneness with God, their Creator.

Note that Archangel Michael did ask, in one of our later readings, that we do rise up in consciousness as high as we can to make it easier to get his sword under us, between us and the Earth to which this habit attaches us; but this was offered in a very lighthearted way. The insight given me at the time was that some of us are so tightly attached to our Earthbound habits that he would have had to use a violet scalpel rather than his violet sword. So give him a break and raise your consciousness to a little higher and more detached level when you call for his assistance.

---

will see clearly that it was your imaginative powers that inadvertently brought all negativity into your life. Now you may use this power in a positive way to create your soul's desires.

Tool 2: Created by Saint Germain who uses his violet all-consuming flame to remove and transmute any negative energy (that we request to have removed) existing within us back to its original neutral state and to return it to the Universe

Again, in a state of meditation or reverie, of quietness or calm, silently call in Saint Germain. Give him a moment to connect with you. Then ask him to manifest the violet all-consuming (cool) flame of transmutation within, through, and around your body to dissolve and remove all existing negative energy, to transmute it to its original neutral state (of atoms and subatomic particles), and to return it to the Universe (so it can be recycled for higher purposes). Here is an example of the way I have done it for years.

> I call upon Saint Germain. (Short pause). I ask Saint Germain to manifest the violet flame of transmutation within, through, and around my body to dissolve and remove all the negative energy (that I desire to release), to transmute it back to its original neutral state, and to return it to the Universe.

If you wish to state the nature of the negative energy you wish to have removed from your systems in more detail, that is fine. You could say, "I wish to remove from all my systems all negative energy related to that which Archangel Michael has just severed all cords of attachment." Or you might say, "I ask that the violet flame remove all negative energy related in any way to my previous fears of opening my heart to others or in the presence of others." There is no right or wrong way to do this and no need for specific verbiage. We are each on our own when it comes to our relationship with these Beings of Light in the heavens above. I offer these examples only to indicate that nothing fancy is required. The idea is simply to make clear, in your own way and in your own words, what kind of assistance you desire.

If you use it somewhat as described, this spiritual tool, with the help of Saint Germain and his many assistants, will dissolve and remove any and all types of negative etheric energy from your system. However, if your intuition tells you to focus on a particular type of negative energy (that which your higher self or soul may deem a high priority at the moment), then ask for that specific type to be dissolved and removed, and it will be done.

Tool 3: A breathwork tool maintained by Augmenton and many other Beings of Light

With the use of the first two tools you will have released and severed your psychic attachments to a negative earthbound habit, and you will have caused that negative energy to be dissolved and removed from your systems, transmuted to its neutral state (of atoms and subatomic particles) and returned to the Universe (for recycling). You now have set yourself up to bring in the new positive habit pattern(s) with which you wish to replace the old. You have in essence released the old and created a void into which you will wish to move your positive replacement habits.

This is an excerpt from a reading by Cathy, on spiritual tools, received from Augmenton on 4/13/97.

Breathwork

The breathwork tool that we are discussing was indeed given in a previous reading.

There is the breathing in, the drawing in, of breath as if sucking in through a straw until the entire being is filled. Be certain to breathe it into all of the extremities, as well as into the lungs and the abdominal area, so that every cell within the body is filled with the breath, until there is literally no more room for breath within the being. And while there is the breathing in, there is the stating (silently is fine) *and the visualizing* (using your highest powers of imagination) *of breathing in that which will fill the void created by what is being breathed out.*

Once the being is entirely filled and this air has been drawn in rather forcefully, then there is the relaxation and the allowing of the air to escape. It is not blown out. It is not forced out, but rather it is allowed to escape very gently, very peacefully.

Now, in the process of releasing, call upon the violet flame of transmutation prior to the releasing process so that that which is being released can be burned (in the cool violet flame) *and transmuted.*

*And breathe in whatever you wish as **a replacement** for that which you are releasing, but primarily you will find that breathing in divine love, breathing in divine harmony, and breathing in serenity are quite sufficient replacements. It depends very much on what the issue is that the entity wants to release. If the issue is stress and frustration, then the breathing in can be the breathing in of divine peace, the breathing in of divine harmony.*

*If the issue is something on the order of anger or another negative emotion of some sort, then there can be the breathing in of divine love and the breathing out of the specific emotion. Though it **does not** have to be totally specific you understand, but merely the breathing out of whatever it is that is making the entity uncomfortable.*

There can be the breathing in of the divine light, the breathing in of divine purity, whatever comes through the intuition or feels appropriate to the entity as that with which they would like to replace the negative that they are releasing.

Continuing with my personal example from above, I might have breathed in divine love for God, for self, and for others. I might have breathed in the courage to be defenseless relative to outer world influences (no longer needing my personality's outer world defense mechanisms) and greater trust and faith in the power of my connection to the Creative Forces of God for my higher world protection. I might have breathed in the increased courage and capacity to be my true self, my soul self, and my Divine Self in all my daily activities.

Breathwork Tools

Breathwork is an easy way to replace our old habits with those the Universe can use as a new blueprint from which to create what we truly desire in our lives. Breathwork tools are maintained by other Archangels and Ascended Masters also. All these Beings of Light work together on the same larger mission of assisting in the spiritual evolution of humankind.

Why are breathwork tools so effective, so Universally efficient? One reason is because they are so simple and easy to use regardless of where you are and whatever you happen to be doing. No one need know that you are carrying out an internal discipline that will change your life and bring you to greater inner harmony and Oneness with God. Another is because one of the ways to move your consciousness higher, closer to the level of your soul, is to consciously watch your breath and your breathing.

Why is this so? Because for all of your life in a physical body your soul, not your personality, has controlled your breathing while you sleep and stabilized many of the other homeostatic processes of your body's systems such as blood pressure and body temperature. So if you want an easy way to move up toward being your higher self or soul for a while, focus your consciousness on controlling your breathing. *Cause* your body to breathe in a way that *you* wish it to (i.e., perhaps using a three count or four count for each in-breath and out-breath), and you automatically will be raising your consciousness closer to the level of your higher self or soul. See for yourself how this helps you to be able to observe yourself from above, rather than merely being and identifying with your physical body and its personality, while carrying out your daily activities.

Benefits of the New Ways

Using the newer tools, we can release many old negative habit patterns and replace them with positives, without the psychological requirement of knowing all the miniscule painful details of how and why we originally adopted them. We need only know that we have discovered within us a habit pattern that we no longer desire to have. We need only recognize that it is a habit pattern that is a hindrance to our progress on our path now. This offers us a tremendous saving in time and effort as opposed to the detailed, analytical, and torturous way.

As mentioned in the case of Saul of Tarsus in the chapter on the Universal Law of Grace, what happened in our past is not important in the higher realms of God once we have awakened and made a personal commitment to the spiritual path. At that point the Earth School experience has done its job, and all that is important is merely that the new feelings, thoughts, attitudes, beliefs, and actions we continue to manifest are positive and that they are in harmony with our soul. By experiencing our new inner harmony and manifesting it into the world around us, we evolve ourselves back to conscious Oneness with God.

There is another important point that my soul and Goddess Within wish me to make at this time. In the replacement of the old with the new, there is a period of time (around thirty days) wherein we must practice the new desired habit in our outer world activities before it will truly become ours.

Practicing the New Habits

Practicing the new habit while involved in our daily activities includes practicing the *feelings* that go with the actions or the words. These are not merely intellectual exercises as might be provided by a human teacher in a public school. On the contrary, they are the antithesis of intellectual exercises and if practiced in a rote manner (thinking rather than feeling) without invoking and experiencing your true inner intentions and your related inner feelings, they will have little or no permanent positive effect.

In my example above for instance, I would only actually be protected by the Creative Forces of the Universe if I caused myself to *feel* that I was protected from above. *Feelings* provide the power behind the Universal Laws of Manifestation. We must change from the way we previously felt, as our personality self, to what we desire to feel as our ideal self, our soul self. Then the Universal Laws of Manifestation will create in our own little worlds that which is in harmony with our new ways. Changing our feelings as well as our thoughts marks the beginning of self-mastery.

These spiritual tools help us to cut the psychic cords of attachment to our old ways. They remove any residual etheric negativity that may exist in our bodies as a result of our old habitual ways. This sets us up with a new page on which we can begin to write the remainder of our lives. This makes it as easy as possible for us to replace the old with the new and to move ahead on our own spiritual path.

In literally any situation we can simply breathe in all the new divine feelings, thoughts, attitudes, beliefs, and actions with which we wish to replace the old. Nevertheless, if we wish to adopt a new way of being, we are responsible for actually practicing (for thirty days or so) the positive actions and feelings of the new way until they become as habitual and unconscious as were the negative feelings of the old way. Feelings, positive feelings are required!

The new way is wonderful! The new tools are wonderful. They are efficient. They are expedient. They are powerful. From my own experience (as one who once felt, thought, and believed sincerely that super macho was good and great), I highly recommend the new spiritual tools to the souls of all who are incarnated in the Earth School today.

They help us to realize our personal empowerment, our inner power to change ourselves. They help us to increase our awareness of the higher-dimensional assistance available to all of humankind who wish to return to conscious Oneness with God. They help us to regain our understanding of the creative power of our imagination to visualize (with feeling) that which will cause the Universal Law of Manifestation to bring us what our soul, our true self, truly desires in our own little world. They help us to become our new selves, or better said, to return to being our soul selves once more in conscious Oneness with our Spark of God Within.

For additional spiritual tools, see appendix A.

CHAPTER 22

Dreams

Understanding Our Soul's Nightly Messages to Our Personality

For those readers who do not regularly remember their dreams or who do not care to learn how to interpret them, I offer this excerpt from a reading that corrected a misunderstanding on my part. For well over thirty years I have thought that dreams were one of the best ways for everyone to discover and understand the hidden or unconscious parts of their personalities. I had completed this chapter on dreams before I asked for a reading on attachments. Archangel Michael responded. In his session on attachments I also asked the following question about dreams and received a quite surprising answer.

This is an excerpt from a reading by Cathy received from Archangel Michael on 08/27/00.

✦ I often use dreams as a way to discover, to identify, and to know my unconscious disharmonious habit patterns, those habits that we humans have, but are completely blind about having, those to which we are quite oblivious as parts of our personalities. For myself, my dreams have seemed to be the best indicators of disharmonious habit patterns because I know they are given to me by the soul, and I know my soul wants harmony between my personality and itself more than anything. So I use dreams a lot to know what my soul is telling me about that which is causing any disharmony in my inner world. My question is, are dreams especially good just for me or is this true for everyone?

It is true of you. It is true of many. ***It is not true of all.*** *It is true of all that the soul uses dreams in this way, but it is not true that this is an effective technique for all.*

✦ Oh.

And a part of that is because working with dreams perhaps takes more time, more commitment. They are not always straightforward. You do not get a message that says you get too angry too often. It is not written out in the sky or on a blackboard. Often there are symbols that must be interpreted because there is resistance to hearing, or knowing, or understanding these things about self.

Many are better served by ***intuitive flashes****. Or better served by something they read in a book that strikes them. Better served by whatever their soul can use. And while the soul will use dreams, many souls must be more creative. Do you understand?*

✦ Only partially. By more creative do you mean—

Many souls must be more creative in finding other ways (i.e., intuitive flashes) *to get the message to the consciousness of the personality or through the consciousness of the personality.*

✦ Okay. Well I thank you for this.

So if you do not care to understand how dreams work, or how our souls use them, you can save yourself some time by skipping this chapter. If you skip it, you can rest assured from Archangel Michael's reading, that your soul will find other ways to help your personality join it in harmony.

I am leaving it in the book because I believe it is both interesting and valuable to some. The idea of dreams being provided by our souls certainly fits comfortably into the context of what has been described as the Universal Spiritual Picture. Personally (or rather, impersonally) I have been able to receive and to journal information (intuitively and claircognizantly) from and through the awareness and perspective of my soul and Divinity Within for over ten years now but dreams are still one of the most valuable daily report cards my personality receives in this Earth School.

Dreams are there every morning, and in a sense they may cover a broader base of information, because dreams are not limited to the questions I might consciously think to ask my soul of my own free will. The reason this seemingly unrequested[1] information does not conflict with the

---

[1] Of course we may also request dream answers to our conscious questions too. Just before dropping off to sleep, we may simply pose any question we may have, and our soul will comply by presenting us with the symbolic answer as we sleep. It may

Universal Law of Free Will is that the information in dreams is provided in symbolic form. We show our free will to receive the information by our willingness to interpret the dreams.

Dreams Are a Means of Communication

Dreams were included in the Earth School's design so that the personality self of each entrapped soul would have an easy way of receiving spiritual guidance from its own higher aspects, most commonly from its soul, but now and then from the Divinity that lives within our souls. Through dreams anyone and everyone has the natural means to receive higher guidance or to ignore it as their personalities choose.

Dreams provide one of the easiest ways for ordinary humankind (and doggies too) to receive input from the higher aspects of our Beingness. You can even do it in your sleep. Well, at least you can do the receiving part in your sleep. The interpretation is usually done in the conscious state or better yet a meditative state and then only if your personality desires and chooses to do so.

Dreams are messages, like little picture shows or movies, sometimes in black and white, sometimes in color. Our soul is the creator of all but a very few of our dreams and the Divinity Within the soul creates the rest. In general, a very small percent of our nightly dreams may be actual experiences in other dimensions, to expand our consciousness by giving us glimpses of other worlds, or precognitive dreams providing probabilities of future events in our lives. However, the overwhelming majority of ordinary dreams are little scenarios representing our personality's daily activities and how our soul feels about those activities relative to creating harmony between it and the personality.

By activities I mean to include all the feelings, thoughts, attitudes, beliefs, and actions that our personality puts out into the outer world while carrying out its normal affairs. Dream information is provided by the soul for the personality's educational benefit. It provides a person, the personality of a person, with information about itself straight from its own soul. In essence, this information helps the personality to know itself better. It helps the personality to know which of its subpersonalities are causing inner disharmony and also which habit patterns of those subpersonalities need to be changed to bring them into harmony with the soul and its God Within.

---

present us with one dream or perhaps a series of several dreams all related to the question we asked. The dream content in each segment may have a different appearance, but if the themes are similar, then the theme is probably the answer to our question. If in doubt, ask for it to be repeated, and it will be. Your soul is very interested in creating harmony with your personality.

Dreams Help Us Discover Blind Spots

This is an extremely valuable feature for anyone on the spiritual path, for we humans all have blind spots about ourselves. We all have habit patterns to which we are so accustomed that we have become quite unconscious of having them, quite oblivious to their existence, even though we may act them out each day of our lives (in the same way that we are quite unconscious of the way we breathe, or feel, or react to certain outer world situations). In other cases, we may be conscious of having them but unconscious of their effects on our spiritual progress.[2]

Without dreams we may not be consciously aware of what it is within ourselves that needs changing, for mostly we will not take the advice of our outer world friends about our behavior. At present, the common desire of most humans is to hide from others the disharmony we carry within, pretending to the outer world always to be happy and living behind our façade of happiness. Our dreams cut through our façade.

This information comes from our very own soul. There is no form of life on Earth that knows our personality more intimately, thoroughly, and accurately than our own soul. This is the aspect of our Beingness that has breathed for us, handled all our body's internal functions day and night for all our mortal life. It knows all our unconscious habit patterns, all our day-to-day ways of feeling about things, the habitual ways we have of thinking about things, all our common attitudes about things, and all our beliefs about things that we have adopted from our outer world experiences, which so crucially influence our daily lives. No form of life on Earth has a greater interest in our personality's moving back to a state of conscious Oneness with God. Our soul and our Divinity Within are the closest true friends it is possible for our personality to have down here, for even the Beings of Light in the higher dimensions of Godness above must come to us through them.

Remember here how the Universal Law of Manifestation uses all the feelings, thoughts, attitudes, and beliefs (about life) that we hold inside as a blueprint from which to create our own little worlds. For this reason alone, it is critical to our personality's well being to know which of its subpersonality's habit patterns are in need of greater harmony with our soul.

---

[2] A personal example of this was my ignorance of the effects that my super macho attitudes had upon my spiritual progress. I was aware that I had these attitudes but I thought they were great (like those of many movie heroes). In some ways these attitudes helped my personality's daily outer world life as a youth on the streets of a big city, but they also caused me to be extremely imbalanced with masculine energy and this in turn prevented my ability to receive divine intuitive guidance from above at a much earlier age.

Dreams are there for everyone because everyone has dreams, but in accordance with the Universal Law of Free Will, no one forces us to use them. It is probable that only when our desire and yearning for greater inner peace, harmony, and unconditional love in our lives is sufficient to cause us to become seekers along the path that we will take the trouble to learn to interpret and use our dreams to change our lives for our own higher good.

The important message here is simply that dreams are a very important vehicle that can help any human who wishes to use them to move more efficiently toward a loving harmony with its soul, with the Spark of God Within the soul, and therefore also with God, the All That Is.

Day-to-Day Dreams Have a Simple Format

An overwhelming percent of all our dreams have a simple format that anyone can learn to use in about thirty minutes. This will be the format described here. This description assumes knowledge of the meaning and purpose of life on Earth (as it has been presented in this book), and so it will be much shorter than if this were not the case.

Most humans do not at present know the meaning and purpose of life on Earth. Dream interpretation for them is a very complicated task. By this I mean to say that if a personality knows only of third-dimensional life and attempts to place the meaning of his or her dreams in just that context, tries to make sense out of the nonsense of the outer, man-made world, they will be missing the larger and most important spiritual and philosophical meaning. This is why most humans today are able to see little meaning in their dreams. They are not placing them in the context of the much larger Universal Spiritual Picture. They are trying to find meaning by relating their soul's dream messages to a meaningless third-dimensional world.

The true purpose of all dream messages is to provide us humans with information that will assist all of us here on Earth in creating greater harmony among our personality, our soul (or true self), and the Divine Spark of God that lives within our soul. In other words, the deepest or highest purpose in all dreams is that of assisting us all on our spiritual evolutionary path back to conscious Oneness with God. By placing them in this context, dreams are much easier to understand. We need only look for those things in our dreams that are shown to be out of harmony with our soul and replace them (in our daily lives) with those that are in harmony.

Review of the nature of the spiritual path

As the subtitle for part IV infers, the spiritual path back to Oneness with God for everyone of us here on Earth, is simply the path of creating harmony among our personality, our soul, and our Spark of God within our soul. We do this by discovering those habit patterns within our personality that cause and maintain inner disharmony, by releasing them, and by replacing them with new habit patterns that create and maintain inner harmony.

Before going any further in dreams, I will repeat here four paragraphs that I offered in chapter 9 relative to our generic, human, spiritual evolution. Skip them if you feel you don't need a reminder.

Individual evolution

Habit patterns include the unconscious, habitual ways (of feeling and thinking about certain things) that we, as our personality selves, have acquired, as well as the habitual attitudes and beliefs that we express in our daily activities. These we have learned and adopted from our personality's external world education and conditioning. Habit patterns that create, maintain, or increase disharmony between our personality, our soul, and our Spark of God Within obviously hinder or block our progress along the path toward Oneness.

Our individual spiritual evolution consists of *discovering* personality habit patterns that cause disharmony with our soul and our Spark of God Within. It includes the *releasing* of personality habit patterns that cause disharmony with our soul and Divinity Within. Our evolution also includes our *replacing* disharmonious habit patterns with new habits, which create and maintain increased harmony among our personality, our soul, and our Divinity Within.

In this way we are spiritualizing the physical body we chose to inhabit. We are automatically expanding and raising the consciousness of our personality to that of our soul. We are becoming our soul again and returning to conscious Oneness with our Spark of God Within while still in our physical body experiencing physical life.

By divesting ourselves of negatives we are returning to the condition our souls once knew in our original heavenly state, where we can once more experience eternal unconditional love, meaning, purpose, and fulfillment. These are the things we have missed and found lacking in our physical life experiences. These are the things we have searched for but could never find in our physical outer world existence.

End of the review and back to dreams.

Dream Messages

One of the critically important messages that our soul provides us in the dreams it creates for our personality is how it perceives and feels about the habit patterns our personality expresses or manifests in our daily lives. By showing us those habits which cause disharmony with it, we can know which habits need to be replaced if and when we make the choice to move along the spiritual path.

Remember that our soul is a part of God and due to the Universal Law of Free Will we, as our personality selves, cannot be coerced into following the spiritual path by any aspects of God above us. We absolutely must make the choice to evolve ourselves spiritually of our own free will.

This is the very reason that our dream messages are most often given in symbolic form as opposed to being given to us directly in our native languages. By providing only dream symbols, the Universe knows that the only way our personality can derive meaning from our soul's messages is through a process of interpretation, and this is done of our own free will. If the messages were given to us verbally, we could mistake them for commands from above or orders from God. This could be interpreted as a type of coercion, which is counter to the Universal Law of Free Will created by God. God would love to have all entrapped souls back in conscious Oneness with Him/Her as companions, but God desires only true, loving, and willing companions, not those who have been coerced and do not really wish to be there.

A simple way to understand most of the dreams our soul provides us each day

What follows is the format that the soul most often uses in the design of our personal dreams to help us understand when and how we are creating inner harmony or disharmony.

Dream Characters: A Brief Symbol Format

You, Your Soul

In the little dream scenarios that our soul presents to us in common dreams, the character that is "you" in the dream story is your soul, or symbolizes your soul self, the real you (before the fall in consciousness). For this reason it is very important to remember your feelings about all the other characters, actions, and symbols. It is the emotional part of the dream that tells you how the real you, the higher you, the soul *feels* about your personality's daily outer world activities.

People We Know

The other people who appear in our dream movies represent different parts of our personality, or subpersonalities. If these characters are people we happen to know in our waking life, it is easy to understand the nature of the subpersonality they represent in us. We need only to write out a one-sentence description of this person, what he or she represents to us in our waking state, daily activities. That one-sentence description will convey the nature of the part of us that is being referred to by our soul in our dream. It may be a lovely and loving subpersonality, or a mean-minded, abusive one, but either way it is a part of our personality or it would not have appeared in our dream!

Further, it is probably a part of our personality that we expressed into our outer world "yesterday," for most often our soul gives us feedback about our daily activities as soon as possible.

I had nearly all male subpersonalities until I became partially successful in my attempts to integrate more divine feminine energy into my daily life. Most of these males were inconsiderate, dominating, unfeeling, tough-guy subpersonalities. Some were judgmental and demanding. Others were kinder, gentler, more understanding, and willing to offer assistance to others.

Almost all my few feminine subpersonalities were kind, gentle, considerate, thoughtful, and loving but, as I said for me, these did not appear nearly as often as the overly masculine, aggressive males.

People We Don't Know

Sometimes a person will appear in our dreams who we really do not know, someone we have never met. Again, write out a one-sentence description of the way you felt in the dream about the way he or she acted (gentle and kind, or obnoxious in some way). That is the description your soul intended for you to see in this character and to recognize as a subpersonality, a part of your total personality self.

This is truly the way you, (at the higher conscious level of your true self, your deeper self, your soul self) feel about that unknown aspect of your personality. It is this *feeling* about your personality's habitual ways that indicates whether the ways of that subpersonality are creating inner harmony or disharmony.

If we were still being our souls in heaven above guided by and one with our Divinity Within, there would be no feelings of inner disharmony. But our personality at the current stage of human evolution in the Earth School, is guided in many ways from without, by the many feelings, thoughts, attitudes, beliefs, and actions we have learned and accepted from our man-made outer world environment. It is some of this adopted and learned outer world guidance that now causes the inner disharmony we wish to replace. You can easily see how tremendously beneficial our dreams can be to any who choose the way back to Oneness with God.

We are told from above that we are not to attempt to kill off, or destroy the subpersonalities that display these disharmonious traits. We are merely to assist them in maturing, in growing up, in awakening to the larger spiritual picture and harmonizing with the soul. This we do by replacing the negative habit patterns that we were shown through our dreams with new harmonious habits. These new habits will change the nature and character of this subpersonality so that we may not recognize it in our dreams any longer. When we have changed the nature of a subpersonality to the point where it no longer shows up in our dreams, we know our soul is telling us that that particular subpersonality is no longer a hindrance to our spiritual path. In this way we can understand when we are making progress.

Dream Animals

Animals that play a role in our dreams represent our emotions (those we probably displayed yesterday). These too may be called positive or negative depending on whether they create harmony or disharmony with our soul. Again, write out a one-sentence description of how you personally perceive and feel about that type of animal and you will know the nature of the emotion in your personality to which your soul is referring.

In my past dreams I have had Kodiak bears that would have weighed five to ten thousand pounds or more come in and threaten me. To me they represented negative emotions that could kill me, quickly and easily. They symbolized for me the initial emotion of *fear* and then the emotion of *anger* at that which caused the fear. Manifesting the emotions of either fear or anger in my daily life could and did, quickly and easily, kill any harmony I had going between my soul and my personality; whereas the positive emotions of understanding, compassion, forgiveness, and love never did.

This does not mean we are to repress or suppress our awareness of having negative emotions. To do so would only create another obstacle in our path, which itself would require releasing and replacing. Our challenge is to release the negatives as something we no longer desire in our lives and to replace them with positives we know will assist us along our spiritual path.

Another beauty of a negative emotion I had in a dream was symbolized by a badger. The badger represented to me an emotion that I knew was extremely defensive and extraordinarily vicious in its defensiveness. About this symbol I had to ask, "Who, me?"

We all have blind spots and in the incident that triggered this particular dream I really believed I was only "sticking up for my rights." Well, the soul doesn't care about any such foolish man-made beliefs that we may have acquired naturally from our illusion-filled outer world. The soul is interested only in helping our personality in every way allowed by Universal Law to understand how to free itself from the illusions of the outer world and from our mistaken identity as only a body and its personality, so we can harmonize with our soul and return to conscious Oneness with God. To replace my extreme (badger-like) defensiveness I used its opposite of defenselessness. This required an increase in my trust in God as an inner and higher form of defense, rather than believing I must always defend myself, but it worked out just fine.

What were the results of my awakening to and understanding the meaning of my bear and badger emotions? Due to my releasing and replacing efforts, it has been about ten years since I last saw my defensive dream badger. The gigantic angry bear was a little tougher for me to replace. The huge one hasn't been around for several years and, when last seen, was about the size of a teddy bear and quite harmless.

My favorite dream animals are dogs (always representing for me the positive emotions of unconditional love and loyalty beyond measure). I also like to see other wild animals in my dreams, like deer, that are harmless to others (symbolizing to me the emotions of being free and unfettered by the outer world, with intentions of harm to no one).

Inanimate Objects

There are thousands of inanimate objects in our outer world life that our soul can use in our dreams as symbols in a message. For any of these that appear in our dreams we can follow the same approach. If we are in doubt as to what our soul intended a symbol to mean to our personality, we can simply write out a one-sentence description of what the object personally means to us in our daily lives. If we ever see it again, we can know that our definition is the meaning our soul will have intended us to see and use. Our soul knows our every feeling and thought and always has.

Special Cases: Vehicles That Carry Us

In the larger spiritual picture there are a few inanimate objects that generally have a more important meaning than the rest. One category includes any objects that act as vehicles to carry us along the path, the road, to wherever we are headed.

Cars, tricycles, airplanes, rockets all were created for the purpose of carrying humans somewhere. Some are more efficient than others. Airplanes are faster than cars, rockets can go higher than airplanes, and bicycles are more efficient than tricycles (which can be very poor transportation on rocky roads).

In our dreams these vehicles are often shown carrying "me" or "you," (representing our soul self) in the dream. These vehicles, which carry our soul, often represent the way our soul sees and feels about our personality's momentary ability to carry our soul along the path. An old, rusty, beat-up automobile as compared to a bright, shiny, attractive one certainly could give us a hint that we might want to pay a little more attention to our personality's condition. This would be especially true if, in the dream, we really preferred the shiny attractive vehicle and had merely let the old one fall into a state of disrepair.

Flying in a rocket may be our soul telling us that we are really moving our consciousness upward and outward in space at the moment. The tricycle could show us that our current rate of progress is slow and we might want to upgrade our personality if we prefer to move more swiftly along the path.

Another valuable relationship these vehicles may show us is the driver. Who is in the driver's seat in our daily lives? The optimum would be that our soul is always shown as driving, choosing the way while our various subpersonalities are simply coming along as passengers who may be helpful in fulfilling whatever our current mission might be. However, it has often been very helpful to me to receive the message that one of my subpersonalities was now at the wheel and I (my soul) was merely a passenger. Such a dream message may allow me to take stock of myself and prevent my subpersonality from causing a crash (perhaps with another human personality) in my daily life.

A few animals (i.e., horses, elephants, camels) can also serve the same purpose of representing our momentary personality as a vehicle for our soul, but only when they are shown carrying us in the dream. Otherwise they probably represent just the emotions we would normally attribute to them.

Special Cases: Clothing That Shows Our Public Attitudes

Very common is the dream where we find ourselves out in public without clothing. An experience in our daily lives that probably or possibly could have triggered this type of dream is one where we were suddenly placed in a surprise situation for which we were not prepared attitudinally. In our daily activities we may find ourselves "naked before others," unprepared for public attention. For example, if we had known beforehand that we might be asked to speak to a crowd, we could have created a suit of attitudinal clothing that affirmed to ourselves that we were quite adequate speakers and that we knew the subject matter in depth. If we had clothed ourselves in such a manner beforehand and had handled the situation without personal embarrassment, we would not have been given this dream as an explanation to us.

Further Generic Information About Dreams

Hopefully you have noted that in working with your soul, trying to understand your dreams, the format above uses our personal definitions for people (known and unknown) for animals, and for inanimate objects. Many dream books go into great detail describing fixed meanings for various symbols. The above format allows you to develop your own meanings as these symbols come up in your dream life. Using symbols that may have been appropriate for some other human who has an entirely different personality and has led an entirely different life from yours can waste a great deal more time than creating our own meanings, for their symbols may have represented something quite the opposite of what the same symbol means to you.

Strawberries are a favorite food of mine. If they were ever to appear in one of my dreams, I would give them some sort of a positive meaning. However, strawberries might have quite a negative connotation to those who are allergic to them and break out in hives or suffer from swollen tongues. Dream symbols mean different things to different personalities. It is mostly our very own personal meaning that our soul wishes to use in conveying its ordinary daily messages to our personality.[3]

Are we allowed to create our own meanings for symbols? Is this permitted? Indeed it is for all ordinary, everyday, personal symbols. Our soul knows beforehand that our personality may not understand just what it intended for us to see about ourselves. Suppose your soul gives you a dream that contains a symbol that is, for you, quite ambiguous. It could mean this, or it might mean that, or still again it may mean something else. Don't fret for a minute!

In silent dialog with your soul about the dream (while you are interpreting), tell your soul that you are confused and that in the future you are going to interpret this symbol to mean ______. If you ever get that symbol in another dream, you can rest assured that it will mean just what you defined to your soul that it means to you.

Souls are not dumb! Souls are not rigid! The soul has the greatest interest in the personality's movement into harmony with it. Our souls will be happy to use any and all the meanings we care to attribute to any symbol in our dreams. Your soul will be overjoyed merely to see that you understand that it is a part of your Beingness that you can talk to and work with. In the matter of attempting to create increased harmony with it, you will find your soul to be your most flexible, helpful, and loving higher friend.

Interpreting Your Dreams

Now you know the symbol format most commonly used by the soul in creating our ordinary dreams. Here is a simple way to put that knowledge to use in interpreting your dream messages.

---

[3] The exception here is that of archetypal or archetypical dream symbols. These are symbols that would have the same meaning for all of humankind. A description of these would be too extensive for inclusion in this chapter but may be found in any book totally focused on dreams.

1. **Recording your dream**

   First, write out the dream as soon as you awaken. Don't talk and don't walk! Don't let your feet touch the floor! When you awaken from a dream state, you are still at your soul level of consciousness (the alpha state), and it is easy to recall your dreams and your feelings. However, if you talk to someone, or get up and put your feet on the floor and find it to be cold to the touch, you probably will have shifted your level of consciousness down to that of your personality (the beta state), making it far more difficult to remember the dream. Shifting the focus of one's attention from your inner world to the outer world is the most common cause of not being able to remember dreams.

   If you have time to write only a single brief sentence, do so (i.e., the cow jumped over the moon). Then briefly write out the feelings you remember having had while in the dream. Many times these two items are all that are needed later to trigger a complete recall of all the dream's content, people, places, actions, and feelings.

2. **Interpreting the dream's theme, condensing the dream content into a one-sentence theme**

   Later, when you have the time to interpret, pull out your notes and reread the dream. Keep in mind that the primary reason for the soul to provide these messages to the personality is to help us understand how we can best create harmony with it and the Spark of God Within it. In a relaxed state of meditation or peaceful reverie, put yourself in your highest philosophical frame of mind.

   From this perspective write out a one-sentence generic theme describing just this particular dream. Regardless of whether it was a long dream or a short one, or whether it contains many details and many different parts, the idea here is to melt it all down into a spiritually philosophical theme sentence that condenses all the detail into the mere essence of a spiritual story line (for example, a woman is trying courageously to _______ but finds herself frustrated by _______).

3. **Bringing the one-sentence theme into the context of the Universal Spiritual Picture**

   Place this dream's theme into the context of your understanding of the Universal Spiritual Picture (i.e., a consciously entrapped soul is providing its personality aspect with a greater understanding of the personality's unconscious habit patterns in order to facilitate the creation of greater harmony between them). Then view this dream's one-sentence theme in the context of what your soul is trying to show you about yourself.

At this point you should have an understanding of the general theme of this dream. You should also have placed that theme in the context of the very purpose and meaning of life on Earth itself, that of creating harmony among our personality, our soul, and the Spark of God within the soul.

4. **Interpreting the dream symbols, one by one**

   Now you are ready to go through the dream symbols, substituting for each just what they mean to you. If you record your dream content on just one side of a page, you will have space to place your meanings and interpretations alongside each symbol. By the time you have completed this, within the context of the Universal Spiritual Picture, you should be receiving a very good idea about which specific habits and which of your subpersonalities are causing inner disharmony.

5. **Forming your understanding of the meaning of the dream and adding your idea of the circumstances that triggered it**

   Having a good idea of the meaning of the dream and knowing that your soul gives you feedback on your actions as quickly as possible, try to determine what circumstances in your daily life (those that occurred the day before you received the dream) caused your soul to offer you this message. It is important to know the outer world situations that cause your various subpersonalities to come out to defend you or help you in some way that now creates negativity with your soul.

6. **Practicing the new habit**

   After you understand the meaning of the dream, you must actually put that understanding into practice or there will be no change in your personality, no increase in inner harmony, and no progress along the path. This must include practicing the related *feelings* that are part of the new habit pattern.

   When you are practicing the new replacement habits in your daily life, you can better prepare yourself beforehand if you recognize and understand which sets of outer world circumstances have previously led to actions on your part that caused you inner disharmony. If you know you are going into such a situation again, you can prepare by clothing yourself in divine attitudes. You can call upon angelic help in remaining centered and in harmony. Forewarned is forearmed.

Summary

As I became familiar with the symbol format and the meanings associated with the appearance of the various subpersonalities in my dreams, my initial reaction to a new character would be something like, "Oh, no! Don't tell me that part of me is somehow like him!" At first it seemed difficult to see certain connections until I learned to get out of my personality, to send my consciousness upward, and to view the scene from above as my higher self or soul. The objectivity that came by choosing such a high, detached perspective made it much easier to see with clear vision which parts of the new character's way of being (that I disliked so much) were also parts of my own personality's behavior patterns at times. The distance (and detachment) created by viewing it from above made it easier to see and accept.

Once we have recognized our negative habits (whether we identify them by using our dreams or some other way), it is now much easier to replace them than I had once believed. Using the new spiritual tools created for the new millennium by some of the Archangels and Ascended Masters in the divine dimensions above makes the releasing and replacement process far easier, smoother, and quicker than it has ever been.

This chapter briefly shows an easy way to understand our common, everyday dreams and to discover the hidden aspects of our personality if we choose to do so. It also shows how our soul works at providing our personality with information that will lead us to create greater inner harmony, peace, and joy.

PART V

Our Changing Perspectives, Seeing From Above

Viewing the Earth School from the perspective of our soul and our Divinity Within

CHAPTER 23

Our Earth School Life as a Theatrical Play

Incarnation in the Third-Dimensional World of Illusion

From the higher perspective of our soul, our Earth School can be seen as a God-created improvisational theatrical stage upon which we have each been given the free will to act out our parts, our lives, in any way we choose. We are permitted to do this over and over again until we find through our own personal experience that we really prefer a divine life, a life of inner harmony, peace, unconditional love, true meaning, and purpose as opposed to that which we have found in any part that we have chosen to play in our repeated performances in the illusion of our Earth School stage.

We may play as many parts as we wish in pursuit of one that brings us the lasting joy and unconditional love we have always wanted. We can try out the experience of fame, perhaps competing with others and being named the greatest whatever in the world. We may try out the experiences of having great beauty, great power, great wealth, or great intellect only to discover before each play is over that none of these roles brought us the lasting unconditional love, meaning, and fulfillment we desired. Each play in which we participate may be very short or very long, but we always know that it will come to an end (due to our false identification as a mortal body and its personality). All life on the Earth School stage is illusory and temporal. None of it is lasting or true.

With the reincarnation feature of the Earth School, all the experiences our personality gains during each play are stored in our real self, our off-stage self, our observer self, our eternal soul self, until the next play begins. Then once again our on-stage personality can utilize all our stored skills and strengths and/or overcome fears and weaknesses that have accumulated from our experiences in our past plays. Again we can choose some part, try out a new role, and learn new skills and abilities that help us on the stage. However, before the play is over our personality always learns that even the new role, which we were so certain would bring us lasting unconditional love and inner joy, did not fulfill our inner needs.

All this is repeated over and over and over again until our personality gains enough wisdom from all the experiences that have been accumulated in its soul to awaken to the Universal Spiritual Picture, to realize, and to know in its heart that in light of all its disillusioning, disharmonious, and painful experiences on the third-dimensional stage, what it most desires of its own free will that which is real, eternal, and divine.

Consciously Creating Inner Harmony

When the personality has awakened to this degree, the soul becomes much more active in the life of the personality, using all its skills and abilities (always in harmony with the Universal Spiritual Laws) to fully awaken the personality to its presence as the personality's Real Self, its True Self, and as an eternal part of God, desiring to return to conscious harmony and love with God once more. The soul will provide the personality with intuitive flashes and nightly dreams that communicate how the soul feels about the personality's daily activities. This provides the personality with the information needed to understand which habit patterns it has unconsciously adopted that cause inner disharmony so that (if it chooses to do so) it can take measures to release them and replace them with new habits that create inner harmony (between the soul and personality).

> *Harmony among our personality, our soul, and the Spark of God within our soul allows us to manifest our Divinity into the outer world while fulfilling our soul's purpose*

As greater harmony is reached among these aspects of our Beingness, the personality begins to know it can receive from its soul, and from the Spark of God within the soul, divine guidance and assistance in all it does. As the personality uses its knowledge of the spiritual path to create greater harmony among itself, its soul, and the Divine Spark of God that lives within the soul: it blends with the soul to such a degree that it becomes relatively transparent to the soul; it becomes One with the soul. At this point the soul is able to manifest the Divinity Within it into the outer world through its harmonious personality with little or no negative discoloring.

In this case the consciousness of the evolved personality has risen and expanded to blend in harmony with the higher consciousness of the soul.

In turn, the soul has been cleared of sufficient residual negativity to bring it into conscious Oneness with the Spark of God Within.

This entity, now living its physical life as a soul guided always by its God/Goddess Within, manifests its divinity into the physical world in its own unique way. Most often this is done in some manner of helping others to help themselves back to conscious Oneness with God. This entity has evolved and become a channel of God's light, God's unconditional love, and God's divine will transmitting these qualities into the outer world, in whatever way fits this unique soul's purpose. This may be by providing help to others in the form of inspiration, higher knowledge, mapping out the way back, or any other of an infinite number of ways. The graduate of the Earth School does this while still having a physical body here on Earth. This entity has evolved consciously to the state of being in this world but no longer of it.

After the death of the mortal body to which the soul was last attached, this evolved soul will Ascend to its natural soul state, the state it knew before it became entrapped in the physical world, the stage world, the third-dimensional world of illusion. The prodigal son or daughter will have returned to his or her true home in the joyful, blissful, unconditionally loving state of conscious Oneness with its God Within, and therefore also with God, the All That Is, including all of God's many minions in the heavenly dimensions above. There this soul will further experience the continuing spiritual evolution of all life while fulfilling various divine missions of its own choosing, perhaps here around Earth or in other parts of the ever-expanding Cosmos.

This entity has now tamed the beast it chose to enter long, long ago and has brought its consciousness up to the level of the soul, freeing itself from its entrapment in the physical world. This one-time actor has now quit the physical world stage that she or he has found to be nothing but illusion and has found a real job, a permanent job in the divine life it once had and lost.

CHAPTER 24

Time, Space, and Reincarnation

Real or Unreal?

Time and space were created by God and God's many minions as necessary aspects for inclusion in the Earth School. Without time and space the Earth School's educational environment could not have included reincarnation or the free will choice of all students to determine when we are ready to return to conscious Oneness with God.

In the reality of the heavenly dimensions above our Earth plane there is no time or space. There is only the present eternal moment. So now and then, while one is down here, the question may arise: are time and space real?

Well, they certainly are real, or seem real, from the perspective of the personalities of those of us incarnated in our physical Earth School world with our third-dimensional perception of life. From the perspective of our identity with our body and its personality, we are born at a specific date and time and in a specific place. A year later we are told that we are one year old even though we may not understand what that means. Later on we can remember things that happened to us when we were at various ages of our lives that we judged as good or bad or just experiences. Forty short years later we are in the midst of our midlife crisis wondering where did it all go, what has it all meant, where is the lasting joy, the unconditional love, and the inner happiness I have been looking for all my life. Where is the true meaning and purpose in my life?

A little while later our mortal body dies and with it dies our temporal personality. Then all our exceptional aptitudes and skills, all our traumatic fears and phobias, and all the other habitual feelings, thoughts, attitudes, beliefs, and actions that we adopted from our outer world learning and conditioning are stored in our eternal soul. A few decades later our soul reincarnates again into the physical body of a new little baby human and we do the physical world life cycle all over again. So, common to us humans is our belief that time and space are real, and from the perspective of our personality selves, from our identity with our body and its personality, time and space do appear to be real, seem to be real, and feel as though they are real.

Time, space, and reincarnation were required for our Earth School environment

The concept of reincarnation first requires the presence of both time and space. The aspects of time, space, and reincarnation together provide us students with unlimited repetitious experiences of disillusionment with the actions and activities of other students who, like us, have not yet evolved to the point of being consistently guided by the God/Goddess Within. The reincarnation cycle continues, whether or not our personality self knows it or believes it, until we awaken at last, in our own good time and of our own free will, to the fact that we really prefer, above all other attractions in the physical world, life in divine conscious Oneness with God again. (The faint memory of our divine life remains stored in our eternal soul.)

When we awaken to the Universal Spiritual Picture, of which our Earth School life is only a tiny part, to the realization that considering all our Earth School experiences we truly prefer the divine life we once knew as souls while we were still in conscious Oneness with God (and all the other many minions of God in the higher divine dimensions), we will be ready to make our free will choice to return to that divine life. We will be ready to make our choice and our commitment to the spiritual path that will help us to evolve more quickly and easily and to return to our rightful place in conscious Oneness with God, in the divine, higher dimensions of heaven above while still having a physical body.

As we progress along our spiritual path, we will evolve our way back to our original, natural soul state of higher consciousness by increasing the harmony among our body's temporal personality, our eternal soul, and the divine Spark of God within our soul. As we move along this path to our soul's higher, more expanded consciousness, we will see and understand from that higher perspective, that time, space, and reincarnation are not real and do not exist in the higher realms of Godness. From that point of view we can see that they were merely created as illusory parts of the third-dimensional Earth School for the benefit of providing us with the personal, painful, experiential evidence we needed in order to make our free will decision to return. We will be able to see that they were created just for us entrapped souls, who without them in our school environment, would have had to remain consciously separated and "lost" from God for all of eternity. Then we will also be able to see, from our own soul's perspective, that they did the job for us.

So, are time and space and reincarnation real?

Yes, from the perspective of us Earth School students, for they were created as part of our third-dimensional, educational environment. They give us the illusions that help us to experience, to grow, to change, and to learn what it is that we truly desire. Of course, they also certainly feel real while we are down here.

No, from the perspective of the souls who have always remained in the higher realms of the Hierarchy of God or those who have graduated from the Earth School and returned to the higher realms of God above. Time, space, and reincarnation are *not* part of the reality of that divine environment. In the heavenly realms of the higher dimensions, there is only the present eternal moment of bliss and harmony, experienced while carrying out various soul missions within the Universe and Cosmos.

Changes in Perspective

During this process, when we have made our choice to return to the divine life in harmony and Oneness with God and when we have made a little progress along the path, we will become increasingly grateful for the existence of the Earth School. We will be increasingly grateful that God created this school environment, just for us, to allow us to come into contact with all the rough and painful experiences inherent in the lower conscious life of a physical body that finally brought us to our conscious awakening of our true preference for our return to the divine life.

As we move further along the path, creating a greater degree of harmony among our human personality, our eternal spiritual soul, and our divine Spark of God Within the soul, we continue to move our consciousness higher and higher. Our perspective changes accordingly. The higher our consciousness, the higher our perspective, and the larger and clearer becomes our vision of the Universal Picture of Life.

When we have moved high enough in consciousness, we can simultaneously see both our life as a human personality in the Earth School (gaining the experience necessary to cause us to move back to conscious Oneness with God) and our life as a soul, as a part of God carrying out our soul's current mission or life purpose through our refined personality.

CHAPTER 25

An Exercize in Awareness

Offered by Melchizedek

Prior to the close of all our readings I always open the door (of free will) to anything the Being of Light who is the source of information for that reading would offer either Cathy or myself for our own higher good on our spiritual path. In chapter 13 I omitted Melchizedek's response to my personal request so I could include it separately as he had suggested. Though this information was given specifically to Cathy and me to help us at the point where we happened to be at that moment on our separate spiritual paths, Melchizedek made it clear that a portion of it would be a useful exercise for *anyone* on the spiritual path.

This is another of the spiritual tools that the higher Beings of Light have created that can be used by us humans to help us through various phases along the path. The creators of such tools watch over them and see that any of us who use them receive the support, from themselves and other Beings of Light, sufficient and appropriate to our specific needs.

After Melchizedek ended the reading I told him that I would put this into practice in my own life, and I would also put it somewhere in the book.

His reply was, *"Put it wherever you feel that it fits best, but it should be blocked* (separated from the rest of the text of the reading) *and given as an exercise in awareness."* So most of the reading is included in chapter 13, but the exercise portion is inserted here.

This is a brief excerpt from a reading by Cathy, on the subject of validating and expanding upon what I had already journaled for chapter 13, from Melchizedek on 03/11/2000.

An exercise in awareness offered by Melchizedek

Indeed, you will do well to remember to call upon all of the assistance that is available including the Angelic Realm and to choose as often as you can to bring joy and lightheartedness into your experience. And when you perceive through your personality or your ego or even through the eyes of your higher self that it is not a particularly joyful experience, then choose to make it one. And do that by simply letting go (of the attempt to control outer world happenings through the personality level of consciousness).

Do not make the attempt to control this phase (of the path). *Allow the highest parts of your own consciousness* (your soul and your Divinity Within) *and those who are in attendance with you, your guides and your Angels, to assist you in flowing through this phase.*

Whenever you find yourself tensing up or feeling frustration or anger or fear or pain, recognize that you are attempting to control (your outer world) *and just stop. Just let go. Step back in consciousness to the core of your being, become your soul, and know that none of these outer world activities have any importance whatsoever in the grand scheme. This is a clue and you may wish to put this in your document. This is a great clue.*

If you are experiencing physical tension, or pain, or disease and if you are experiencing frustration, anger, fear, any level of these, then you are personally, from your personality and your ego, attempting to control that experience (and probably failing in your attempt).

The quickest, most effective solution is to step back, let go, and find the core of your being, for when you are at your core and attuned to your soul so that you are viewing, hearing, feeling, touching, and tasting life through your soul, you will find that there is no importance in the activities that are occurring. You will find that they are not worthy of your focus.

If you will let go and trust to flow through that which is occurring, the Universe in its various manifestations of Angels, Higher Guides, etc. will make the trip smoother, more comfortable, infinitely more peaceful, and more harmonious, and if you will allow it and call upon it, more joyful and joyous as well. Remember that if you are indeed living in the moment, ***THE moment****, you are not likely to be attempting to be in control.*

In This World, but Not Of It

What Melchizidek describes here is a way in which we can shift our personality's consciousness from a focus on unpleasant outer world events or circumstances upward to our soul's higher level of consciousness and perspective. From our soul's perspective, all outer worldly things are experienced as being quite meaningless (in the context of the Universal Spiritual Picture). Our souls are already familiar with this divine, detached state of Being, and it is only our personalities that at first (perhaps) may be out-of-sync.

There are other spiritual tools that will do similar things in meditative states. However, Melchizedek's exercise works while we are out and about in our daily activities in the outer world where our physical body lives.

This is how Christ was able to be "in this world, but not of this world." This is how it is when anyone moves along the path and becomes able to be his or her soul once more, at will, while yet having a physical body. It is like being multidimensional and being aware of all your dimensions, or all your states of consciousness, simultaneously. Being your soul in this way is like being weightless, feeling light and lighthearted, and feeling and being above your body in awareness and understanding.

When we are being our soul, at our soul's level of consciousness, our soul understands that the physical outer world in which our body lives consists primarily of man-made things, circumstances, places, activities, events, etc. The only meaning that any of these outer world things have is what our personality has given them. From the heavenly realms of God, none of these outer world things are seen to have any innate, intrinsic, eternal meaning whatsoever. The only purpose of the outer world is to provide us students with the experiential evidence that in time will cause us to desire to seek to return to conscious Oneness with God.

Melchizedek has provided an exercise that will help those of us who are already on the path, or any who choose the path, to experience a way to resolve the generic human problem of focusing too much upon outer world circumstances that seem to cause us to be fearful, angry, aggressive, defensive, etc. When we practice this exercise enough to make it into a new habit, a new habitual way of being, we too can be in this world and not of it.

We too can become our souls again, gaining mastery of ourselves, mastery of our emotions, and mastery of our thoughts, living in harmony and Oneness with our Goddess/God Within, knowing our purpose in life and fulfilling it in joy and wonder all while still having a physical body. As we learn greater self-mastery, and create greater harmony between our personality and our soul, we can then, through the Universal Laws of Manifestation, cause the Universe to bring that which is in accord with our higher good into our own little world.

When we can do this consistently, we will understand why Christ told us always to turn the other cheek. Forgiving the trespasses of others is the only way to remain at the blissful, detached level of our soul's consciousness attuned to our God/Goddess within. If we permit ourselves to become angry and to focus our attention on the outer world circumstance that seemingly caused our anger, we will already have allowed ourselves to drop down to the level of our personality consciousness again. In doing so we will have immediately lost the blissful feelings of our soul's higher consciousness state of Being.

Our soul knows that no outer world event is worth the loss of the inner bliss. Our personality may not yet understand this because of what it has previously been taught from the outer world to believe, feel, and think. However, our soul certainly understands and if we choose to harmonize the two, our personality can learn it too. Our personality will learn that inner harmony is also for its benefit in the sense that it too will experience the divine feelings of the soul and of the Divinity Within that are part of the greater harmony with the higher aspects within. All aspects of our Beingness experience the benefits of inner harmony.

At our soul level we can recognize the lack of meaning and importance in the transient man-made habit patterns and things of the outer world as compared to the value of the eternal heavenly feelings we experience in our soul state living in harmony with the guidance we receive from our Goddess/God within our soul. Our soul knows that in the real world of the heavens above from whence we all came, one of these states is worthless and the other is priceless. And we are all free to choose which we prefer.

CHAPTER 26

The World Is Perfect

Just As It Is?

For as long as I can remember I have always wanted to be doing something that would make the world a better place rather than just working at a survival job. In one of Cathy's readings by Saint Germain I happened to mention this as a side issue, not directly connected to a question. Nevertheless, Saint Germain replied to my comment saying, "The world is perfect just as it is!"

Well, I didn't think so. From my personality's level of consciousness I could see many things that were obviously "wrong" with the world. Differing degrees of man-made "justice," depending on the wealth of those in court, was only one of perhaps hundreds of other situations that I was certain were "wrong." However, after I mentioned a few of these Saint Germain's reply remained, "The world is perfect as it is."

What did he mean by this? How could the world be perfect when even I could see so many things that were far from perfect?

The Earth School is perfectly fulfilling its mission

His answer to my question was that the Earth School is *perfectly fulfilling its mission.* The mission is and has been to contain an educational environment that would eventually bring the personalities of all humans, to which entrapped souls are attached, to the free will realization that they indeed prefer divine life in the higher consciousness of the heavens within and above over that which they can experience here on Earth.

I could immediately understand this intellectually, but I could not get the consistent feeling of its truth, while carrying out my daily activities, for several years. Why? From the very beginning, eleven years ago, I was able to receive higher information, from within, in a relaxed meditative state of consciousness. However, when I came out of my meditative state I would return (drop down) to my normal personality consciousness again. It took several years of releasing and replacing one set of negative habits after another, creating increased harmony between my personality and my soul, until I could experience being at my soul state of consciousness while carrying out at least some of my daily activities.

The nature of my spiritual progress has been very gradual. My inner harmony has increased by degrees, eventually allowing me to experience my soul's level of higher consciousness while being involved in some outer world activities. These days I can choose to be at my soul state at will and from that higher perspective I can understand, from the feeling level of my soul, precisely what Saint Germain was saying.[1] It may be similar for any human who sincerely chooses to take the path back to conscious Oneness with God.

Pause for a divine note

Before I go on, there is an important point here that my Divinity Within wishes me to make. Just because it took me several years to shift to my soul state while carrying out some of my daily activities does not mean it will take you or anyone else several years. I was extremely overbalanced on the masculine energy side. I was fearful of feeling gentle emotions. I had built many tough shells around my heart to protect me from emotional pain. I could go on, but you can see what I'm saying.

Thenous and Athenarious have stated in a couple of their readings that I am the perfect author for this book. To many readers this may sound like a compliment, but looking at the situation from above, from my soul's detached perspective, I perceive it to mean that I am merely an honest example of some of the benefits that can accrue to anyone, *even from a worst case starting point.*

Some readers will awaken to the Universal Spiritual Picture and almost immediately be able to harmonize their personalities with their respective souls and Sparks of God Within. We are all connected to God and we are all One in God, but we are also each unique in our background experiences. No two souls have ever had the same precise, identical series of experiences. For this reason it is extremely important that you do *not* create a belief inside to the effect that it will take you several years to shift your consciousness upward to your soul. It could happen immediately (as it did in the example of

---

[1] This is not intended to imply that I am able to remain at my soul state at all times, in all places, and in all circumstances. Not yet. I might be able to stay at my soul level most of the time, and I might be able to move up to it at any time but I haven't yet been able to make it a permanent shift and it is not my intention to imply that I have done so. (Though I wish it would happen now!)

Saul of Tarsus). It would be very wise to remain open to the possibility of a rapid shift.

Whether the world is seen as perfect or not depends totally upon the altitude of one's perspective (which, hopefully, is always increasing)

It is easy to see hundreds of things that our personalities would like to be different, to be "better" here on Earth. However, from the higher consciousness and the expanded awareness of our soul's perspective, we can always see, feel, understand, know, and be aware of, the very purpose for which the Earth School environment was created.

Our souls know that if our Earth School life brought us everything that our personalities desired (at their lower level of consciousness) there would be no impetus, no motivation whatsoever to encourage humanity to grow back to Oneness with God. Our souls know that it is a combination of all the seeming "injustices, wrongs, and hurts" that we have experienced at our outer world personality level of consciousness that has motivated us to seek within to find a way to regain our higher consciousness experience with the divine life that we once knew and can still remember in our dream states. Our souls know that it is when we have exhausted our search for divinity in the outer world and still have found it lacking in truth and unconditional love, that we are ready to seek within. It is the pain and disillusionment with the outer world that eventually brings us to the realization that we truly prefer something more divine.

Pain is the great educator (in the school of hard knocks)

The Ancient Wisdom says, "Pain is the great educator." However, the pain of the Earth School is not brought to us by God.

The pain of the Earth School is merely the natural result of unevolved, disharmonious personalities of mortal physical bodies being in contact with and "working out" on other disharmonious personalities. The self-centeredness of the mortal body is the only "evil" on Earth, and that self-centeredness is a natural effect of our being reared as physical beings consciously separated from God. It is the natural effect of not knowing ourselves to be parts of God and connected to God. It is the effect of our having entrapped our souls by playfully allowing them to enter lower conscious mortal, physical bodies long ago.

No pain was artificially added to the Earth School or needed to be. The mere fact of living life as though we were not parts of God, as though we were not capable of being attuned to God and guided by God, is sufficient to create all the discord and "wrongs" we see around us. This predictable discord was seen to be sufficient to cause the disillusionment and pain, which would naturally motivate us all (in time) to desire to return to the Divinity we could still faintly remember.

Earth School pain is brought to us by other humans who, like us, are not yet evolved enough to have brought their personalities into harmony with their souls and their Divinity Within. When any entity reaches the point of evolution in which they have brought their personality into harmony with their soul and with their Divinity Within, they will have changed. At that point they would consciously do nothing to bring harm to themselves or others, for that would immediately diminish or destroy the blissful inner feelings of the peace and unconditional love that are inherent parts of their inner harmony with their Divinity Within.

Rather than causing us pain, it is God and the many minions of God above, who have provided us, the entrapped souls, with a way out from the pain we inadvertently brought to ourselves long ago. Without their gift of evolution, we would have no way to return to our original higher conscious Oneness with God and we would remain lost to God forever.

The most basic Universal Law of the Earth School is that of free will. At any point in time we inhabitants each have the free will to awaken to the Universal Spiritual Picture and to choose the spiritual path back to Oneness and harmony with God, which frees us from the pain. As students we also have the free will to remain in school and to experience anything and everything we desire in our attempt to find divine life in the physical world (where it does not yet exist at humanity's present stage of evolution). Free will allows us to stay here and to experience as much of the pain and disillusionment as we wish until we awaken and are absolutely certain that we desire to return to the divine life in harmony and conscious Oneness with God.

Our soul is real. It is our original and true identity. It is a part of God, and it is eternal. The Divine Spark of God within our soul is also real and eternal. It is our Holy Spirit.

Humankind's bodies and personalities are not eternal. They were unintentionally created by our soul's playful activities with physical life long, long ago. At today's stage of evolution humans still generally identify with their short-lived physical bodies and believe that this is all there is to life. Because of the lack of understanding of a Universal Spiritual Picture across the globe, we humans still behave in quite self-centered manners, bringing pain to ourselves and others while doing whatever our personalities perceive is for our personality's benefit.

We behave in this manner because, in general, we do not yet know the blissful feelings of living in harmony among our personality, our soul, and our Divinity Within. We behave in this manner because, being unaware of the nature of the Universal Laws, we are also largely unaware that by creating inner harmony among our personality, our soul, and our Divinity

Within we achieve the power to create everything our souls desire. This is what living in attunement with God brings us.

Our perspective changes as we awaken and move our personality's consciousness up to the higher consciousness of our soul

As we move into this attunement, we are moving our consciousness upward and becoming our souls once more. We are changing our perspective. We are changing the way we see both ourselves and others. We are changing the way we see life on Earth and the way we see the assistance available in the heavenly realms within and above. In essence, we are changing the way we see and experience everything.

Entities who have evolved and made the transition to being their soul selves again will have no grievances relating to any of the so called "wrongs" ever done against them in their Earth School life, for they will see the effect of these "wrongs" as the factor which motivated their personalities to seek divine conscious Oneness again.[2] These enlightened souls will feel gratitude for all the "wrongs" and will joyfully express their forgiveness to everyone for bringing them the painful, outer world circumstances which helped motivate their personality to choose, of its own free will, to seek the path back to conscious Oneness with God. These souls will forgive and bless everyone for bringing their personalities the painful but supremely beneficial lessons which provided them with the impetus to desire to return to being their soul self, their true self, complete and whole once more in divine harmony with God.

Again and again you will find a tremendous difference between the perspective of your (accidentally created) personality and your God-created eternal soul. The values of the personality have been largely man-made. The values of your soul are in harmony with those of God. God has given us all the free will to choose either.

The Earth School challenge, if we choose of our own free will to accept it, is to bring our short-lived personality into harmony with our eternal soul and with our Spark of God Within and then, by receiving divine intuitive guidance from our Spark of God Within, to manifest that divinity into the outer world in the joyful and meaningful fulfillment of our soul's purpose. Our bringing more divinity into our Earth School will change its atmosphere toward the devine.

When we have created sufficient harmony between our personality and our soul to make the shift to higher consciousness, we will see and

[2] This would be similar to someone who had been cured of a lifelong, disabling infection, by an antibiotic injection, complaining about the pain of the needle.

experience everything in a different light because of our higher perspective and our more expansive consciousness. All the events experienced and perceived by our personality as wrong, unjust, painful, and unfair will be seen by our soul as the painful blessings that motivated our personality to awaken and to choose the spiritual path back to the Divine Life.

So, is the world, the Earth School, perfect just as it is?

No, from the perspective of the *personality,* for from its limited consciousness we still experience and see many things in our environment that are unfair, painful, and unjust.

Yes, from the perspective of our *soul* (and its *Divinity Within*), for the Earth School environment is perfectly fulfilling its mission. The Earth School can be seen to allow for the free will evolution of the personality into harmony with the soul and with the Divinity Within and thus for our return to conscious Oneness with God, while still having a physical body.

The Earth School environment encourages, permits, and assists us to make progress along our spiritual evolutionary path, to find our way back to our original soul state in conscious Oneness with God, and to become conscious companions with God again.

As we find our way home as our soul selves, we become conscious companions with our own God/Goddess Within and with God, the All That Is. We become companions with God and all the other minions of God (i.e., the Angels, Archangels, Higher Guides, Ascended Masters, and all other Beings of Light in the Hierarchy of God), who are also in the state of conscious Oneness. We expand our awareness and realize that we now have all these Beings of Light as our true divine friends. They help us whenever we ask.

As we find our way home by bringing our personality into harmony with our soul, we become able to receive divine guidance from our God/Goddess Within. Then we can know and joyfully fulfill our soul's purpose while manifesting the Divinity Within our soul into our outer world. Manifesting our divinity while fulfilling our soul's purpose here on Earth is part of the spiritual path.

Ultimately, the Earth School permits us to evolve to the state of Ascension where, after the death of our mortal body, we, as our souls living in our Bodies of Light, can once more joyfully carry out and fulfill our choice of the various missions, which are available in the Universe or Cosmos, and do so in the blissful, divine states of Oneness with God, the All That Is.

Yes, the Earth School is perfect just as it is. And we can make it even better!

If it is perfect now, how can we possibly make it better?

As more humans awaken to the existence of the Universal Spiritual Picture and understand the true meaning and purpose of human lives on Earth, more will choose the spiritual path back to conscious Oneness with God. The spiritual path creates harmony between the personality and the soul. The personality's increasing awareness of and harmony with the soul expand its consciousness and raise it to the level of our soul's higher consciousness.

At our soul's level of consciousness, we can all receive divine guidance from the Spark of God within our soul. We can learn the nature of our soul's purpose or mission in life. As we fulfill our soul's mission in the harmony we create among our personality, soul, and Divinity Within, we manifest divinity into the Earth School. Each evolving entity brings more divinity into the Earth School and simultaneously reduces the disharmony and pain its unevolved, uncleared, and disharmonious personality formerly caused.

So, in a decade or two, there will be much less pain on Earth caused by disharmonious personalities and much more divinity manifested by those who have achieved harmony and conscious Oneness with God. *This is how we humans can make the perfect Earth School better!*

Another major factor that will dramatically change the Earth School toward the divine

The Earth School is evolving just as are its inhabitants. The soul of the planet Earth itself is evolving and moving from the third to the fourth dimension. Because of this, its aura is increasing in its vibrational rate. This increasing vibrational rate brings the Earth and all its inhabitants closer to the vibrational rate of the heavens above. This is why so many more humans (who desire it) find it easier now to receive divine guidance from above, through their natural intuitional paths.

But, besides making it easier to receive divine guidance and true information from the higher realms within and above, the increasing vibrational rate has another very dramatic effect on the inhabitants of the Earth School. Each human lives (or exists) at its own unique level of vibration. That level of vibration is perfectly proportional to the level of inner harmony the entity has created between its personality and its soul (and the divinity within the soul). The higher the degree of harmony between the personality and the soul, the higher the vibrational level of the individual.

The vibrational rate of the planet is increasing and will continue to increase until it has moved fully into the fourth dimension, perhaps two decades from now. This means that humans who choose to do nothing to increase their own inner harmony by bringing the personality into harmony with the soul (and Divinity Within) will lose ground, relative to the increasing vibrational rate of the planet, causing them even greater inner disharmony and resultant disease. (All disease is caused by disharmony between the personality and the soul.) By making the choice to do nothing, these entities, of their own free will, will be increasing the disparity between the vibrational level of the planet and themselves.

What does this situation mean to human life on Earth? Only that within the next decade or so many humans will find themselves unable to sustain life on Earth. Many will experience greater inner disharmony in the form of various diseases. This will not occur as an edict from above. The evolution of a planet is similar to the evolution of any other soul. To evolve upward, it must naturally increase its vibrational rate to become closer to that of the divine dimensions above.

Viewed from above, regarding humanity, there is no coercion in this matter. All humans are given the free will to live life as they choose. It is perfectly okay to choose to do nothing to create harmony between the personality and the soul.

It has already occurred that souls of a lower evolutionary vibrational rate can no longer incarnate in the Earth School. To be able to sustain life in a new baby body, a soul must already be well past its involutionary stage and well into its evolutionary stage. This situation will continue for the next one thousand years.

The net effect of all this is that due to the increasing vibratory rate of the planet there will be more harmony in the Earth School in the future because souls still in the involutionary stage will not be able to sustain life here; they will not be able to incarnate. In the future here in the Earth School, there will be much less pain caused by disharmonious personalities (i.e., those with habit patterns of aggression, competition, fear, anger, judgment, impatience, etc.). There will be much more kindness, gentleness, and unconditional love manifested by those who have achieved harmony and conscious Oneness with the God/Goddess Within.

But if it was the pain experienced in the Earth School that provided the impetus that caused us to seek the divine, what happens when the disharmony and pain are diminished?

As evolution continues, the impetus, the motivation will change. As those who evolve manifest the attributes of divinity in fulfilling the soul's purpose, their demonstrations of divinity and their daily expressions of inner joy, unconditional love, and soul fulfillment will inspire and attract others to emulate that divinity in their own lives, in their own unique ways.

As opposed to the motivation of pain, which drives us away from that which is painful toward seeking something more divine, it will be the demonstrations of divinity manifested by evolved souls that motivate, inspire, and attract others to seek the benefits of conscious Oneness for themselvees. With evolution in place, everything evolves, including methods of motivation.

So all in all, these are the ways the Earth School will change for the "better" in the future. And as it evolves and changes it will always be "perfect just as it is" for it will always be fulfilling its Universal Spiritual Mission to provide an educational environment that allows us entrapped souls a way to evolve ourselves from the lower consciousness of the physical bodies to which we attached ourselves long ago back to complete conscious Oneness with our Spark of God within, and God, the All That Is.

APPENDIX A

More on Spiritual Tools

A spiritual tool is a method or process created by Ascended Masters, Archangels, or other Beings of Light to make it easier for us humans to free ourselves of our negative habit patterns and our Earthbound attachments. The Beings of Light who create these tools always stand behind them and see that the necessary etheric and spiritual dynamics are taken care of whenever any human uses them.

It is recommended by all Beings of Light that in all such exercises and in all meditations we use our very highest imaginative powers. Some readers may have to go back in time to recall the strength of the imagination that was perfected before seven years of age, when we were still living as our souls and before we became "educated" by our outer world environment to believe that we are only our body and its personality. If use of the imagination seems strange to you, please remember Christ's saying that unless we become as little children again we shall not enter into the Kingdom of Heaven. It is not well known to the masses of humankind, but the imagination is one of the most powerful tools that we can use for creation through the Universal Laws of Manifestation.

If we were still our souls, living in our bodies of light instead of these physical bodies, we would have no use for these spiritual tools. Whatever we wished to create, we would create using our soul's natural skills and abilities in harmony with our Spark of God Within, and with God, the All That Is. But as humans, we have been consciously separated from those abilities for—well,—a long, long time. As our personality selves we have no remembrance of those creative skills.

Use of these spiritual tools (of our own free will) helps us to refresh our memories relating to our soul's creative powers. They give us experience in using our imagination to visualize what is described in the tool and to declare our inner intentions to our Divinity Within and God's many minions. If we were already being our soul selves, that is all that would be required to manifest anything that was in harmony with the higher good, the Universal Good.

However, living as our personalities we lack awareness of many of our soul's innate abilities, as yet. Use of these various tools does more than bring us the releasing and replacing results we seek. It also gives us the practice we need in focusing on our faith, our belief that we are indeed parts of God, and the realization that God and God's minions have the power to bring us what we seek when we are on the path back. The tools give us practice in rediscovering the power of our imagination in the act of creation.

Using our imaginative powers, we can visualize in our mind that which the spiritual tool describes. This will immediately create it in the ethers, in the etheric realm (above the physical realm). If we can hold that visualization long enough and strong enough, the Universe can use it in accordance with the Universal Law of Manifestation to create it in our own little world down here in the third dimension.

Note that *visualization* here includes holding the feelings, thoughts, attitudes, and beliefs associated with that image. In the act of creation, it is our feelings that provide the power and our thoughts that hold the image.

Note also that *Universe* includes the Archangels, Ascended Masters, and other Beings of Light whose missions are to assist humankind's spiritual evolution back to Oneness.

In this way we are gaining awareness of our old innate soul skills and abilities. We are growing in our awareness of who we really are and of the assistance available from a much larger spiritual world than we learned of down here. We are learning or relearning the power, the value of our imagination, which our outer world has taught us to be valueless but which the Universal Law of Manifestation uses to bring us that which we hold in our hearts and minds. In short, we are getting practice in many things that will make the path back to harmony with our soul and Oneness with our God/Goddess Within so much easier and quicker.

Enough on that. Here are some of the tools that did not fit in as part of the book itself, but that I wanted to include because of their usefulness. I am adding them here for reference purposes.

This is an excerpt from a reading by Cathy, on spiritual tools, received from Saint Germain on 9/04/00.

Welcome beloved and blessings be upon you. This is St. Germain.

In the time in which you now find yourself on the planet, it is useful and accepted perhaps to release and replace single items, single thought processes, single emotional responses. But in truth, it is much more appropriate and much simpler perhaps to release negativity or to release attachments generically, without focusing on a particular one. Do you understand?

✦ Yes.

And so here are two exercises that are quite beneficial.

The vacuum tool of Archangel Michael, a very generic tool for releasing and replacing

One is that of calling upon Archangel Michael. Call him to come to you and to remove all negativity from your being. And you can choose to have him do this from the physical, and then the emotional, and then the mental, or you can choose to have him do this from the entire being at one time.

It is helpful to visualize or to experience (to feel), *if one is not proficient in visualization at the time, Archangel Michael's presence above the head and inserting through the crown chakra something on the order of a vacuum cleaner hose. Have him vacuum out all negativity, all grayness, and all darkness within the body, the emotions, the mind, and the entire aura.*

Be certain that there is the experience (feeling) *or visualization of this clearing, this cleansing being done all the way down into the toes and into the fingers, so that there is an entire clearing, an entire cleansing of the physical being, the emotional body, the mental body, and the entire aura when this is being accomplished. This may actually take a very brief time.*

Afterwards, do whatever is most comfortable for self in terms of visualizing this activity being completed. Once that is done, then the power is reversed (using your imagination, flip the switch and have it blow the other way) *and white light, pure white light, flows into the being at all levels from the same hose. Do you understand?*

✦ Yes.

And in this way there is the clearing not only of attachments per se but of all negative thought patterns, negative feelings, and negative emotions, perhaps even those that are unconscious to the entity.

Another breathwork tool, also very generic

Another tool is to simply breathe in with some force. Breathe in through the crown chakra. Breathe in pure white light and as that light circulates through the being, on the out breath, breathe out all negativity. Breathe out anything untoward, anything out of harmony with the divinity within.

Be certain to breathe out through the feet, through the soles of the feet and down into the Earth, for the Earth itself is a great neutralizer. It takes negativity and neutralizes it totally, turning it into a positive energy force.

This breathwork tool can be used as often as one feels it is necessary, but there is a recommendation that it be done at least each morning for a period of ten to fourteen days and if that does not seem complete enough, then for a period of thirty days.

Now both of these tools can be used to cleanse the whole being but they are both also effective if a particular emotion, thought pattern, or even a physical ill is troubling one. And then the breath can be used to specifically expel through the feet that thought pattern, emotional feeling or blockage, or physical issue.

Also Archangel Michael can be called upon to remove just one particular issue.

A tool for relaxing and centering

Often prior to either of the tools being used, if there is time and if the place is appropriate, then can the breath be drawn in through the nose until the lungs are completely full with some force. And then allow the breath to simply slip out. Do not breathe it out. Do not push it out. Simply, in the process of relaxing the being, allow the breath to escape. Do this three to ten times and you will find yourself quite relaxed, quite at peace, and generally quite centered.

Now the tools for releasing can be used in any setting. It does not have to be one of quiet or even one where the entity can close his or her eyes. As soon as there is the awareness of negativity, sadness, anger, fear, there can be the releasing of that through the breathwork, and through calling upon Archangel Michael.

Another releasing and replacing tool recommended by Saint Germain

And there is another tool that is quite helpful and that is the tape, the cassette tape, made by Doreen Virtue, which is called "Healing With the Angels." This is a guided meditation. But the process described on the tape may be used without the tape and without the time of the guided meditation, which is approximately twenty-five minutes.

The process is to call upon the angels to be with you and to request them to place in a silver bucket that they hold, anything that you wish to release. And the angels then take that bucket away.

The angels either disperse that material into the ethers or into the violet flame, where it is transmuted into more positive substance. And having given this to the angels, you then ask the angels to surround you with white or golden light and you breathe that into your entire being. You may breathe this in through your heart chakra or through your crown chakra, whichever seems most appropriate to you intuitively.

There are in fact as many variances of these spiritual tools as there are beings. And we recommend that there be the trying of them all. For it depends entirely on what the entity responds to best. Try them on and see how they work. See how comfortable one is with them.

And it may be that one particular tool is better at one time and another for another instance. But the entity should allow intuition to guide this. And if there is the stress (and there may be in some, over choosing a tool), be aware that it does not really matter what you use because the important factor is the intent, the intent to release and the intent to replace negativity with something that is akin to the divinity within.

Indeed. One could merely say "I release this and I replace it with divine love or divine peace or divine wisdom," whatever feels most appropriate. (If we were already living as our soul selves, this is all that would be required.) *The point of the tools is to have something in which the entity can have faith and trust. For if there is not the* ***inner faith****, if there is not the* ***inner belief*** *that in fact there has been the releasing and the replacing,* ***then whatever exercise is used is an exercise in futility****. There must be the faith.*[1]

Habit patterns can grow back

It is also important to understand that using these tools does not mean that these things will be gone forever because the (personality) *mind will allow them to return if it is a habit pattern. And they may need to be released again. In fact, it is not unusual when an entity is working on something such as anger or fear that there will be as many as fifty releases in a day.*

The important thing is to know that whenever the entity again experiences that from which he or she desires to release or detach, it is time once more to verbalize, whether internally or in spoken words, the releasing and replacing of that thought, feeling, or whatever. Replacing can always be done by simply breathing in the white light, the violet light, the golden light, and in some cases the emerald green light if this is a healing process. Do you understand?

✦ Absolutely.

It is also important that people be given every shred of information that will allow them not to judge themselves. It is so very important for them to understand that after using an exercise, any particular exercise, if a sense of anger or fear comes up again in the next day or the same day or the next week, they have not failed. It merely means that this is a strong habit pattern and it needs more application of the healing tool.

Another tool on tape by Doreen Virtue

For those who are working on clearing, cleansing, detaching, severing attachments, or healing, we also highly recommend the use of the tape "Chakra Clearing" by Doreen Virtue. Using side number 1 in the morning and side number 2 in the evening as a discipline activity over a period of fourteen days is extremely helpful, together with all other tools. It is also helpful when one

---

1 If you remember, faith was also a key factor in the healings of Christ. He would always ask those who would be healed if they *believed* he could heal them, if they had *faith* in the healing process. For if they did not, there was no reason to go further. Their lack of faith would preclude any healing he might do.

is working on moving forward along the path of spiritual growth and finds oneself temporarily blocked or finds oneself in the illusion of being blocked.

***Forgiveness** is one of the most advantageous activities that an entity can use, and forgiving **self** has great importance. For indeed we find that it is difficult to truly forgive others if one is not able or in the habit of forgiving self.*

✦ Archangel Michael spoke at length on the fact that, in my own words, if a person wants to create an attachment they need only to hold a grievance of some sort.

Indeed.

✦ And if they want to get rid of it they need only forgive the grievance.

*Correct. And with your forgiveness, **replace the grievance with love** for there is nothing stronger and nothing more healing than love given out to the heart chakra of him with whom you have a grievance, or one who causes you to feel aggrieved.*

*For know this and know it well; never, never is an emotion or a thought process that comes from you truly based on **anything external** to self.* (Meaning that always, always the reaction habit pattern of negativity lies **within us**.) *If there is an activity or something external to self that brings up a sense of fear or anger or grievance, then look **within self** to see why this is true. For that which is occurring externally is not the cause of that which occurs internally. One must always look within self. Healing is always within one's own power because the entire healing process is done within self.*

Note to the Reader

I am inserting here a short journaling from my soul that attempts to clarify Saint Germain's point before we go on.

The true, real, and original cause of all our internal negative reactions to external situations (that we commonly consider the "cause") is a negative habit pattern of some sort that we have picked up and adopted from our outer world, man-made education and conditioning. Our personality may consider this unconscious inner reaction our natural way. It is not!

It may be seen from above as the learned way of the personality but it is not the way of our soul attuned to its Divinity Within. This difference is the root cause of our inner disharmony whenever we allow our personality's anger habit (or other negative habits) to explode.

We are truly parts of God and therefore we have the ability and the power to respond to external occurrences in Godlike and Goddess-like ways if we so choose. We have the power to create within ourselves these new divine ways. In choosing to create these, we are moving ourselves upward in consciousness toward becoming our souls again, attuned to and guided by our God/Goddess Within.

This ends the formal journaling on this matter and we return back to Saint Germain's original excerpt.

Empowerment

It is important for the reader to understand that he or she has within himself or herself all that is needed to complete the inner healing or the severing of attachments. There is nothing external that is required (because our God/Goddess lies within us). *Each entity is empowered to heal his or her own life experience, entirely.*

And so ***there is empowerment****. This is extremely important. It is something that those new on the path often are unable to recognize, realize, conceive of, or have an awareness of.* ***There is empowerment.*** *No other living entity, or even one who is not in the flesh, not incarnated at the time, has control except when that is* ***allowed*** *to occur and even that is a choice and a function of the entity herself or himself.*

In other words, if we had already awakened to the realization that we are truly souls who are parts of God, it would be clear to us that no external influence could ever have the power to overcome our soul's will or the will of our Spark of God Within. It is only our personality's consciousness that still believes in victimization due to its man-made education and conditioning. It is also only our personality that may believe that external assistance is required to release the old habits and replace them with the new. However, while we are still in our personality's level of consciousness here in the Earth School, these spiritual tools can be of great help in moving us upward, quickly and easily.

This begins a series of excerpts from a reading by Cathy,
on spiritual tools, received from Augmenton
(an Ascended Master) on 4/13/97.

A fatigue tool

Another tool that you may wish to use when you are fatigued, when you are tired, particularly when you are feeling a sense of falling asleep (and you do not wish to do so) is to breathe in through the mouth, something like (a steam engine)*—in, out, in, out, in, out, in, out—in a more rapid manner. This will energize the body, energize the consciousness, and is much more beneficial than caffeine for staying awake, for increasing energy.*

A four-way forgiveness tool

Then there will be the one of forgiveness. This is a very powerful tool and one that is very useful to entities in this time in your third dimension. And this would be used in a quiet state (and it need not be a state of meditation; you may offer that these things may be done in a state of reverie, for those who are not currently meditators).

In the quiet state, visualize being with an entity from whom you need forgiveness or to whom you feel that you should offer forgiveness. Say to that other entity "I forgive you for (whatever the offense has been)." Then also ask for forgiveness of self for taking offense, or for holding a grudge, a negative thought, or a pain of any kind, in relationship to this other entity. So there is forgiveness given to the other and sought for self from the other.

Then ask forgiveness from the Godhead, from the Universal Consciousness, for both yourself and the other person.

And you can make these words more attractive, more flowing.

✦ So in the forgiveness tool, there is:

- *our forgiveness of the other person*
- *forgiveness sought from the other person*
- *forgiveness sought from the Godhead for ourselves*
- *forgiveness sought from the Godhead for the other person*

✦ I understand that it doesn't really matter whether the other person forgives us or not.

It matters only in your visualization. You visualize that they ***do*** *forgive you! And then that is, in effect, the* ***truth*** *in the etheric realm. In the third dimension it matters not. Also, as offered by Saint Germain, it is highly beneficial to send love with the forgiveness as an additional healing agent.*

A self-esteem tool

Another tool, which is quite effective and very simple to use, is to stand before the mirror and look self directly into the eye, and state with clarity, "I love myself unconditionally. I love myself without reservation" And do this (repeat this) perhaps ten times, preferably in the morning upon arising but at any time during the day that it occurs to the entity to use this.

For we find that for most of those who are incarnated in the third dimension at this time there is a lacking of self-love and self-appreciation. Self-worth, if you will.

✦ Yes, it seems as though anyone who does not have that problem is truly an exception.

Indeed, that is quite correct.

Summary

So now you have the latest on the quickest and easiest ways to make progress along the spiritual path, the easiest ways to release and replace negative attachments, negative habit patterns that no longer suit who you are now and who you are becoming. As Saint Germain has said "There are as many variations of these as there are beings, so it matters little which you use. Whatever you find most comfortable is best for you."

Using these shortcut methods as opposed to those involving voluminous, detailed, personality mind analysis and the understanding of all the negatives from all our past lifetimes (just to discover the reasons that we adopted them) can reduce the time required to return to Oneness with God by many decades, perhaps by many lifetimes, and can reduce the pain factor to an absolute minimum. As it has been given, at this point so near the New Age changes, there is no longer time for the slower approach.

We must play our part in the process by our practice of the new positive replacement habits. The new tools can and will remove any and all past life negativity. However, you and I are the only ones who can create the new habits in ourselves that bring our personality closer in harmony with our soul and our God/Goddess Within.

APPENDIX B

Books and Other Materials

Recommended by the Archangels and Ascended Masters in our readings

The following materials will be beneficial to those who are seeking additional information:

1. Sanaya Roman's book, *Opening to Channel.*
2. Sanaya Roman's book, *Soul Love*
3. Doreen Virtue's tapes, *Chakra Clearing and Healing With The Angels.*
4. *A Course in Miracles*

This is an excerpt from a reading by Cathy from Saint Germain on 03/31/01.

Welcome Beloved, this is Saint Germain.

✦ Good afternoon, Saint Germain. I am finishing up book one, *Who Am I and Why Am I Here?* The only part I feel is not finished is appendix B. There are only a few books mentioned. Would you like to mention more to the readers?

A complete list would be extremely long for there is much information that has been provided that is relevant and useful to the seeker. Keep in mind that different entities, different beings are drawn to different sources. They will be drawn to those that are most compatible to the path they are taking or with their current state of consciousness and perspective. And so you must caveat any list that you put into your book, ***by saying that it is not all-inclusive****.*

Certainly we would recommend the works of H.P. Blavatsky, Alice Bailey, the Theosophical Society, Leadbeater, and Besant.

The books of Rudolph Steiner.

The works of Deepak Chopra.

All the books by Sanaya Roman. Everything that has been published by Sanaya Roman or by her in conjunction with Duane Packer fits exceedingly well. Also we would specifically mention their tape series on "Divine Will" (there are two parts to that now), and their tape series on "Awakening the Light Body." Recommend the Luminescence newsletter (created by Sanaya and Duane). All of the Luminescence material is applicable and it depends on the particular inclinations of the entity who is seeking such material.

The Light Shall Set You Free.

Also the works of Dan Millman, Neale Donald Walsch, and Wayne Dyer in his later offerings, particularly his cassette tape album of "Manifest Your Destiny," and his books, You'll See It When You Believe It, Real Magic, *and* Your Sacred Self.

Any and all of the myriad books on Angels that have been provided. Especially the books titled, The Angels Within Us, *and* Ask Your Angels. *The angelic books by Taylor.*

*All the books by Doreen Virtue—*Divine Guidance, The Lightworkers Way, *and* Divine Prescriptions *as well as her tapes.*

The books of Chris Griscom and those of Shirley MacLaine.

There are a number of books by Mark Thurston available from the A.R.E. (Association for Research and Enlightenment) bookstore in Virginia Beach, Virginia. Also the biography of Edgar Cayce by Thomas Sugrue, There Is a River. *You might recommend the A.R.E. bookstore (the Metaphysical and the Angelic sections) for there are many who would pursue dreams, as a part of their path.*

Those who would pursue healing will find Hands of Light *and* Light Emerging *to be beneficial. Also the books by the McGareys, both physicians.*

Books on Reiki

All of the Saint Germain books that have been published

Jesus and Mastership

The Celestine Prophecy *will appeal to many.*

Books on Shamanism and drumming

You Can't Afford the Luxury of a Negative Thought *and* Love, Medicine, and Miracles

The Impersonal Life, The Way Out, The Way to the Kingdom

Books by Benjamin Crème will appeal to many.

Joel Goldsmith's Practicing the Presence *and his other books on* Meditation *and* Spiritual Growth.

And these truly are only samples of the vast array of printed material. Is that sufficient?

✦ Oh, sure. Whatever you think.

Each seeker has a unique path and many will have different interests. The most important information to offer is that an entity should follow his or her intuition and any synchronicity that appears in their experience, such as a

book that jumps out at them, one that is given to them, or perhaps one that they stumble across.

✦ Okay. Well, I thank you.

You are very welcome and if you have no further questions we offer you our light and our love and our assistance as you wish it. And we are through for now.

APPENDIX C

An Abbreviated Version of the Universal Spiritual Picture

The Meaning and Purpose of Human Life in the Earth School

God's Creation of All Souls

In the beginning there was only God, the All That Is. God was spirit. God was everywhere, in all Galaxies and all Universes within the entire Cosmos, not just on planet Earth. God was everything. There was only God.

Creation occurred before the individuation of souls. All of creation had occurred throughout the Universe and the Cosmos before the individuation of souls. The planet Earth had been created and already contained the mineral, vegetable, and animal kingdoms.

And after all of this had been completed, God still found it unsatisfying because it did not provide companionship with Beings of like minds and hearts. Therefore, as the last of the major creations and for the purpose of companionship, God created individuated souls.

God desired to have companionship with those who had the opportunity to choose to be One with the Father, One with the Creator. For this reason God created all souls with free will.

God created all souls from God's Beingness, so all souls have a divine Spark of God, of Godness, of Goddessness, of absolute Goodness at the center of their beings. God individuated Itself to create souls. All souls were perfect and divine, whole and complete. All souls knew themselves to be parts of God. All souls were completely aware of the Spark of God within them and lived in perfect harmony with that Divinity Within. All were aware of their individual connection to God and also to all other facets or aspects or minions of God. All souls were etheric, spiritual, not having physical bodies. They lived in individual bodies comprised of light.

Most of these individuated souls remained in conscious Oneness with God in the higher dimensions of divine life as Angels and Archangels, volunteering for and carrying out various missions that happened to come up around the Universe. However, some souls chose to play with existing physical animal life to see how it would feel to be physical. These playful souls inserted themselves into existing animal bodies. At first the game was just temporary and there was no harm done, no permanent loss of consciousness. However, some stayed in the physical bodies too long.

The Entrapment

These latter souls began to *identify* consciously with their newly acquired physical bodies and the personalities of those bodies. They began to take on the lower consciousness of the personality minds of the physical bodies to which they had lightheartedly attached themselves. They began to forget their true nature and character as divine Beings of Light, as parts of God in the Hierarchy of God's minions. Eventually, they lost all conscious memory of their true identities as souls and of how to get back to their original soul identities.

At this point they totally identified with the physical body and personality. Now they were consciously entrapped in physical life, feeling separated in consciousness from God (as opposed to feeling the rapport of the higher conscious Oneness they had experienced as souls). This was the nature of the inadvertent, unintentional "fall" of humankind.

It was like any group of children whose only intent was to play, having a wonderful time enjoying a new experience, but eventually finding themselves in a situation from which they could not escape without higher help—perhaps like finding themselves accidentally locked in their basement play area after they tired of their play.

Having forgotten their original identities as souls and also of the way to return to their original state, these souls were totally, hopelessly entrapped in the lower consciousness of the personality minds of the physical bodies with which they now identified. This was not part of God's plan!

God's Design and Creation of the Earth School

When God, and God's many minions in the heavens above, saw the dilemma into which these souls had entrapped themselves and from which there was now a *zero possibility* for any to return without assistance, they designed and created an educational environment which would allow all entrapped souls eventually to free themselves from their limited physical life, if and when they chose to do so.

The design of the educational environment was required to include the *free will* choice of each entrapped soul to return to his or her true state of conscious Oneness with God (or not) because God had given souls free will at their original creation.

The way out of our conscious entrapment also required God's creation of the cycles of involution and evolution placed within an educational environment (the Earth School). The educational environment would allow us entrapped souls eventually to learn, through our own free will experiences, whether we truly preferred our limited, illusory, and pain-filled physical world life or the Divine Life we had once known in our bodies of light, in full conscious Oneness and harmony with God in our original soul state.

Involution is the path of increasing involvement with and attachment to all aspects of the material, outer world, physical life with which we choose to experiment in our predictable search for lasting joy, unconditional love, meaning, purpose, and fulfillment. Evolution is the path of awakening to the larger Universal Spiritual Picture followed by the ever decreasing involvement and attachment to outer world physical life and the increasing involvement with our inner world spiritual growth back to conscious Oneness with God.

A planet was chosen to play the part of the educational environment. To make the story as short as possible, I will say here that the planet Earth was chosen to become the school for entrapped souls. In addition to the major concepts of involution and evolution, several Universal Laws and other features were added to the environment as educational devices to assist all entrapped inhabitants to find their way back to conscious Oneness with God. Among these were the Universal Laws of Free Will, Manifestation, and Grace, together with other educational features such as reincarnation, Karma, prayer, meditation, and so forth.

Together these features would assist the Earth School students to experience all they ever desired to experience of physical life, lifetime after lifetime. They could then determine for themselves, of their own free will, from the *personal evidence* provided by their mortal life experiences, whether they preferred the limited physical world life they now knew or the eternal, unlimited, higher conscious, divine life as souls in conscious Oneness with God.

Involution

Involution could be called the "way in" to total involvement with physical world life. It is the path of increasing involvement and attachment to all aspects of physical, outer world life on Earth.

The entrapment took place millions of years ago in third-dimensional time. In essence, the entrapment created what were to become human animals as opposed to true animals. It took place before there were any human animals. If you object to the term human animal being used to describe our physical bodies and their personalities, please consider that there are only three generally recognized categories of physical existence: animal, vegetable, and mineral. However, humans are now distinguished from true animals.

The entrapment of divine souls in existing physical animal bodies had created a new form of physical life on Earth. True animals are all created having group souls (i.e., the group of all otters share one "otter" soul, the group of all zebras share one common "zebra" soul, etc.). The entrapment created a form in which an eternal, divine, individuated soul was now attached to a mortal animal body (which had an ego and was not divine). The difference in souls is the primary difference between true animals and humans.

It was God's creation of the Earth School's features of involution and evolution, that provided us entrapped individuated souls with a separate path of evolution from that of the existing true animals. While the true animals kept their own path of evolution (with a group soul as their connection to the higher realms), we were given a new evolutionary path (due to our already having an entrapped, individuated soul attached). Except for the creation of this new path of evolution, we humans would have been lost to God forever.

Not that it means much, but by today's standards we humans are much more beautiful than we once were, thanks to evolution. I add this just to bring a touch of realism to the picture of our original entrapment and the enormous length of third-dimensional time involved. We have evolved physically, emotionally, and consciously. We have arrived at the point where we are now (at the beginning of the Golden Age) ready to make a quantum leap upward in consciousness, moving our evolving consciousness from the level of our body's personality mind upward to that of our original soul's mind. (See the front cover for a symbolic representation of this transition.)

The story of involution continues with the entrapped souls identifying with the bodies and the personalities to which they had attached themselves, becoming totally focused on the many aspects of the outer world life going on around them, and losing conscious awareness of their inner connection to God. Involution allows for all humans to experiment with and to experience, lifetime after lifetime, of their own free will, every possible outer world way of finding lasting unconditional love, inner joy, fulfillment, and meaning in life here in the Earth School. Obvious experimental attempts may include the seeking of fame, glory, riches, alcohol, drugs, sex, and other hobbies.

However, all of these outer world experiments are futile and doomed to disillusionment and failure, for that which humankind seeks can be found only in the soul's higher consciousness in Oneness with God. In general, humankind is currently living at the personality level of consciousness where the source of lasting unconditional love does not yet exist. In the Earth School, even when an entrapped soul finds what is called outer world "success" of the grandest nature, he or she eventually finds that particular type of success to be hollow, superficial, short-lived, and without true meaning and purpose in and of itself. (Our bodies and our personalities all age and die).

Nevertheless, this futile outer world search fulfills a need of all Earth School students. Over time, it provides each human with the personal, experiential evidence needed to cause her or him to cease the seeking of eternal unconditional love, joy, meaning, and purpose in outer world activities and to begin seeking them in the only place that hasn't yet been searched, the world within. The world within is the door to the soul's higher consciousness where unconditional love and enlightenment exist.

When, through many lifetimes of searching in the outer world, the personality of the entrapped soul has tried it all and found all outer world activities lacking in lasting unconditional love, joy, and fulfillment, the personality may, in its disappointment and disillusionment, give up the outer world search for a moment.

It is just such a moment of a personality's giving up the outer world search, that allows one's soul an opening through which to make its presence known to the personality and to attempt to influence the personality to awaken to the vast spiritual life that exists behind and above the Earth School's outer world activity. Repeated personal experience with disillusionment can cause the personality to cease or to pause in its search for lasting happiness in the outer world and to allow itself, at last, to be influenced by the soul to seek eternal happiness within.

When this decision has been made, the student has completed his or her involution phase of experience.

Evolution

This is the point where the Earth School student begins to evolve back toward conscious Oneness with God.

Because, through involution, the personality has learned the lesson of disillusionment and no longer sees the third-dimensional, physical world as a potential source of lasting unconditional love, joy, and fulfillment, it is now more amenable to listening to its soul. In this stage, the soul attempts to help the personality to awaken to the Universal Spiritual Picture of the meaning and purpose of human life on Earth in whatever ways it can. The soul may, with the help of the entity's Guardian Angel or Higher Guide, bring to the personality of the individual a book, a poem, a serendipitous event, or some synchronistic experience, which the personality finds emotionally moving in a particularly powerful and positive way.

Regardless of the methods it uses, the soul's efforts are always involved with its attempts to bring the personality to an awakening, to an expanded awareness of the existence of the Universal Spiritual Picture. Once the soul is successful and the personality awakens to the fact that there may be a higher meaning to life on Earth, the soul will continue to do all that it can to elicit the personality's help in moving along the spiritual path, which is the path of bringing the personality into harmony with the soul and the Divinity Within the soul.

Increased inner harmony is created by the personality's release of attachments to Earthly ways and habit patterns (of feelings, thoughts, attitudes, beliefs, and actions) that it has learned from its outer world environment, which cause inner disharmony with its soul self. These disharmonious habit patterns are then replaced with new habits, which create and maintain inner harmony with the soul and with the Spark of God within the soul. It is this releasing and replacing activity, that brings us into increased inner harmony with our soul.

The newly created inner harmony between our personality and our soul automatically raises our personality's consciousness up to the level of the higher consciousness of our soul. It is this inner harmony among our personality, our soul, and our Divinity Within, that allows our soul to pass divine intuitive guidance and information, which it constantly receives from the Spark of God Within, down to our personality mind where we can use it in our daily activities.

There is another category of harmony to be achieved that also enhances our natural ability to receive divine intuitive guidance. It is the inner harmony that derives from having an equal balance of divine feminine energy and divine masculine energy integrated within us. Consider Divine Feminine Energy here to be the inner *passivity* of mind, which opens the door allowing us to receive divine intuitive guidance, and consider Divine Masculine Energy to be the *activity*, which allows us to carry out that divine guidance in the outer world.

As we move further along the path, we continue to release attachments and habit patterns (that we discover to have created any inner disharmony) and to replace them with new habits, which create inner harmony. We continue to focus our attention on our integration of more divine feminine energy and more divine masculine energy as we release and replace the negative or disharmonious type of third-dimensional feminine and masculine energy, which we have learned from our outer world experiences.

Moving along the path in this way, we are moving our heart (our ability to love unconditionally) and our consciousness (our ability to see and understand the non-physical aspects of life) upward and outward in the Universe, experiencing the expanded levels of our soul. With our experience of the increased inner harmony, we are beginning to remember what it was like, how it felt, to be our soul in attunement with our God/Goddess Within for our soul can feel and transmit unconditional love and receive divine guidance constantly.

Moving along the path continues the refinement and clearing of our personality selves. The spiritual path is indeed the path of the refinement of our personality. When the soul has refined or spiritualized the personality (and itself) to a certain degree and has reached a certain level of harmony with its Divinity Within, the soul begins to manifest that Divinity into the outer world while carrying out its life purpose. Because of the refinement process, the personality moves into such harmony with the soul, and the Spark of God Within, that the soul can now manifest its Divinity into the outer world without the personality discoloring it. The personality, through the releasing and replacing process, has, in effect, become transparent relative to the soul.

Such an entity has evolved itself into becoming its soul self again. It still has a physical body with a personality, but the personality has been spiritualized. Through the practice of meditative exercises, it can now begin to feel, to experience the light body of its soul again. This individual may not look any different but it will *be* different in its actions. It will tend never to do that which it knows will bring it down from the inner harmony it has created Within. This entity has become multidimensional; able to move its perspective **at will**, from that of the body's personality upward to that of the soul or even to that of the Divinity Within. As it shifts upward in its perspective, it also shifts upward to the higher, more expanded consciousness and awareness of the soul. Further, it shifts its heart upward to the higher, more divine feeling capabilities of the soul where it can once more experience the receiving and transmitting of pure unconditional love that it has missed for so long.

This being, as it manifests its divinity into the outer world, has achieved a high degree of conscious Oneness with God, again. It knows itself to be a soul (which happens to have a physical body attached) guided by the Divinity Within. It knows itself to be One with its God/Goddess Within and also with God, the All That Is. This entity knows itself to be One with all other aspects and minions of God in the Hierarchy of God throughout the Universe (and the Cosmos). It knows that it and these are all parts of the One God. Its consciousness has been raised, its perspective has been raised, and its feelings about the world have also been raised accordingly.

Ascension

Even while living as a soul, carrying out what it has discovered to be its soul's purpose, contract, or mission and enjoying the rapture of the new inner harmony with God, this entity will continue to evolve and refine its personality until it reaches the culmination of humankind's spiritual journey, Ascension. Ascension is the final result of a soul moving from the position of being entrapped in a consciously limited physical body, in a third-dimensional world culture, feeling separated from God—spiritually evolving itself and returning to the divine state of consciousness from which it came. In evolving itself in this way, this soul has brought Godness, Goddessness, Divinity, and Divine Goodness into the third-dimensional world where it hadn't been before.

After the death of the body (and the personality) of this harmonized soul, it Ascends to the fifth dimension (or higher). It has freed itself from the wheel of physical life on Earth. It has freed itself from the Earth School cycles of reincarnation, birth, death, and Karma. It has rejoined the other minions of God in the Hierarchy of God. This soul is now free to choose from the various missions available in the Universe. It may choose to go elsewhere, far, far away, or it may choose to use its experiential knowledge and understanding of Earthly ways to join the Archangels and Ascended Masters in assisting humankind's evolution back to conscious Oneness with God.

Either way, as the prodigal son or daughter, this soul has found its way back **home**.

GLOSSARY

Note: The first items in this Glossary are listed in groups rather than appearing in alphabetical order. Their meanings or definitions are better understood when considered in relation to each other rather than separately.

Angels, Guardian Angels, Archangels

Angels Angels are individuated souls who have never been incarnated in an existing physical body since their original creation by God at the beginning. They remain in their pure state of conscious Oneness with God as they carry out their various missions related to assisting humankind's spiritual evolution back to harmony and conscious Oneness. Angels live complete and whole in Bodies of Light. They have the ability to materialize a short-term body (appearing to be physical) in order to carry out a particular work or mission that requires or is made easier through such, perhaps as in assisting a human in distress. However, they have never been incarnated, so they have never known the experience of being or feeling consciously separated from God as we humans have.

Guardian Angels Guardian Angels are angels who have been assigned as guardians to a human during the human's incarnation. All humans are assigned at least one Guardian Angel and one Higher Guide at birth. The mission of these guardians is both to protect their assigned human from danger and to assist her or him along the evolutionary spiritual path back to conscious Oneness with the Spark of God Within. This they do always in accordance with Universal Spiritual Law, but because they have the special *guardian* mission they are permitted to offer warnings of danger without specifically being requested to do so.

Archangels Archangels are angels who have evolved themselves into positions of higher authority/responsibility (relative to the mission of assisting humankind's evolution) within the Angelic Realm. (All life everywhere is always evolving.) There are seven other major levels of angelic beings in the Angelic Realms, but those named Angels and Archangels are the two most closely, most directly associated with assisting humans in their evolution back to conscious Oneness with God.

A list of Archangels who have contributed information or other service in the co-creation of this book over the years includes Archangel Melchizedek, Archangel Michael, Archangel Ariel, Archangel Uriel, Archangel Gabriel, and Archangel Raphael. Melchizedek is the Archangel who is currently presiding over all of the Archangels and Angels.

Ascended Masters, the Great White Brotherhood, and Higher Guides

Ascended Masters Ascended Masters are souls who have been incarnated into physical human bodies and who have completed their path of spiritual evolution back to conscious Oneness with God. These were volunteers (i.e., lightworkers, wayshowers, starseeds) for the mission of becoming human and showing the way back home to all entrapped humankind.

They have ascended. They have evolved and freed themselves from the limited Earth life existence and have again taken their rightful places as minions of God in the Hierarchy of God in the fifth and higher dimensions above the physical Earth plane. Their general missions, like those of the Archangels, are all related to assisting humans to evolve themselves back to conscious Oneness with the Spark of God Within and to return to the freedom of the heavens above.

A list of Ascended Masters who have contributed information or other services in the co-creation of this book includes Sananda (the soul name of the one who was called Jesus in his last incarnation), Saint Germain, Lady Mary (Mother Mary, or Mary, who was the mother of Jesus), Augmenton, Kuthumi, Athenarious, and Thenous. Sananda, the soul of the human personality who manifested the Christ Spirit of God two thousand years ago, is now the head of the Great White Brotherhood of all Ascended Masters.

The Great White Brotherhood The Great White Brotherhood is the ancient name of the group consisting of all souls who have become Ascended Masters.

This is an excerpt from a reading by Cathy, on definitions, from Saint Germain on 02/11/01.

The term ***white*** *here relates to the color of light, the higher vibratory rate of light, the energy of the God Force being seen as light* (as opposed to darkness). *And then you may state that multiple members of the Hierarchy of the Great White Brotherhood, when they appear in physical form, generally do so in the form of their most recent or last incarnation, and many of them appear as other than white, other than Caucasian shall we say.*

Higher Guides Higher Guides are souls that have been incarnated in existing physical bodies in the third dimension Earth plane. They may have volunteered to enter into the Earth School cycles of involution and evolution as lightworkers or wayshowers to show others the way back to conscious Oneness with God, or they may be among those souls who were originally consciously entrapped in play. Regardless, Higher Guides are those who have evolved themselves to the degree where they now are permitted to provide humans with information from higher levels of consciousness than exist on the third-dimensional Earth plane. Higher Guides and Guardian Angels work in harmony to assist their assigned human to evolve him or herself along the spiritual path.

What is the difference in the kind of help they offer? Why is it that one of each is assigned? As given above, Angels have never been incarnated into existing physical bodies and Higher Guides have. It was determined by God when the Earth School was created that the perspectives of both types of advanced souls would be more beneficial than only one in understanding how best to assist their human. Both are Beings of Light perfectly competent to help the one to whom they are assigned.

Excerpt from a reading by Cathy, on definitions,
from Saint Germain on 02/11/01.

No assignments are made to incompetents!

God and the Hierarchy of God, comprised of all God's Minions

God, Godness, Goddessness For the purposes of this book, the terms God, Godness, Goddessness, Absolute Goodness, and a few others are used synonymously. God, and all the Beings of Light, who are minions of God in the Hierarchy of God in the higher dimensions of life, are comprised of an *equal balance* of Divine Feminine Energy (which consists of unconditional love and the ability to receive divine intuitive knowing of all things) and Divine Masculine Energy (consisting of the ability to put the divine intuitive guidance and information received through the feminine, into powerful but gentle, respectful, unconditionally loving action or manifestation).

For this reason, using only a masculine term for God is misleading and therefore quite inappropriate to offer to any who have chosen the spiritual path back to conscious Oneness with God. The higher truth behind the situation is that no one can reach conscious Oneness with God unless they have achieved a certain degree of divine masculine/feminine balance. This is a Universal Requirement for entrance into the higher realms (fifth dimension and higher). Why? What higher good could come from an entity who is incapable of receiving divine guidance and information from God? Receiving divine guidance is possible only through one's Divine Feminine Energy.

All Beings of Light in the fifth and higher dimensions have achieved (evolved themselves into) a balance in their Divine Masculine and Divine Feminine Energy, abilities, and qualities. At any moment, they can choose to Be and to manifest either their Divine Feminine Energy or their Divine Masculine Energy or both together.

Hierarchy of God The Hierarchy of God comprises all Beings of Light, all minions of God, who live in the higher realms of divine life above our physical, third-dimensional Earth world. In this Hierarchy, there are levels and there are divisions of responsibility and of purpose or mission. Suffice it to say that all Beings of Light in the vast Hierarchy of God in the higher realms above (fifth dimension and higher) are competent in their positions.

Note: The remainder of the Glossary is in alphabetical order, to some degree.

Ascension Ascension is the culmination of the soul's evolutionary journey from the point of entrapment in a physical body having a limited consciousness and understanding, along the spiritual path back to full conscious Oneness with the Spark of God Within the soul and thus also with God, the All That Is. Ascension marks the return of the human prodigal son or daughter back home, as a soul, to the conscious Oneness with the Divinity Within from which it unintentionally fell long, long ago. Ascension marks the end of the birth/death/reincarnation cycles required of all Earth School students.

Beings of Light Angels, Archangels, Ascended Masters, and others, are all Beings of Light. Beings of Light are souls who either have never been incarnated into physical human bodies or who have evolved themselves back to divine, higher conscious Oneness with God. This qualifies them, as members of the Hierarchy of God, to choose to participate in the mission of assisting with humankind's spiritual evolution and return to conscious Oneness with God. Beings of Light live in a state of divine wisdom, divine love, and divine will in bodies comprised of light.

Being (the state of) "Being" is a state of soul consciousness in which an entity is living in the eternal moment, attuned and consciously At-One with her or his God/Goddess Within. Being is achieved only by the stilling of the personality mind and the shifting of one's consciousness upward to the level of the soul. This is the state of Being one's Real Self, True Self, or Soul Self in harmony with the Divinity Within and above.

Being is not a state of thinking, for thinking is of the personality level of consciousness. Being, therefore, does not include thinking, either of the past or of the future. Rather, it includes only the instant intuitive knowings and understandings constantly received from one's Divinity Within related to one's focus of attention.

Below is an excerpt from a reading by Cathy from Otheus on 06/01/94 that was very helpful to me in my struggle to understand that which I then believed to be quite foreign to me.

✦ Is "Being" a feminine activity?

It is that which comes from the feminine attributes, to be sure.

✦ How so?

Because it is a matter of passivity in quieting self and opening self and extending love and opening the heart to the object with which you are to be one, and these are feminine activities.

✦ Aren't they masculine, because of this projection?

*It is **not** a projection into; rather it is an opening of self to allow that to come into your own Being. You become "one-with," by inviting that essence* (with which you wish to be One) *into your own Being.*

Chakras

This is an excerpt from a reading by Cathy, on definitions, from Saint Germain on 02/11/01.

Chakras are personal energy vortexes; centers that connect human beings with Universal energy, energetic forces. We would say that the goal is to have the chakras in balance, each balanced within itself. And we would say that there are seven such energy vortexes connected to the physical body of the incarnated being.

✦ Okay.

And you may choose to name them, giving their positions and color if you choose. It is not necessary to do so within the scope of your current volume. We would also say that there are other energy vortexes numbering up to 24 that are not directly connected to the physical being. And we would not go into details on the others in this book.

These are the locations and the colors of the seven chakras connected to the physical body.

- The crown chakra is located at the top of the head, and its color is violet.
- The brow chakra is situated between and slightly above the eyebrows. Its color is purple.
- The throat chakra exists in the throat area and is blue in color.
- The heart chakra is positioned at and around the heart area. Its color is emerald green.
- The solar plexus chakra is in the area of the navel and its color is yellow (or perhaps golden if one has evolved to a more angelic state).
- The sacral chakra exists in the general area of the sex organs (slightly above) and is orange in color.
- The base chakra is at the base of the spine and is red.

Dimensions All beings and all life, everywhere in the Cosmos, evolve(s) upward into life at higher levels of consciousness, awareness, and refinement.

First Dimension The first dimension comprises the mineral life of a planet. The larger forms must break down into smaller bits and pieces to form soil suitable for plant life. The highest forms of evolutionary life in the mineral kingdom include the gems that we humans often treasure.

Second Dimension The second dimension includes all plant life, the conscious life of the entire vegetable or plant kingdom. Without this kingdom there would be nothing for physical creatures of a higher nature (and greater mobility) to feed upon. Evolution here can be toward more beautiful, more fragrant flowers or more useful roots, fruits, and seeds.

Third Dimension The third dimension is the physical plane. The third dimension is the world of material "things" in which we, identifying ourselves as humans, currently live. Reference to the third dimension focuses upon our outer world life of physical matter and physical activities as opposed to our inner spiritual world life of "Being" in the more divine dimensions and the higher levels of consciousness that are available within.

The third dimension, at humankind's current phase of evolution, consists of a great deal of negative (self-centered, disharmonious) energy mixed with a smaller proportion of positive (divine, harmonious) energy. The term third dimension is used to qualify everything in the physical world of incarnated humans. Therefore, we may have third-dimensional habit patterns, which cause inner disharmony between our personality and our higher conscious soul with its Divinity Within. These third-dimensional habits include all of the habitual ways of feeling, thinking, believing, and acting that we have learned from our outer world since we were born, as opposed to the divine, higher ways that our eternal soul and Divinity Within know will bring to us the heavenly feelings of inner harmony with God.

Our soul was perfect at creation (without a physical body) in its divine body of light that allowed it to be anywhere, at any moment, complete and whole, and joyfully fulfilled as it carried out various missions in the Universe. This is the way of the Angels today and will be the way of our souls (again) in the future.

Fourth Dimension The fourth dimension consists of life at a higher level of consciousness than that of our physical third dimension, but like our third-dimensional, physical world, it also includes both negative and positive energy. This is the astral plane where the souls of most humans reside between incarnations until they have evolved themselves to the point of Ascension (where they return to conscious Oneness with God and free themselves from the cycles of reincarnation, birth, death, and Karma).

The fourth dimension is nearly divine at the higher end and nearly third-dimensional at the lower.

Fifth Dimension The fifth dimension is the first of the divine dimensions. Here there is only harmonious, divine, positive energy. This is the first dimension of the heavenly, blissful vibrational levels of divine life as a soul, in a body of light, as a Being of Light, in conscious Oneness with God. This is the dimension to which an incarnated soul Ascends when it has managed to evolve the personality of the physical body to which it had been attached, to the required degree of harmony with the soul and the Divinity Within.

Sixth and Higher Dimensions The sixth dimension includes life continuing to evolve to higher degrees of soul refinement and greater areas of responsibility. Issues to be further refined might include, for example, the creation of an even more perfect balance of Divine Feminine and Divine Masculine Energy within the soul. Regardless, evolution continues. All life everywhere is always evolving.

Ego and Personality

When the original, perfect, divine souls playfully attached themselves to physical animal bodies, they not only acquired the limited *personality consciousness* of the third-dimensional animal to which they attached, they also acquired an ***ego***, the self-centered survival element present in the personality of all mortal bodies.

The ego element is appropriate to the third-dimensional animal life, to which we originally attached our souls, because animal life is mortal. Animals grow old and die. The self-centered ego of animals helps them to survive life in the midst of other mortal animals, each of which also has an ego element in their personality. So it is the nature of physical animals to be self-centered in order to keep themselves alive in the physical world.

However, it is definitely ***not*** the nature of souls to be self-centered for they were created as (perfect, divine, and) ***eternal*** and cannot die. Souls have no need for a self-centered survival element (nor the competitiveness and aggression that go with it).

The presence of the ego element within the human personality is the basic cause of disharmony between the nature and character of our (more or less self-centered) human personalities and the divine nature of our souls. It is the ego element that is the primary cause for our personality's adoption of habit patterns that are not in harmony with the divine nature and character of our soul. This is why the spiritual path is described as the path of releasing disharmonious (self-centered) habit patterns and replacing them with new habits that are in harmony with the Divinity Within our soul.

In this way we create harmony between our personality and our soul, and also with the Spark of God within our soul, on our return to conscious Oneness with God, and Ascension.

This is an excerpt from a reading by Cathy from Saint Germain on 01/28/01.

✦ Is it okay to use personality as synonymous with ego? Are they one and the same?

You may use the terms synonymously. It is not inappropriate so long as you make it clear you are doing so.

✦ Okay.

However, you will find that there are entities who are moving along the path of spiritual development who have ***personalities*** *and manifest* ***personalities*** *that are not entirely* ***ego*** *controlled. It depends on how you use the term, how you define the term.*

✦ Okay. Well, those personalities that are not ego controlled (not entirely selfish or self centered) are probably rather transparent (transparent in a good way) and are manifesting more the divine character of the soul. These would be entities who have already evolved their personalities into a greater harmony with their souls and are now manifesting more of the divine nature of the soul.

Correct.

Readings and Channelings (verbal or journaled)

Below is an excerpt from a reading by Cathy, on definitions, from Archangel Michael on 10/15/00.

For your purposes channeling is the attuning of self to the divine within and to the highest level of consciousness which the channel is capable of reaching, and this varies from channel to channel. The information is received primarily through the crown chakra and also through the brow chakra (the third eye) and is then transmitted through the throat chakra. It is not a one-definition experience in the sense that often the heart chakra is also involved, but channeling for your purposes involves only the higher four chakras, the crown, the brow, the throat, and the heart.

✦ Thank you.

The process is one of having attuned self to the highest level within. Then the information is received much like the tuning in of a radio or television signal. The example of a radio is probably the more acceptable. And the channel may experience receipt of the information at a particular point in the area of the crown chakra, and this may vary depending on the channel itself, and it may also vary depending on the information being received.

It is also important to note that all channeled material in this definition, comes through the higher self of the entity who is serving as the channel.

Spark of God This is the Spark of God's Beingness placed within each of our eternal etheric souls at the moment of our original creation by God. In spite of our personality's involvement with physical world life, the Spark of God within our soul remains untainted, pure, perfect, and divine.

Spiritual Tools A spiritual tool is a method or process created by Archangels, Ascended Masters, or other appropriate Beings of Light that makes it easier for us humans to release and to free ourselves of our discordant negative habit patterns and to replace them with those that bring harmony between our personality and our soul. These tools were designed to speed up the evolutionary process by making the releasing and replacing procedure much quicker and easier than it has ever been. The Beings of Light who create these tools always stand behind them and see that the necessary etheric and spiritual dynamics are taken care of whenever any human uses them. For more on spiritual tools see chapter 21, and appendix A.